DISCARD

DUE

PROGRESSIVE EDUCATION: A MARXIST INTERPRETATION

STUDIES IN MARXISM, Vol. 8

PROGRESSIVE EDUCATION: A MARXIST INTERPRETATION

by
Gilbert G. Gonzalez
University of California, Irvine

University of Charleston Library
Charleston, WV 25304

Marxist Educational Press
Minneapolis

Marxist Educational Press
c/o Anthropology Department
University of Minnesota
215 Ford Hall, 224 Church St. S.E.
Minneapolis, Minnesota 55455

Copyright © Gilbert G. Gonzalez 1982
All rights reserved.

Library of Congress Cataloging in Publication Data

Gonzalez, Gilbert G., 1941-
    Progressive education.

    (Studies in Marxism ; v. 8)
    Includes index.
    1. Progressive education—United States—History.
2. Communism and education. I. Title. II. Series:
Studies in Marxism (Marxist Educational Press) ; v. 8.
LA216.G66   370'.973   81-5787
ISBN 0-930656-15-6   AACR2
ISBN 0-930656-16-4 (pbk.)

Printed in the United States of America

CONTENTS

Foreword	7
CHAPTER ONE. A Methodological Introduction	9
1. The Marxist Method	10
2. Lenin's Contribution to Marxist Methodology	17
3. A Marxist Critique of Educational Historiography	29
4. Summary and Overview	37
CHAPTER TWO. The Roots of Progressive Education: Educational Theory and the Rise of the Bourgeoisie	39
1. The Educational Thought of Locke, Rousseau, and Smith	40
2. Ideology and Social Relations of Production	51
CHAPTER THREE. Monopoly Capitalism and Progressive Reformism	53
1. The Evolution of Capitalism and Nineteenth-Century Educational Reform	53
2. Background to Progressivism: Monopoly and the Intensification of Class Conflict	59
3. Progressivism: The Politics of Monopoly Capitalism	63
CHAPTER FOUR. John Dewey, Theoretician of Progressive Education	85
1. Instinct Theory and Dewey's Educational Psychology	87
2. Society as Organism: Social Harmony in Dewey's Educational Purpose	94
3. Relations of Production and Dewey's Educational Scheme	100
CHAPTER FIVE. The Rise of Intelligence Testing	105
1. Classical Psychology vs. the "New" Psychology	106
2. The Concept of "Intelligence" as an Ideological Construct	116
3. The Materialization of "Intelligence" in Testing Instruments	118
4. Racism and the Concept of Intelligence	122
5. The Role of Intelligence Testing in the Schools	125

CHAPTER SIX. Mass Education and the Forces of Production   127
  1. Technological Change and Child Labor   127
  2. Monopoly Capital and Agitation for Mass Compulsory Education   130
  3. Education in Labor-Intensive and Capital-Intensive Forms of Production   132

CONCLUSION. A Marxist-Leninist Analysis of Modern Education   139

CASE STUDY. Educational Reform in Los Angeles and Its Effect on the Chicano Community, 1900-1930   151
  1. Background for Educational Reform   152
  2. The Mexican Problem   155
  3. The Scientific Method: The Department of Psychology and Educational Research   157
  4. The Educational Technicians: The Counselors   159
  5. Curriculum Development and Vocational Education in the High Schools   165
  6. Conclusion   170

NOTES   173

INDEX OF NAMES   195

PUBLISHER'S FOREWORD

Although there has been much controversy about Progressive education, the vehemence of the arguments has rarely been accompanied by clarity and fundamental analysis. The critiques of Progressivism have by and large been superficial and have not examined the integral connection between its tenets and the rise of monopoly capitalism, a dominant factor in the development of society in the United States during the twentieth century. There has long been a need for a consistent Marxist analysis of the ideological role of Progressivism in the shaping of education in this century.

Professor Gonzalez's book provides a refreshingly perceptive and penetrating analysis of the ideological nexus between the growth of monopoly capitalism and the development of Progressive educational theory and practice. He begins by outlining the basic principles of Marxist analysis and providing a Marxist critique of educational historiography. This is followed by an exposition of the ideological bases of early bourgeois educational theory: Locke, Rousseau, Adam Smith. He then describes the evolution of capitalism in the United States and the concomitant changes which occurred in education in the nineteenth century. The central role of John Dewey in articulating a new educational theory adapted to the needs of monopoly capitalism is then discussed in detail. Gonzalez then places the role of intelligence testing in social and ideological perspective. He concludes with an analysis of educational theory and its relation to the forces of production. A case study, in which he describes the evolution of theory and practice in the Los Angeles schools, provides a concrete application of his theoretical analysis.

This book illumines and clarifies many issues which are currently subjects of debate and controversy, such as the role of intelligence testing in education, the new emphasis on vocationalism, the purposes and goals of the schools in the United States, racism in the schools, the differences between demands on the schools made by the petty bourgeoisie and monopoly capitalism. The Marxist Educational Press believes that this book will contribute new insights into a frequently misunderstood epoch in the history of U.S. education and will throw new light on the relationships between the socioeconomic context and the functions of schools in capitalist society.

University of Minnesota Gerald M. Erickson
November, 1981

Chapter One
A METHODOLOGICAL INTRODUCTION

This is a study of the theory of education as it emerged during the late nineteenth and early twentieth centuries in the United States. My purpose is twofold. First, I propose to sketch the Marxist method for studying the educational process. Rather than verifying this method empirically, I shall outline its content and its application. The methodological approach includes the contributions made by Lenin to Marxist theory, especially his theory of monopoly capitalism. A Marxist-Leninist framework of analysis has not been applied in any of the numerous studies on education in the United States. It is the absence of this methodological approach in the literature which compels me to present this approach to educational history. In applying Marx and Lenin to the study of educational history, I realize that I am at the disadvantage of cutting a new trail without recourse to previous works which would have elaborated this theory and documented its correspondance with the important economic, social and political data of this history. My first task then must be to present and develop this alternative approach for the study of education.

Secondly, I shall present an interpretation of Progressive education based upon Marxist methodology. Within this methodological framework, I shall do three things. First, I shall analyze the nature of the political and ideological changes during the late nineteenth and early twentieth centuries. Secondly, I shall examine the relationship between these changes and modifications in the system of capitalist production. And lastly, I shall examine the relationship between these political, economic, and ideological changes and educational theory. This study will confront the political phenomenon known as Progressivism and, in particular, the chief tenets of Progressive education. This study is not intended to be an exhaustive examination of educational thinkers, of Progressives, or of the economic and political forces which pushed Progressivism to the political surface. To repeat: My purpose is to develop the Marxist method for the study of educational theory and to posit an interpretation of the Progressive education based upon this method. Such a scope and purpose invites further research and methodological study.

Because Marxist theory is seldom applied to the study of American history, and also because it is so often misinterpreted, it will be fruitful in the following portion of this introduction to describe its principal aspects. In addition, I will synthesize Lenin's contribution to Marxism and analyze the application to major questions confronting the study of Progressive education. Finally, utilizing Marxist theory, I will analyze and critique the three main tendencies comprising the historiography of American education. I hope to show the importance of two key ideas. First, that Marxist theory and its further elaboration by Lenin has not been applied to the study of Progressivism nor to Progressive education; and secondly, that this Marxist theoretical system is a viable alternative to the study of Progressive education.

1. The Marxist Method

The key links in any analysis of a social formation must include the interaction of economics, politics, and ideology. All Marxist analysis inherently recognizes the relationship between the economic basis of society* and the superstructure (politics and ideology). Without such a methodology, one inevitably utilizes a pluralist approach which considers phenomena only in their separateness, not in their actual relationships. In the analysis of the political process, one must *always* investigate the relationship of the state to production. Any approach that separates the superstructure from the base is non-Marxist.

---

*According to Marx's materialist conception of history, the economic basis of society is the social relations of production, principally the property relations under which the forces of production are set into motion. The forces of production and the relations of production that determine how they are used constitute the mode of production.
—Ed.

The material world of production is the key to understanding the political, social, and cultural organization of society. Production is the basis for the existence of any social group. According to classical Marxist political economy, the system of production is the base upon which a social and political structure rests. Without the ability of a society to carry on production, the means for its survival collapse. Everything in the society in which we live was created in the processes of production. Production is key. The minute production stops, society begins to die. Therefore, without production there is no social order.

The manner in which production is carried out is crucial; not all societies have had identical systems of production. Production has an economic ring to it, yet production is social in nature for it requires that individual members of a society come together and socially perform the various tasks in the productive process. In the historical development of human societies a number of distinct systems of production have appeared, and each has had a particular level of technology and a particular social, or organizational, formation. The relationship of the social organization to the organization of production is extremely important. The social sphere, in the final analysis, corresponds to the social relationships of production. How people come together for the sake of production will determine how people relate to one another in the political and social sphere. Furthermore, the prevailing ideology of any given society is ultimately a reflection of its particular system of production and forms an element of the social relations characteristic of the daily life of society.

Capitalism is a particular system of production based upon private (or individual, rather than social) ownership of the means of production. The fact that the productive instruments are owned individually, or privately—yet are of such a high technological character so as to demand mass forms of production (e.g., factories)—is the material basis for the existence of socially distinct groups or classes. This study is based upon the objective existence of classes, that is, of owners of productive property, the bourgeoisie, and of propertyless workers, the proletariat.[1] Classes reflect the private appropriation of the means for society's production of goods for the market. Not everyone owns productive property. This is the objective basis for the existence of a class of owners of the means of production. Indeed, ownership of the basic and overwhelmingly important productive establishments—i.e., banks, industry, businesses, transportation, land—are in the hands of relatively few private individuals. This class of owners, in order that their property be productive, employ labor. Actually, they purchase the labor capacity of individuals in the marketplace and realize that capacity within the productive process. Thus, private owners of the means of production become not only owners of the means of production but also owners of the laboring capacity of individuals.

This productive relationship is a social relationship which is the essence of capitalist production. Without the owners of the means of production and the laborers who put that production into action, there would be no capitalism; and capitalism creates, of itself, the two fundamental classes: the bourgeoisie and the working class. This social relationship exists independently of the "consciousness" of either the workers or the capitalists. By virtue of capitalist production, classes become inescapable, a reality which is nothing more than the social reflection of the manner in which production is carried out.

Classes and class society are often considered to be a relic of some bygone era, the vestigial remains of European feudalism.[2] There is a well-traveled argument that the absence of feudalism has determined the social organization of capitalism in the United States. Thus the proponents argue that the lack of a class-conscious aristocracy has "pulled the rug," so to speak, from under the feet of the class "model" along "European" lines. This narrow understanding of classes as a rigid heritage from the past ignores the fact that distinct groups with particular relations to property and to each other in production continued to exist and evolve into ever more concentrated poles in the United States. The latter half of the nineteenth century was continuously racked by violent labor-capital struggles (as is documented in chapter 3). The proponents of a classless interpretation of U.S. history might perhaps argue that the workers in their struggle with capital were duped by agitators into believing that classes existed and that only through struggle could they emancipate themselves. To some extent radical ideas did come from foreign workers, but the labor struggles that have characterized much of nineteenth and twentieth century American history were a phenomenon that sprang spontaneously from the nature of capitalist production. The consequence was a long history of intermittent violent, bloody, system-threatening confrontations. Nevertheless, the myth persists that classes along "European lines" have failed to materialize in the United States. The fact is that they have materialized and that capitalist-labor conflict has been the principal factor in determining domestic social policy, especially in schooling.

If class struggle has not been at least feared by property owners in the United States, why (as it shall be shown in chapter 2 through chapter 4), has there been such a determined effort to stamp it out?[3]

Why did Josiah Strong articulate sociological principles of class solidarity nearly ten years before Emile Durkheim pronounced the necessity for a corporate society in *De la Division du Travail Social*? Questions such as these have received little attention from those who have devoted themselves to the model of "American Exceptionalism." Each case of national capitalism has its pecularities, but also its fundamental similarities. What is similar between capitalism in the United States and capitalism anywhere is that some individuals own the means of production, while others are hired as wage labor to perform the tasks required in production. There is no other way for objectively determining economic classes under capitalism. Those who own the instruments of production also own the products of that production. Those who perform the labor own nothing but the power to work, which they sell to the capitalist. Capitalism, as an economic system of individual profit-making enterprises, cannot be capitalism unless it be characterized by these two classes coming together for purposes of production.

This social relationship has a significant corresponding political and ideological foundation. There is a link between the state and the interests of capitalists. For example, the capitalist state enforces the sanctity of private property and intervenes in the economy to speed it along (or slow it down) and to create measures for social controls. Furthermore, the state, especially in organizing and directing the educational system, trains bureaucrats, technicians, executives and workers for the economy. Most importantly, the state's educational system does not merely train personnel in the skills required in production. The ideological structure necessary to maintain the hierarchy and absolutism of factories, businesses and banks, etc., is a part of the state's educational curriculum. On the one hand, the state's power enforces the social relations of production through laws limiting the activities of unions, court injunctions against strikes, etc. On the other hand, the state steadily socializes the population into an ideology that makes the existing class structure, the distribution of wealth and political power, wholly legitimate. Thus, the state is not a neutral agency, but a bulwark in the defense of capitalism. Corresponding to the state's power of enforcement is an ideological structure. Both intervene to maintain the economic structure and its social relationships. Furthermore, the prevailing ideology is the core of the cultural system of society. Culture and ideology are, as a rule, in correspondence with the social relations of production. One task of the state is constantly to monitor and control the correspondence between social stability and the ideology of the population.

Thus, we can diagram one aspect of the relationship of base and superstructure in this manner:

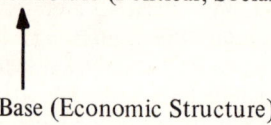

Superstructure (Political, Social and Ideological Structure)

Base (Economic Structure)

In the investigation of the base and superstructure, one must refrain from a mechanical interpretation of seeing only a one-way response from economics towards politics or ideology. Marx certainly was never an economic determinist, and Engels declared that such an interpretation of Marx was in serious error. Marxists argue that production and changes in the form of production are in the long run the foundation upon which political action and ideological views rest. Marx never thought that things occur in such a way that politics are mechanically determined by economics. It is a two-way street. What Marxists posit is that, of the two, economics is key over the long run and that in any given social formation there is a general correspondence between economics and politics. In a social formation, politics and economics are in interaction. For example: the ideological outlook of the capitalist (i.e., individualism) does affect the economy, through, for instance, the individualistic profit motive of the capitalist which propels mechanization in industry (superstructure → base), or, the other way around (base → superstructure), economics (i.e., social production in factories) results in class consciousness, unionization and, eventually, the political activity of working people. This enhances our understanding of the relationship between base and superstructure:

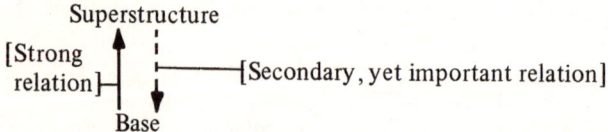

No system of production remains static. There is a tendency for economic development to outpace political and ideological structures. At such times the close correspondence between the two spheres breaks down, and struggle ensues at the superstructural level until a new correspondence with the changed economic conditions is again attained (or, in some cases, a temporary retrogression of the economy is forced by the old superstructure). Therefore, politics must likewise undergo changes which correspond with changes in the economic structure, or in political realignments or relationships. As the economy undergoes changes, the old superstructure continues to influence the new superstructural developments. For example, Marxism as a new theory of society, although developed as a challenge to bourgeois social theory and political economy, could only have developed *on the basis of* those very theories. Marx once ironically stated that the classical concept "class," so much identified with Marxism, was to be credited to bourgeois political economy.

As regards the base, Marxism finds the principal generator for development in the base to be the contradictions inherent in the mode of production. That change with which we will be concerned within capitalist production is the movement from nonmonopolistic to a monopolistic form of production. This can be seen as two distinct stages. Thus, we can add to the diagram of the relationship of base and superstructure the following:

$$\begin{array}{ccc} \text{Superstructure}^1 & \longrightarrow & \text{Superstructure}^2 \\ | & & | \\ \text{Base}^1 & \longrightarrow & \text{Base}^2 \end{array}$$

These diagrams do not depict the actual thoroughness with which Marxist theory studies society. Interrelationships continue between old ideological forms and new determining forms of production and between old nondetermining forms of production and new ideological forms. In incorporating these situations into our previous diagrams we arrive at this methodological generalization:

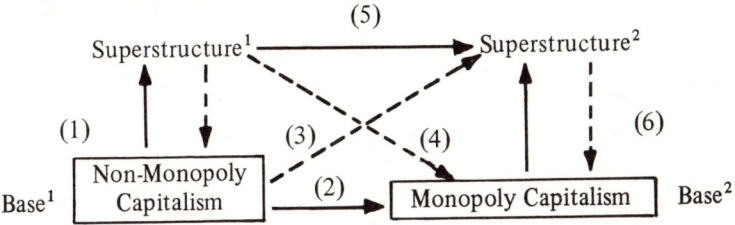

We have a model of the interrelationship between base and superstructure that is certainly not guided blindly by economics, but shows the complexity with which Marxist methodology views its subject matter. In (1) we see the actual correspondence and interaction between the base and superstructure at the stage of nonmonopoly capitalism; in (2) the effects of production in stage one impel change in the economy leading to stage two (monopoly capitalism); (3) the old form of production still persists to a degree, and therefore continues to find a political and ideological expression in the new stage; (4) the former ideological and political structures still play a role and continue to affect the changed economic develoment; (5) the old superstructure continues to play a role influencing the manner in which the new dominant ideology and political structure develop; and lastly, (6) the correspondence between the base and the superstructure is reattained in the stage of monopoly capitalism.

In this historical analysis of the educational system, I will be especially concerned with three aspects of the diagram: those changes in the base, that is, the changes from nonmonopoly to monopoly capitalism (2); secondly, in changes in the superstructure affected by base, from an ideology corresponding to nonmonopoly to an ideology corresponding to monopoly (6); thirdly, the continuum in educational ideas of early capitalism to monopoly capitalism—relationship (5), from the old superstructure to the new. Many principal ideas of the earlier capitalist period continue into later capitalism, and several different formulations of the era of monopoly appear influenced by the earlier ideological forms.

Marxist methodology runs counter to the empiricist approach which enjoys predominance in most historical studies. Marxists begin with a plan, an approach to the data, with an understanding of how society functions. The problem for the Marxist is to cut through the maze of data, the complexity of any historical phenomenon. Every historical situation presents two aspects: it is complex, and it is simple. However, the essential aspect is its simplicity, the complexity always shrouding the essence. Empiricists generally focus upon the complex. For them things become so complex that the forest is sacrificed for the trees. Marxists, on the other hand, do not deny that phenomena are complex. What they deny is that this complexity is the principal focus of analysis. Marxists hold that there are laws or tendencies guiding social development, and that it is the task of Marxism as a scientific theory of society to uncover these laws. Thus the purpose of my methodological discussion is to define the tool with which the essence, the basic aspects of Progressivism, can be uncovered and analyzed. For it is the essence of Progressive thought which is really important; the complex is not negated, but viewed in perspective. I shall not investigate each major thinker, every idea, each change in the base. My purpose is to sketch a new approach to the study of the educational changes occurring in the Progressive period. As such, I shall delineate the principal ideas developed during the Progressive period, the material basis for those ideas, and cite instances of their expression. I warn the reader not to expect an empiricist "proof." However, I shall ask the reader to recognize the relationship between methodology and the evidence.

The question of simple versus complex is handled in this fashion: I recognize the diversity of thought during the Progressive period, but I also wish to show that, in spite of diversity, there were key ideas which gave Progressivism a central purpose. It was these key ideas which interest us; conflict between politicians, or among scholars, does not define Progressivism. I shall argue that there were significant ideas which joined individuals who—though at times in opposition over particular issues—were by and large in agreement with regard to key ideas consonant with the prevailing economic system. In the last instance, Progressivism in education was not in opposition to monopoly capitalism, as prevalent interpretations would have it, but was firmly joined to it.

2. Lenin's Contribution to Marxist Methodology

By the end of the nineteenth century, capitalism had evolved into a qualitatively new form, monopoly capitalism. The essence of capitalism remained (i.e., a system of production based on private ownership of the means of production and on wage labor), but in form it was radically altered. For a traditionally competitive capitalist production had come under the domination of huge monopolistic enterprises. It is of fundamental importance to distinguish between monpoly and premonopoly stages of capitalism because, if no recognition is given to the superstructural changes caused by monopoly capitalism, Progressivism and Progressive education lose their principal significance. Historiography on Progressivism does not recognize the importance played by monopoly capitalism in shaping the politics of the late nineteenth and twentieth centuries. This absence reflects an indifference to the possibility of applying Lenin's contribution to Marxist theory to American history.[4] *My fundamental argument in this study is that the political phenomenon known as Progressivism—as well as one of its particular manifestations, Progressive education—was a direct consequence of the rise of monopoly capitalism.*

Lenin, for the most part, has been ignored by American historians. Lenin's theoretical contributions to Marxism have not been applied to U.S. history. Indeed, a work on the United States paralleling Lenin's *The Development of Capitalism in Russia* has not yet appeared. Although a few writers have used a general Marxist framework, the tendency is to argue that the American experience is an exception to classical Marxist theory. An alternative approach and view of Progressive education is therefore in order.

Lenin's contribution has three principal aspects: economic, political, and ideological. These three do not exist independently, but interact and react upon each other. Of the three, economics is the principal force in determining the other two. Lenin, as well as Marx, argued that the inherent tendencies within capitalist production guide it toward the increasing concentration of production. The tendencies which Lenin saw maturing as monopoly capitalism were in their infant stages when Marx wrote *Capital* and, therefore, were understandably not elaborated in Marx's formulation. However, Lenin based his thesis upon Marx and derived fundamental economic and political insights into modern capitalism.

a. Lenin: The Economics of Monopoly Capitalism

Monopoly capitalism exhibits, as do all stages in every mode of production, particular political and ideological manifestations. We therefore begin the discussion with the economic aspects and proceed to the political and ideological. Lenin synthesized five principal economic characteristics of the highest stage of capitalism:

1. The concentration of production and capital developed to such a high stage that it created monopolies which play a decisive role in economic life.
2. Bank capital merged with industrial capital creating the finance capital of a "financial oligarchy."
3. The export of capital becomes extremely important as distinguished from the export of commodities.
4. International capitalist monopolies were formed, and shared the world among themselves.
5. The territorial division of the entire world among the greatest capitalist powers was completed.[5]

These five characteristics need not be present in each country simultaneously, but these are the general tendencies within capitalism beginning in the latter part of the nineteenth century. These tendencies develop unevenly; there are periods of sharp upswings, at other times slowdowns, and perhaps even temporary regressions. Nevertheless, over the long run a process of increasing monopolization of production characterizes modern capitalism.

Lenin did not conjure up an independent theory of monopoly capitalism. He based it entirely upon four fundamental attributes (uncovered by Marx) peculiar to industrial (or competitive) capitalism. These were: a tendency of the rate of profit to fall, a tendency toward concentration of production, a tendency toward periodic crises of increasing intensity, and a tendency toward the progressive impoverishment and relative increase in numbers of the proletariat. Competitive capitalism was constantly exhibiting tendencies that threatened its very existence. The economic consequence of these contradictions is monopoly capitalism.

As mentioned earlier, capitalism is a particular form of production which relies upon the labor of workers as the principal element in the derivation of profits. The "congealed" surplus labor within a commodity determines its value over and above the costs accrued in the process of production. Thus, the survival of the capitalist *qua* capitalist requires that, of the total labor constituting the value of a commodity, only a portion of the value of that labor be paid to the laborer. The remainder is pocketed in the exchange process. Since capitalists exist in a society where numerous capitals produce for the same market, a competitive relationship with other capitals is established. Competition inevitably brings ruin for the many as well as success for the few. Marx noted that "competition rages in direct proportion to the number, and in inverse proportion to the magnitudes of the antagonistic capitals."[6] The consequences led to the "ruin of many small capitalists, whose capitals pass into the hands of their conquerors."[7]

The tendency of the rate of profit to fall is the principal impulse to monopoly and occurs for a number of interrelated reasons. First, the amount of labor incorporated into a commodity will determine its value and price level on the market. (The value of labor is determined by the value of goods and services needed to reproduce it on a daily basis. The price of the commodity fluctuates about, and in the last instance is determined by, the value of the commodity.) Each capitalist sells commodities, whose price is determined, in general, by the value of the labor incorporated into the commodity. That value is set socially; that is, in a society a value for a given commodity is set by the general level of labor necessary to produce the commodity. Thus, in a given society (and under conditions of competitive capitalism) the general price is ultimately determined by the amount of labor socially necessary to produce the object.

Secondly, since prices (and value) are determined by labor, a capitalist, in seeking advantage in competition with other capitalists, will incorporate labor-saving machinery. This measure will cut his labor costs and increase the productivity of labor. Meanwhile the socially determined price will remain (if wage goods are not affected in the same way). One capitalist seeking a means to gain profit advantage will cut costs (incorporate new technique, machinery, etc.), yet sell at the socially determined price (or slightly below) to gain market advantages.

Profit is thus determined by the unpaid labor accruing to the capitalist. In determining an advantage over other capitalists, one capitalist will incorporate labor-saving techniques which increase profits by outselling and underpricing the commodity (in relation to socially determined price). However, the moment other capitalists incorporate that same machinery, the value of the object will socially fall. Thus, the labor taken to produce a commodity is socially less and the general value, price and rate of profit will be correspondingly less. The result is that throughout the competitive stage of capitalism the price level gradually descends. The capitalist attempts to counter this tendency by constantly expanding and investing. The final consequence of the pressure to counter this tendency is monopolization in the economy. Constant pressure to mechanize, the steadily rising costs of technology, the raging competition destroying one then another capitalist, result finally in fewer producers but on a larger scale. When one, two, or a few giants finally come to dominate in an industry, the price is not determined by the competition between them, or by the value of labor incorporated into a commodity, but by the price they determine to be profitable. In this way the tendency of the rate of profit to fall is countered, but not destroyed, by monopoly.

The constant tendency, indeed the very logic of capitalism, impels larger scales of production as a technique for greater productivity. Yet competition is proportional to the number of capitals in a particular branch of industry. *Once monopolies are established, the power to control competition simultaneously manifests itself.* And thus the competition of numerous capitals is revealed as the competition and cooperation between monopolies. Competition remains but is restrained by cooperation through pools, trusts, and mergers. Classical competitive capitalism eventually became obsolete, an anachronism within a "reality of massive corporations acting cooperatively to maximize their profits."[8]

Monopoly capitalism, then, is a direct consequence of developing competitive capitalism. Lenin described monopolistic production as large scale production in any particular branch of industry; monopoly included cartels, pools, trusts—what are now referred to as oligopolies, i.e., combinations of all types which transformed free competition into the monopoly of a handful of giants. "Competition," Lenin concluded, "becomes transformed into monopoly." He added: "This is something quite different from the old free competition between manufacturers, scattered and out of touch with one another, and producing for an unknown market."[9]

The pattern of free competition is transformed through the inevitable tendencies of capitalist production into its opposite. The economic tendency in capitalism is toward large-scale industry as a mechanism for opposing the tendency of the rate of profit to fall. While it can curb the latter only to a degree, this nevertheless requires a constantly encompassing monopolization of production in both the private and state spheres.

Lenin cited numerous statistics from various countries to support his argument. As his statistics for the U.S. are from the period with which we are concerned here, we shall reproduce them. In 1904, large-scale enterprises in the U.S. with an output of $1 million numbered 1,900, or 0.9% of 216,180 total enterprises. These few employed 1,400,000 workers (of 5,500,000), or 25.6% of the total workforce. Their output was 38% of the combined output for all industry (or $5,600,000,000 of $14,800,000,000). By 1909, concentration was further along the road: 3,060 enterprises with an output of $1 million (1.1% of 268,491) employed 2,000,000 workers (of 6,600,000) or 30.5%. Its output, $9 billion (of $21 billion) was 43.8% of total production. In the first decade of the century, nearly forty-four percent of the total production was carried out by 1.1% of all industrial enterprises and nearly 1 out of every 3 workers was employed by them.[10]

Monopolization, then, is further socialization of production. Rather than scattered forms of production, and thus more individualized forms of production, large-scale industry demands greater socialization of labor. Greater socialization of labor results simultaneously in an increase in the numbers of laborers exploited by capital and in the actualization of the conditions for large-scale organization by these laborers. Thus, under the extended socialization of production brought on by monopolization, the contradiction between wage labor and capital is intensified to a degree never experienced under competitive capitalism. Monopolization is the extension of production to a national scale, and thus the foundation for mass, national strikes which can paralyze an entire nation. Furthermore, the existing means of production are increasingly concentrated in the hands of a small minority of the population.

Simultaneous with the development of monopoly capitalism is the growth of state monopoly capitalism. Thus, an economic aspect of monopoly is the active role of the state as a "capitalist machine ... the ideal aggregate capitalist." The state in the era of monopoly assumes the functions of a corporation, directly investing money and extracting profits. State capitalism is itself a direct consequence of the tendency of the rate of profit to fall. The survival of private capital dictates that large portions of it become state capital. Therein it survives under a more efficient, powerful and centralized structure. It is, therefore, far better able to command vast resources and labor, and to attempt comprehensive central planning to counter persistent periodic crises.

Laissez faire in this study refers to the role and conception of the state which, under competitive capitalism, is different from the role of the state under monopoly capitalism. The *laissez-faire* state, as defined by Marx, was never a neutral institution but was the *political* instrument of the bourgeoisie to be used in their economic interests.[11] The latter aspect defined the role of the state to be part-time partner, regulator, and investor, but always coordinated with projects in the interests of private capital and generally initiated by the latter. Historian Robert A. Lively concluded that the nineteenth-century state in the United States had always played a role in economic affairs.[12] However, he, like numerous historians, conceives of the term *laissez faire* as a strict hands off policy by the state. This is a too rigid definition; one that no classical political economist would propose. Within the tradition of classical political economy, the state was to be used when needed, and throughout the history of European and American capitalism the state has played an important economic role. However, that role is sporadic and inconsistent. The important point is that the state under nonmonopoly capitalism does not *establish* itself as investor, regulator, banker, planner. It does such things only on a small, sporadic and temporary basis.

Under monopoly capitalism, the state enlarges these tendencies and institutionalizes them into codes of permanent political conduct.[13] The federal government becomes economic planner, regulator, investor, banker (as well as social intervenor) on a *permanent* basis. As such, it does not wait for private initiative to enlarge its conduct temporarily (as was the practice under nonmonopoly capitalism), but does so as an established and permanent practice. The supportive role of the state for capitalism becomes strengthened through the obscuring of the lines separating capital from the state. The state becomes a collective capitalist under monopoly capitalism.

Finally, the full economic characterization of monopoly capitalism would be incomplete without acknowledging the predominance of finance capital. Lenin pointed out that in the period of monopoly capitalism industrial capital is merged with banking capital to form finance capital. Monopoly capitalism is "the domination of finance capital" where "ownership of capital is separated from the application of capital to production." Finance capital reigns supreme "over all other forms of capital [and] means the predominance . . . of the financial oligarchy."[14]

Monopoly capitalism, or imperialism, as Lenin also called it, is not merely large-scale production. It is the intervention of monopolistic banking in this large-scale production. Thus, the "top dog" of the capitalists is the financial (who is often also an industrial) magnate. Ultimately, the economy of monopoly capitalism is an economy of centralized credit and centralized large-scale production. Industrial giants often have their own financial institutions; thus, they have actually merged banking with industrial capital. For example, Standard Oil established the Chase-Manhattan Bank. The Rockefeller and Morgan groups are excellent examples of the financial oligarchy described by Lenin. This centralization of economic power is matched by a thorough centralization of political power.

b. Lenin: Politics and Ideology of Monopoly Capitalism

In Marx's analysis of capitalism he characterized the social relations within the factory as despotic. This was not the case with social relations in general outside the factory, which were characterized by anarchy of production and the vagaries of the market. The workplace was marked by an unbending discipline and control. Outside of the factory, the uncontrolled force of the marketplace ruled the life of the individual. Classical liberalism corresponded to this social anarchy and, therefore, "emphasized individual freedom as the ultimate goal of all policy."[15] Aside from religious restraints very little direct domination, besides their relationship to their employer (and to capitalism in general), intervened in the personal lives of workers. However, under monopoly capitalism the emphasis on "individual freedom" is undermined through an extension of despotism—via the state—to society in general. In effect, the state itself becomes a huge factory.

The most important institution responsible for stabilizing the social order under both competitive and monopoly capitalism is the state. However, under monopoly the unparalleled growth of the state bureaucracy insures that almost no phase of human existence escapes some aspect of the public power. No other institution in society, neither the church nor local governments, could dominate so effectively as the centralized state. In a political sense the effective increase in the bureaucratic police power of the state parallels the massive socialization of production. Lenin quoted Engels to point out this characteristic of monopoly capitalism. The public power, argued Engels, grows stronger, however, in proportion as class antagonisms... become more acute.... We have only to look at our present-day Europe, where class struggles and rivalry in conquest have turned up the public power to such a pitch that it threatens to swallow the whole of society.[16]

This inescapable role is manifested in bureaucracies of every conceivable type, which even enter into personal life. The state has no other recourse than to assume a wider authoritarian role (under the guise of "liberalism"), principally because the class contradictions inherent in capitalism grow intensely acute under monopoly capitalism. This political extension of despotism, Lenin concluded, was reactionary and corresponded to the political needs of monopoly capitalism.[17]

This reaction is in contradiction to classical liberal democracy. In the modern epoch a democratic government is not popularly considered to be "of the people, by the people, and for the people" (majority rule), rather it has become a *method* whereby stability and moderation are maintained *through minority rule*. Political domination is steadily extended and deepened so that it parallels the social relations within the factory. Domination—confined to the factory under competitive capitalism—encompasses all aspects of society under monopoly capitalism. Thus, economic concentration is paralleled by concentration of political power and the extension of domination. This concentration betrays the possibility of popular rule and, under the heightened contradiction between wage labor and capital, creates the necessity for the extension of domination.

This aspect of domination and repression was considered by Max Weber as a necessary consequence of capitalist rationality. Marcuse wrote that Weber's "concept of industrial capitalism becomes concrete in the formal theory of rationality and *domination* which are the two fundamental themes of *Wirtschaft und Gesellschaft*."[18] Weber connected the forms of domination to industrialism itself and not to the exigencies of monopoly capitalism. Lenin however concluded that the centralized domination (which Weber perceived) was one aspect, one tendency, peculiar to the existing stage of capitalist development. Weber argued that domination was inescapable, the fate of modern man, and thus he apotheosized the existing social and political relations. As Marcuse observes:

> The specifically Western idea of reason realizes itself in a system of material and intellectual culture (economy, technology, "conduct of life," science, art) that develops to the full in industrial capitalism and this system tends toward a specific type of domination which becomes the fate of the

contemporary period: total bureaucracy.[19]

What led Weber to apotheosize total domination? Why was the toleration of dissent, central in the political thought of classical liberal thinkers, conspicuously absent in the political theory of Weber (as in the works of Lippmann, Croly, Arons, Dahl, Parsons, Kornhauser, Schumpeter, etc.).[20] Marcuse offers an explanation:

> The liberating force of democracy was the chance it gave to effective dissent, on the individual as well as the social scale, its openness to qualitatively different forms of government, of culture, education, work—of human existence in general. The toleration of free discussion and the equal right of opposites was to define and clarify the different forms of dissent: their direction, content, prospect. But with the concentration of economic and political power and the integration of opposites in a society which uses technology as an instrument of domination, effective dissent is blocked where it could freely emerge; in the formation of opinion, in information and communication, in speech and assembly. Under the rule of monopolistic media—themselves the mere instruments of economic and political power—a mentality is created for which right and wrong, true and false are predefined wherever they affect the vital interests of the society.[21]

Fifty years before Marcuse, Lenin had concluded that monopoly capitalism and democracy were incompatible: "The specific political features of imperialism are reaction all along the line." Finance capital cannot survive on an international scale without militarism; nationally, it cannot survive without a rigid bureaucratic order. It demands a social discipline as a condition for its survival. Lenin considered monopoly capitalism the indisputable "negation" of democracy in general and a movement towards reaction. "The politics of monopoly capitalism," he said, "is the change from democracy to political reaction. Democracy corresponds to free competition. Political reaction corresponds to monopoly."[22]

Originally, the slogan "Liberty, Fraternity, Equality" synthesized the interests of the bourgeoisie and peasantry in battle against feudalism. The slogan remained until the working class was politically capable of demanding for themselves "liberty, freedom and equality." In the era of monopoly capitalism, those popular institutions which made it possible for working people to capture local and even state control for their class interests became intolerable. The political reform in the United States during the late nineteenth and twentieth century effectively eroded popular forms of democracy and substituted a highly centralized political system. The model applied to society was that of "business enterprise." Not only centralization, but centralization modeled after the factory. It was top-down management which attempted to be efficient. Indeed, the "efficiency" movement reached into the remotest spheres of ordinary living. "The model of the efficient business enterprise," wrote Samuel P. Hays, " . . . rather than the New England town meeting, provided the positive inspiration for the municipal reform."[23] The theory of liberal democracy was replaced by the pluralist-elitist methods modeled after factory domination. For the apologists of the new liberalism, politics attained stability through charismatic leadership ruling over an amorphous and emotional mass. The progressive Herbert Croly remarked that the U.S. needed a St. Michael or a St. Francis to dominate society. His close friend and colleague, Walter Lippmann, added a corollary: "Political decision is inevitably the concern of comparatively few people."[24] Lippmann emphatically expressed the purpose of state intervention in society in general. We have to deal with society, he warned, "deliberately, devise its social organization, alter its goals, formulate its method, educate and control it . . . we put intention where custom has reigned. We break up routines, make decisions, choose our ends, select means." A measure of the new liberalism was the use of the state to structure the social process, to dominate it, control it, channel it in a direction which minimized the struggle between capital and labor. "Government," remarked the progressive economist John R. Commons, "is the only supreme authority among men. . . . It is the only means whereby refractory . . . elements of society may be brought into line."[25]

c. *A Leninist Interpretation of Progressivism*

Of all the historians of Progressivism, only Gabriel Kolko analyzes the theoretical question of the relationship of the American economy to the politics of Progressivism. Furthermore, his analysis systematically challenges the viability of Marx's as well as Lenin's thesis on the relationship of politics to economics. I shall thus briefly examine Kolko's analysis of the relationship of Progressivism to the American economy. I do this because it contains the theoretical basis for much of the non-Marxist radical historiography of Progressivism, and also because it is important to differentiate clearly Kolko's radical historiography from Marx's and Lenin's analyses.

   Conventional interpretations of American history postulate the uniqueness of American historial development. This position is exemplified in one of the best critical analyses of Progressivism yet published,

Kolko's *Triumph of Conservatism*. An analysis of Kolko's characterization of the relationship between politics and economics is important in order to show his categorical rejection of classical Marxist theory of politics and, especially, his absolute indifference to Lenin's theoretical contributions. Both of these conditions have shaped his and others' theoretical conclusions about Progressivism. Kolko clearly rejects Marxism: "It was [Marx's and Engels'] failure to discuss the potential role of the state and politics in preserving capitalism that is the really fundamental reason why Marxism is not too useful in comprehending recent American history."[26]

This "failure" of Marx is corrected through a comprehensive theoretical synthesis labeled by Kolko "political capitalism." In essence, Kolko argues that politics guides economic development, and thus Progressivism, as a political movement, shaped the economic aspects of modern American capitalism. Kolko thus argues that Progressivism represented the political domination of the economy, i.e., the determination of the economic by the political. Such a phenomenon is not compatible, he argues, with Marx's understanding of the relationship of the state to the economy, in fact just the opposite, for Marx understood politics to be, in general, subordinated to economics. Kolko's conception of "political capitalism" is concretized through demonstrating the power over the state exerted by big capitalists. Corporate leaders politically manipulated the economy for their own welfare. Ultimately, however, Kolko finds the relationship between economics and politics to be a pluralistic relationship. He sees no causal connection between economics and politics; he concludes that, from the welter of freely contending policies, those of the largest capitalists eventually emerged victorious. He therefore argues that the triumph of Progressivism was not from the necessity of capitalism, "but from conscious needs and decisions of specific men and institutions."[27] He continues to state that any number of options were available to political leaders "and in virtually every case they chose those solutions . . . advocated by . . . business and financial interests."[28] He argues that Progressivism was a *voluntaristic policy* chosen by big businessmen and supported by politicians to further their own class interests. Kolko asserts that he can find nothing in Marx to support his conclusion. He is correct in that Marxist theory would never regard politics as independent of economics, nor would it accept that politics could in the long run independently shape economics. Kolko therefore rejects classical Marxism and thus the Marxist conception of the state, including its elaboration by Lenin. Lenin argued that politics is concentrated economics. Kolko, however, argues that economics is concentrated politics.[29] Kolko therefore finds the initiative for Progressivism in politics.

Allowing, then, that Kolko sees no need to base politics upon economics, it is therefore justifiable in his system to attach no importance to the rise of monopoly capitalism as a force in shaping social and political reality. Thus, he states, "It was not the existence of monopoly that caused the federal government to intervene in the economy, *but the lack of it*"[30] (emphasis added). Consequently, that which we may label "monopoly" did not develop naturally from competitive capitalism, but was an effect of a voluntary policy of business to regulate the economy for greater profit-making possibilities.

In comparing Kolko's and Lenin's theoretical approaches, the principal difference rests in their points of departure. Lenin begins with economics and from there proceeds to politics; Kolko begins from politics and moves to economics. Lenin saw monopoly capitalism as the economic consequence of inherent contradictions in capitalism; Kolko sees monopoly capitalism as the economic consequence of voluntarism, a conscious political choice by corporate capitalists. Lenin would have seen Progressivism as the political consequence of the economics of monopoly capitalism. Kolko interprets Progressivism as the political design by the larger capitalists and thus as one political phenomenon of several possibilities independent of the existence of capitalist tendencies. For Kolko it is conceivable that the process of concentration could have been reversed through politics alone. Lenin, however, would argue that only certain choices were open to capitalism, and these choices were inevitably the policies of monopoly capitalism. Therefore, Progressivism, the gigantic alteration of institutions, structures and ideology, was, in general, the encapsulation of the various policy choices open to monopoly capitalism.

According to the Leninist perspective, the Progressive movement was a political and ideological reformation of society, stemming from the development of monopoly capitalism. The political consequences of monopoly capitalism, that is, the intense conflict between capital and labor that threatened the survival of capitalism, was the basis for the fundamental ideological aspect of Progressivism, the striving towards a harmonious, stable, "organic" society. The bitter struggles waged by labor after the Civil War corresponded with the concentration of capital and the immense socialization of labor. Previous to monopoly capitalism, production was scattered and localized. Union struggles were likewise scattered and only locally organized. With the rise of monopoly, concentrated production under national corporations brought on the conditions for national unions and strikes. Such potential power within the hands of the proletariat seriously challenged capital. This condition led such spokesmen for Progressivism as G. Stanley Hall to remark: "labor today, if it fully realizes its power and can organize, has the world on its hip and can radically reconstruct our entire industrial system."[31]

That situation demanded political action and took the form of the conscious need to create an "organic" unified and peaceful society, thereby strengthening (but not changing) the existing social and economic structure. In placing an organic society as the goal, a break with the previous ideological underpinnings and role of the laissez-faire state was mandated. Anarchistic social relations governed by the marketplace gave way to the constant intervention of the state in the social process that was required to steer society away from class conflict. One particularly important group participating in the formulation of state interventionist policy were the academics, especially the social scientists. To the extent that the Progressive movement attempted to resolve the contradiction between classes, it was forced to foster state intervention to dominate and guide social relations. In so doing it was acting in the interests of monopoly capitalism.

Lastly, the general goals of Progressivism—social harmony, economic stability and growth—were the general goals of the state's educational system. The goals of social harmony and economic growth were also central, of course, to the education system during the nineteenth century. However, what had changed radically was the sharp emphasis upon a *particular* ideological construction: the organic theory of society that postulated an identity of interests between capital and labor. The central purpose of Progressivism and Progressive education was the institutionalization of this theory in society.

3. *A Marxist Critique of Educational Historiography*

The several threads, or strands, of educational historiography all revolve about the question of the essence of the educational process. What are the fundamental attributes of the educational system? Its relationship to society? Its principal function in society? These are the central questions which divide the numerous writers into at least three basic camps: the first is the liberal position, arguing in general for the logic of schools as they exist in practical and ideological terms; the second, a radical school of criticism, confronts the liberal thesis, disputes the "well-being" of education and proposes a radical alternative to the existing school system. Radicals, like the liberals, see no necessary connection between production and education. The third is the Marxist analysis which (like the radicals) severely criticizes the existing educational process, but (unlike the radicals) pinpoints the problem in the functioning of a capitalist economy. The latter, therefore, posits the need to eliminate private ownership of the means of production as a principal step in the final solution of the schooling problem. The Marxist writings, however, have not taken into account Lenin's theory of monopoly capitalism. Because of this, Marxist educational historiography has not observed the relationship between Progressive education and monopoly capitalism. Later in this chapter, I shall show how this failure has led to serious errors of analysis on the part of Marxists.

a. **Liberal and Radical Historiography**

The leading school of thought is colored by a liberalism much like that of Arthur Schlesinger and Louis Hartz and is typified by Lawrence Cremin's *The Transformation of the School*.[32] Cremin praises the major changes created in the late nineteenth and early twentieth centuries in the educational system, argues their logic, and ultimately defends the schooling system as beneficial. Cremin's purpose is as much to praise past leaders such as Dewey, Kilpatrick, Thorndike and the changes they wrought as it is to sing the praises of the great American school of the present. Indeed, there is little to differentiate between Cremin's approach and the prevalent theory and practice of American education. Cremin's scholarship cannot be ideologically separated from the tradition which he describes and, to a limited extent, scrutinizes.

The general character of Cremin's work, like the writings of so many of his persuasion,[33] is to accept the educational changes of this century as representing unequivocal progress. Thus for example, Dewey argued against laissez-faire individualism, and Cremin approves; the Industrial Education Association lobbied for manual training in the schools, and Cremin writes approvingly. In the final analysis, Cremin writes a defense, an apologia, for the schooling system. Inevitably, there is a void of criticism in his work: for he came not to criticize, nor even to analyze critically, but to defend—and in this process the most obvious and clear injustices of the educational system do not even move him to a blink.[34] Cremin's work is in essence not that of a critical, objective observer, but of a direct participant and advocate of those transformations which he describes.

Many critics see Cremin's work as the kind of superficial analysis which ignores the most obvious features of the educational process. Colin Greer criticizes Cremin's naive faith in Progressive clichés, the use of liberal blinders when assessing liberalism itself. Cremin, for example, argues that schools are an independent social force and that they have been the great "social aperture" for upward mobility and have therefore created social equality. Greer, in his major work *The Great School Legend*, shows that if this were the case, poverty would have been eliminated long ago. Greer goes further and demonstrates that schools do not resolve social problems nor act as social equalizers, but rather function not only to preserve but also to reinforce inequality. Greer attacks the "in-house" approach epitomized by Cremin that looks rather uncritically at the schooling system. This counter approach, represented well by Greer, looks beneath the veneer of the rhetoric at real problems and constitutes a radical tendency, the second major stream of contemporary writing.

Greer criticizes others besides Cremin; Ellwood Cubberly, Bernard Bailyn, and Oscar Handlin are carefully "raked over." In this, Greer does an excellent job of cataloging and extracting the essence of their historiography. He summarizes their positions well, and rightfully exposes a vein of thought so commonly accepted and repeated that few historians have bothered to scrutinize it carefully to determine if there is any substance to such persistent beliefs. Simple weighing of evidence has disclosed very convincingly that the work of the vast majority of educational historians (and educators) has been part and parcel of a campaign not to discuss truth, but to promote political rhetoric. That Greer found this to be the case comes as no surprise to many of our nation's poor—but this fact only verifies how well the socializers themselves have been socialized; the mythmakers pay homage to the myths of their antecedents.

This revisionist tendency has an extended field through the works of writers such as Raymond Callahan, Clarence Karier, Joel Spring, Ivan Illich, and Michael Katz. The arguments generally state that the problem of schooling is that it is unequal, antidemocratic, and functions in an antihumanitarian and repressive manner. Greer, Karier, and Spring claim that the cause of these problems is found in the dominance within the educational institutions of the liberalism which Cremin praises. Callahan, however, views the matter quite differently; he sees the problem in the *failure* of liberalism to influence the schools.

Callahan's work depicts the schools as dominated by the principles of the Taylor factory efficiency system and by the principle that, rather than the education of children, the saving of the "almighty" dollar is the foremost concern. Thus all those factors which speed up a production-line educational process were incorporated into schooling after 1900. Callahan writes that "educational discussion and writing was saturated by business and industrial technology and analogy."[35]

He pinpoints the essence of the educational tragedy as the inculcation of business values, which superimposed themselves upon the schools and suffocated the possibility for children to learn in a free atmosphere. Callahan claims that the choice was between a humanitarian concern for children and the dollar: "Their [educators'] models were not the thinkers such as the Deweys, the Beards, or the Veblens but the men of action—the Fords and Carnegies."[36]

Educators made the wrong choice out of weakness. Consequently, Callahan writes that "very much of what has happened in American education since 1900 can be explained on the basis of the extreme vulnerability of our schoolmen to public criticism and pressure."[37] This "vulnerability" thesis is used by others also. For example, Spring (and the Marxists, Bowles and Gintis, on particular issues, such as IQ testing) argues that the schools "capitulated" to the pressures of elite groups and of their particular ideological and economic needs.

Karier writes that the "school, as a formal vehicle of education, exists as an instrument of social and economic power of the most influential elite groups as much as for the political and social organizers through which society is managed." Karier claims that "the educational state that emerged in twentieth-century America did so ultimately as an instrument of those economic and political elites who managed the American corporate state."[38] The images of the elitist version of Progressivism are clear in Karier's summation of the roots of education in the United States. Those elites, however, were representatives of "the managerial middle class."[39] Ivan Illich's entire "de-schooling society" thesis similarly argues that schools have been dominated by erroneous ideas of influential groups. In general, the radical tendency, while very critical of the educational system, focuses upon the educational system as an institution dominated by those policies of elites which have ultimately resulted in the practices described.

Thus the methodological infrastructure of the radical historiography is the same pluralism which guides the work of those historians whom these radicals excoriate (i.e., Cremin, Hofstadter, etc.). It is fundamentally their interpretation of the present practices of education which separate them from the liberal Cremin. Within this methodological framework the resolution of the educational problem has several tendencies. Joel Spring, like Ivan Illich, urges that schools become less powerful in their role as a social institution, that education be returned to the people. Accordingly, Spring states, "The only possible solution is ending the power of the school." Raymond Callahan urges that schools become more powerful: "It seems to me that two major interdependent efforts are needed. One is to change the nature and improve the quality of our graduate work in educational administration, the other is to seek ways and means of reducing the extreme vulnerability of our superintendents in the local school districts."[40] However different their resolutions appear, their viewpoints on the nature of the problem remain quite similar. The point here, however, is that the schooling problem (while connected to society) is seen as principally a problem stemming from incorrect educational *policies*. Thus Greer offers the following statement: "Our proper obligation is to make the school work. To do that we have to acknowledge that we have no models, that we are asking the public school to adopt a new role."

Having demonstrated the gap between the rhetoric of the educational system and the reality of undemocratic schooling, Greer is faced with a vexing question: What new role is needed to resolve the problem? I quote at length his general conclusion to demonstrate that Greer, unlike Spring or Illich, still has faith in the power of schools to change the social world:

> Schools could be an agent for major change in this society. . . . Since the goals in the school's rhetoric are anathema to the organization and theory of a puritan capitalist society, would it not be absurd and what might happen if that rhetoric became more than words? What if teachers succeeded in promoting literacy and the capacity for critical thinking. . . ? And what if we created in our classrooms a less formal, more human environment characterized by excitement, respect, and autonomy—by students' participating in the planning and control of learning? Couldn't we expect this more humane environment to reinforce behavioral styles entirely different from the hostile competitiveness presently rewarded and encouraged in the public school classroom? If we could break the harmony that now exists between the schools and society by provoking a change in one of the major ways society fashions itself, might we not be able to contribute to the radical reformation of that society?[41]

Other critics, e.g., Ivan Illich and Michael Katz, write that a policy disestablishing compulsory schooling and, in so doing, particular institutional structures, is fundamental to changing the schooling programs and therefore society. Katz writes:

> The reformulation of educational purposes cannot be accomplished within current educational structures. Bureaucracy . . . is more than a form of organization, it is the crystallization of particular values. . . . School structure communicates particular norms, the learning of those norms has priority over

learning skills. Those norms . . . reflect the purposes of education . . . Any radical reformulation of educational objectives, it follows, requires a radical restructuring of educational forms.[42]

b. Critique of Radical Historiography

Progressivism was, in general, the ideological as well as political reflection of capitalist economy in its monopoly stage. Failure to make this crucial distinction is one which either implicitly or explicitly characterizes the works of all radical historians such as Joel Spring, Clarence Karier and some Marxists like Herbert Gintis and Samuel Bowles. In general, radical critics of education (as well as liberal apologists) either implicitly or explicitly separate the educational system from the mode of production. Following this pluralist method of analysis utilized by the radicals, schools become an independent institution in society capable of being shaped by any interest which can take hold of it. According to this view, changing the educational system means simply changing those in control of it, without regard to the distribution of property or any other factor relating to the mode of production.

This second tendency has a second characteristic, which derives from the more fundamental one just described. It does not posit an inevitable and logical relationship of education (nor of politics) with capitalism. This is evident by a nearly absolute absence of an awareness of the direct and conscious connection between the schools (as an element of the state) and the system of production. This approach intrinsically views the educational process as connected only generally with the society of which it is part. These critics carefully describe very real attributes of the educational system. They fall short, however, in failing to confront the question of capitalism in general and its relationship to the socialization process.

Within my methodological approach, I incorporate several important points stressed by the radicals. Their cutting critique of Progressive education is warranted. Clarence Karier has written several essays which support my contention (developed in chapter 4) that Dewey's philosophy within education was repressive and antidemocratic. Paul Violas' work on Charles Horton Cooley and E.A. Ross is an important study of the oppressive sociology of social control which characterized Progressive social science.[43] From these radicals I have taken these key points and absorbed them within a wholly different causal explanation. On the one hand, I stand with much of the critique of the radicals, but on the other I disagree fundamentally with their analysis as to why such an educational reality came into being as well as with their solutions to educational problems.

The central question is: Can the schools be changed without changing society? Radicals answer yes. Through separating the educational system from the system of production, schools can in their view become independent institutions with a power of their own. If the materialist approach is taken, schools are regarded as part of an interconnected whole, whose general tasks are rooted in the system of production.[44] Radicals as well as liberals in general, however, begin from the opposite and contend that the schools are potentially independent forces and can indeed change society. Politics again are seen as a matter of choice and as determining economics.

c. Marxist Historiography

The above issue becomes the central question in the work of the few writers on education who can be called Marxists, the most visible being the work of Samuel Bowles and Herbert Gintis. Their work posits a direct relationship between schools and the economy, that schools are not dominated by an arbitrary policy which can be changed without changing society. Bowles and Gintis argue that educational policy is guided by the interests of capitalism, which by its political control of the state also controls schools. The program of the school is not the result of bad policy, elites, nor of bad structures and processes within schools, but rather of the political and labor needs of capitalism. If one wishes to change the schools permanently, one must seek solutions in a revolutionary overhaul of the entire society beginning with the economic and political institutions. Marxist critics look beyond the school itself, or the values and policy of educators; they unequivocally argue that the system of production, or capitalism, is, in the final analysis, the basis for the content of school programs. Bowles and Gintis correctly write: "The roots of repression and inequality lie in the structure and functioning of the capitalist economy."[46] I am in agreement with their general characterization of the schools as ideological and skill-training centers corresponding to the capitalist economy. In arguing this, Bowles and Gintis have capped a long history of educational criticism.

However, even though Bowles and Gintis are arguing that capitalism is the basis for the practice of schooling, there are a few strands of questionable analysis that course through their work. For example, they write that the Progressive education which Greer, Spring, and Karier excoriate was not really the essential educational Progressivism put into practice. They claim that Progressive education was never given a chance: "A historian of Progressivism in education might well echo Gandhi's assessment of Western Civilization: 'It would be a good idea.'"[46] Bowles and Gintis (like the non-Marxist Callahan) argue that the "real" Progressivism of, for example, Dewey (whom Spring places alongside the reactionary Bagley) was never adopted nor put into practice. I shall argue in chapter 4 that Dewey, as several non-Marxist radical historians demonstrate, was a Progressive and fell squarely into the main current of educational theory and practice.

Whereas the other radicals do not fully acknowledge production, the Bowles and Gintis thesis, as outlined in their articles, as well as their book on education in the United States,[47] reveals that they make no clear and systematic distinction between monopoly and nonmonopoly stages in the economy. They therefore see no clear and distinct relationship between Progressive education and monopoly in the mode of production. By not carefully recognizing the social effects of monopoly production, Bowles and Gintis fail to discern fully the relationship between monopoly capitalism and Progressive education. For example, they attribute to Dewey undeserved recognition for allegedly pursuing a "democratic and open education"[48] and therefore write: "Dewey's overall framework seems eminently correct."[49] They have completely missed the essence of Progressive thought in education, because they do not confront the relationship between Progressivism and monopoly. They are, consequently, led to state that, whereas Dewey's "framework" was "correct," his error was the typical error of liberals, i.e., having a firm belief in the power of individuals to better themselves. They write: "Dewey's error lies in characterizing the social system as democratic."[50] This "error" was simply the ideology of Progressivism. Dewey was thoroughly enmeshed in developing an implicitly and essentially undemocratic education which emphasized a form of individualism corresponding to monopoly production.

Whatever error he may have committed, Dewey was "eminently correct" in his overall theory of education for the sake of monopoly production. By not making this recognition, Bowles and Gintis, much like the non-Marxists Joel Spring and Raymond Callahan, can summarize Progressivism in this manner:

> The history of twentieth-century education is the history not of Progressivism but of the imposition upon the schools of "business values." . . . The evolution of U.S. education was not guided by the sanguine statements of John Dewey and Jane Addams . . . rather by the time-motion orientation of Frederick Taylor.[51]

In comparing the two critical approaches, we see some clear differences. On the one hand, the radicals excoriate Progressive education in general and Dewey in particular. However, they make no connections between Progressivism and the capitalist economy. On the other hand, the Marxists link capitalism with education, but do not link Progressivism with the economy or with education. *These contradictions suggest the need, not to synthesize the two positions, but to apply a methodology which neither has utilized.* In so doing I hope to contribute to the resolution of this contradictory understanding of Progressive education.

4. Summary and Overview

I have begun this analysis with an overview of Marxist methodology and of its interpretation of Progressivism. In the following chapters, I hope to demonstrate the relationships between the mode of production and educational theory. In chapter 2, I examine the educational thought of key theoreticians of the bourgeoisie in the late seventeenth and eighteenth centuries: Locke, Rousseau, and Smith. My purpose in this historical departure is to link several major ideas on education with the historical development of capitalism. Although my main focus in the study is the Progressive period, I hope to clarify the historical origins of the core of Progressive education. While monopoly capitalism definitely affected the educational institutions and ideology of capitalism, it did not alter the class essence of the educational theories of these early thinkers. My approach, then, while principally concerned with the changes effected during the Progressive era, will also show the continuity of educational theory under capitalism.

In the third and fourth chapters, I examine the connection between the intense class conflict and the emphasis on the organic unity of the division of labor. I analyze the thought of Josiah Strong, E.A. Ross, Jacob Riis, John Dewey, and William James with parallels drawn between them and John R. Commons, Theodore Roosevelt, and Charles H. Cooley. The thread which links these well-known Progressives was their adherence to the need to establish a harmonious relationship between capital and labor. This emphasis, I argue, finds its source in the class contradictions within a society dominated by monopoly capitalism.

In the fifth chapter, I analyze the rise of the concept of "intelligence," and its importance in the development of intelligence testing. My purpose here is to clarify the link between this major twentieth-century ideological tool within the classroom and the division of labor under monopoly capitalism.

In the sixth chapter, I show the relationship between the development of the forces of production under monopoly capitalism and mass compulsory education. In essence, Progressive education came forward partly in response to the increasing unemployment among young adults. Technological changes demanded fewer laborers per productive unit, making necessary the expansion of education to encompass more children and youth. Mass compulsory eduction, I argue, was a consequence not of Progressive reformism, but of the drive for technological advantage characteristic of capitalist competitiveness in the drive for higher profits.

In conclusion, I hope to present a general sketch of an alternative view of Progressivism and, in particular, of Progressive education. I have followed the conclusion with a case study of the application of Progressive education to the Chicano national minority in Los Angeles, 1900-1930. I include this essay in order to demonstrate the practical application of Progressivism, and also to show the roots of much of the discontent which manifested itself in the Chicano movement of the 1960s and 1970s.

Chapter Two

THE ROOTS OF PROGRESSIVE EDUCATION: EDUCATIONAL THEORY AND THE RISE OF THE BOURGEOISIE

Schools are forces of status quo rather than change: social and economic changes create educational change; and schools are not, as many have thought, independent social forces which can determine the social order. Rather, schools are instruments, at once political and social, created for the survival of the social order. Seen in this perspective, the word "education" takes on a new meaning. Rather than denoting a democratic ideal that education serves universal human goals, or that it serves as a ladder for upward mobility independent of external economic considerations, the capitalist social order has been protected and supported by free popular education. In this context the schools were molded by the needs of a capitalist society.

The social and political order and its fundamental basis, the economic organization, affect the purpose and goals of all formal education—public and private, elementary, secondary and higher. The structure, content, philosophy and goals of education are subtly but quite openly maneuvered into focus with the basic means of society's survival: the economic organization and its ensuing political and social structure. Basic institutions in society should be in accord with one another. If public schools in particular and education in general functioned independently of the "social order," the conflict would be incredible and the results would be institutional anarchism.

Schools are not to be exclusively blamed either for "permissiveness," as conservative critics argue, or for failing to educate minority groups, or for alienating youth, as liberals and radicals often postulate. If the schools have failed, then blame should fall upon the cause and not the effect. The perennial crisis in education is really a crisis emanating from the social order. Democratic reformers in education must always be cognizant of the fundamental relationship between school and society. Nothing could be more absurd or potentially chaotic than to expect a secondary public institution to become the vanguard of a far-reaching social change. Such idealism emerges without foundation, destined surely to be thrown easily aside, or recast into an ugly cynicism.

What has been the foundation of modern mass public education in the United States? What social theories have guided its purposes?

Education, as we know it today in the United States, as well as historically, is a specialized form of socialization that takes its essential content from the prevailing social context. Its principal objective is the political socialization of individuals, or groups, within a specific society. It is one means, employed either by the state (as under monopoly capitalism) or as in John Locke's time (under preindustrial capitalism) by a particular class, which at its base reflects the social distribution of property and the dominant ideas toward property. The relative social development of the concept of property has had a very important, if not the most important, role in the socialization processes of all societies. Private property was a pivotal aspect of the developing bourgeoisie, and the unfettered individual right to private property lay at the basis of its political theories of the state. From these theories were derived its theories of socialization.

1. The Educational Thought of Locke, Rousseau, and Smith

I examine the theories of education of John Locke, Jean Jacques Rousseau, and Adam Smith principally to plot the relationship between their educational ideas and their views on property. We shall see that the foundation for their educational ideas was provided by the bourgeois notion of private property and by the existing social distribution of private property. In the classical liberal tradition, these writers sanctioned the right of individuals to appropriate to themselves instruments of production, that is, tools, land, machines, means of transportation, and so on. In short, they sanctioned the private appropriation of the means of society's production. Thus, they argued that property (and not merely personal belongings, such as clothing, shelter, individual mode of transport, etc.), being a natural right arising from the industry and labor of some, was to be sanctioned by law and protected by the state.

Because the right of private property was the fundamental right around which social communities organized themselves into governed societies, it followed that this right was to be protected and insured from generation to generation. Education in all its evolving forms was *one* means through which the right of private property and of the social relations emanating from the distribution and use of property in production was to be insured. It is essential to bear in mind that these political theorists regarded education as secondary to property; in other words, their educational theories flowed consequently from their theories of property. Never did they consider education as the principal foundation upon which the political and economic organization of society evolved. Education was one politically conscious activity composed of two aspects. The first was the development of general goals, or practical ends, of education. The second, encapsulated in the first, was the methods through which the ends were attained. Both reflect the political content of education, for the first, the end, was directly related to the second, the means. The ends were the political and economic ideals of the bourgeoisie; the means were the best possible methods through which these ideals were reached. We shall see how the bourgeois ideal of the individual was mirrored in the "child-centered" emphasis in the educational method of Locke and Rousseau.[1]

a. John Locke

Locke formulated two sets of ideas toward education. The first, in its emphasis upon formal education and learning, was innovative in comparison to feudal ideas of education and radical in its methods. This set was intended as the model for education for a man of property, a gentleman. The second, hardly radical although somewhat innovative, was intended for the education of the children of the poor and unemployed. Locke thus proposed two kinds of education: one for the nonpropertied poor socioeconomic classes of society; the other for the bourgeoisie. Locke developed at some length the methods and goals of education for the bourgeoisie in a letter addressed to a friend and later published in the late seventeenth century under the title *On Education*; here we have his full expression on education for the bourgeoisie. As to the lower class, we have but one piece of legislation, authored by Locke in 1697, which intended to control, if not resolve, the growing problem of pauperism in England. When we juxtapose the two sets, the fundamental differences in Locke's approach to education for the two classes appear and one sees the purposes education was to serve in the society of the bourgeoisie. Locke, in his principal writing on education, was concerned with a relatively small class of English society, the landed gentry. His educational writings reflected both the old traditional views on pedagogy as well as the modern and innovative. For example, Locke still claimed that dancing was an entirely proper skill for a man of proper breeding, but he also posed the necessity of learning reading and arithmetical calculation for the efficient management of an estate. Locke wove into the fading feudal formality of the nobility the sense of the practical, the useful, in the everyday life of a new class of entrepreneurs. Thus while Locke felt that Latin was necessary for proper refinement, it was to be learned only when of practical use. If one could express his ideas more fully in English, then, of course they should be expressed in English.

Locke also represented a break with the feudal ideas of truth learned scholastically. For Locke, natural laws were to be studied and new laws deduced. Astronomy, geography, and science (natural philosophy) were to be incorporated into the general education of the man of property. He also was a strong believer in religious toleration but believed fervently in Christianity. The important emphases which Locke brought to education were the need to learn practical, useful ideas and skills and the importance of the individual in learning. That the extreme formality of the feudal nobility and the sense of permanent social distinctions (i.e., fixed classes) had lost their hold among the bourgeoisie is reflected in Locke's emphasis upon individual labor as the foundation for the acquisition of property.

The individualism promulgated by the bourgeoisie was an ideological support for the acquired individual ownership of land. Under a feudal economy (and subsequent ideology) land was the principal instrument of production, and ownership was generally communal, with peasants having usufruct rights to plots of land and obligations to the lord, who held title subject to the discretion of the king. Villages were often granted large areas of land and peasants worked allotted plots, regulated by a communal custom and tradition and by homage to the lord. Pasture land was for the free use of the entire village, and no one had the right to appropriate either land held communally (as in pasture land called the commons) or given in usufruct. Use of land was based generally upon inheritance, and therefore birth determined for life whether one was a peasant or noble. Under such strict social bonds a sense of individualism (as we know it today) was nonexistent.

The bourgeoisie were in opposition to feudalism because they began, slowly at first, to appropriate to themselves instruments of production, such as land, and by degrees broke the governing principles of feudal land ownership. Consequently, what was once more or less communal became individual; the old ideology of fixed classes through inheritance of the communal use of land was abandoned. Individualism was the ideology that conformed to the new forms of land ownership gradually evolving out of the ruins of the natural feudal economy.*

The bourgeoisie in the cities, like their counterparts in the countryside, attacked feudalism, broke the age-old customs of the monopolistic guilds, and began to carry out production of commodities for their private benefit rather than be bound by the craft guilds, which were oriented toward cooperation. Guild rules strictly established the number of apprentices to be trained, the number of masters in a trade, and the price of the product. In this way, guilds regulated production. Under guild conditions of production, the consciousness of the producers was steered away from individualism and held in check by the self-interest of the guild itself. The bourgeoisie, some of whom were former guild members themselves, other merchants, combated the feudal craft guilds in order to establish the right to carry out production unhindered by guild regulations. Once the privilege of the guild to regulate production was broken, each producer could produce and market commodities at will. The individualism of the bourgeoisie corresponded to the independent use of private instruments of production (a use acquired in the demise of feudalism and in the rise of capitalism). In that independent use of property, wage labor gradually became a commonly used basis for production.[2]

The theorists of the bourgeoisie in their assault against feudalism waged a constant struggle against feudal ideology. Locke, like his predecessors Comenius and Montaigne, based his theories of the state and of education upon these new forms of production. Bourgeois production and new social relations in the form of wage labor and employer (rather than lord and peasant) were the bases for a corresponding bourgeois ideology. That ideology of liberalism argued for the individual's right to private property based upon the varying individual capacities for industriousness.

The educational theories which accompanied the rise of the bourgeoisie were meant to lend support to its interests. Locke's sense of bourgeois individualism was inseparably a cornerstone of his educational thought. The emerging of the individual as a distinct human being, with unique characteristics, was definitely the foundation of Locke's child-centered theories of education. Locke was not interested in forcing the child into a mold, but in taking the strengths of the child and building upon them. A teacher, he said, "should well study their

* Natural because under such an economy people generally consumed what they produced. What surplus existed was generally exchanged for products produced locally.

natures and aptitudes . . . observe what their native stock is, how it may be improved, and what it is fit for."[3] Thus, in the process of focusing upon individual strengths and weaknesses, "one's natural genius should be carried as far as it could" without "putting another upon him."[4] In Locke's principal work on education the stress is upon the learner: how best to fit the learner to a set of objectives. Yet the learner, like the teacher, lives in a social context which sets the relationships of ends and means. Therefore, political liberalism "ought to be encouraged"; the social rights inherent in nature are to be developed. The concept of private property became crucial at this point. The basic law of society, according to Locke, was the natural law of property:

> Though the earth and all inferior creatures be common to all men, yet every man has a "property" in his own "person." This nobody has any right to but himself. The "labor" of his body and the "work" of his hands, we may say, are properly his. Whatsoever, then he removes out of the state Nature hath provided and left in, he hath mixed his labor with it, and joined to it something that is his own, and thereby makes it his property. . . . The same law of Nature that does by this means give us property, does also bound that property too. . . . But the chief matter of property being now not the fruits of the earth and the beasts that subsist on it, but the earth itself, as that which takes in and carries with it all the rest, I think it is plain that property in that too is acquired as the former. As much land as a man tills . . . and can use the product of, so much is his property. He by his labor does, as it were, enclose it from the common.[5]

The correct comprehension of property, i.e., in its natural existence subject to natural laws, was the content to which the child-centered approach conformed. "Children cannot well comprehend what injustice is, till they understand property, and how particular persons come by it."[6] The teacher must bridge the gap between words and action, and experience, being an important tool, should be brought into use as part of the teacher's methods. Thus, "they may be at first taught not to take or keep anything but what is given them by those whom they take to have a power over it; and as their capacities enlarge, other rules and cases of justice, and rights concerning 'meum' and 'tuum' may be proposed and inculcated."[7] Until the son reached the "capacity of knowing that law"[8] his father or guardian was to guide him and "understand for him." Upon understanding that law, the son, like the father, shall be free.[9]

Locke had already made it clear in his political writing that it was the responsibility of parents to inculcate in their children proper conceptions concerning property, but that it was the state which defended the natural rights of property holders. Thus Locke did not grant the state the right, or the responsibility, to educate the children of the bourgeoisie; he placed that responsibility upon the parents. It was the responsibility of bourgeois parents to socialize their children privately to the proper ideas of the bourgeois state and society. Thus, the ideological conditioning privately done by parents was in correspondence with the function of the state's executive, legislative, and judicial system.

The dawn of the age of capitalism was not by any means pleasant. Mass pauperism made its appearance simultaneously with the country gentleman, yeoman farmer, and city manufacturers, i.e., with private property in land and tools for commodity production. This historical legacy of the capitalist system to this day has not been solved by capitalism, even though it has attracted the attention of serious thinkers through the decades. Locke was not the first, and definitely not the last, statesman to devote a dedicated attention to the problem of the poor. His reflection, understanding and conclusions vis-a-vis the problems of pauperism are edifying for our understanding of his thoughts on education. While commissioner of the London Board of Trade, Locke authored a poor-law reform bill. In it, he expressed his ideas on the causes of poverty and the method for its eradication. In his theory of property, it was labor which gave rise to private wealth; his explanation for those who lacked private property was that idleness caused their poverty: "virtue and industry being as constant companions on the one side as vice and idleness are on the other."[10] The division, then, between the poor and nonpoor was their personal virtues. Lack of the desire to work caused poverty, except for those who absolutely could not work for reasons other than "personal vice." Locke was somewhat flexible and classed the poor into nonworthy and worthy. First, there were those "who pretend they cannot get work and so live by begging or worse," or "drones"; second, were those who could work and were "able to do something."[11] For the first, Locke felt that existent laws only needed enforcement. For the second, he proposed employment for those over 14 years of age, and work schools for children of the poor between the ages of 3 and 14. His revulsion at the poor is reflected in his proposals for eliminating poverty: "If any boy or girl, under fourteen years of age . . . be found begging out of the parish where they dwell . . . they shall be sent to the next working school, there to be soundly whipped and kept at work till evening."[12] If any "poor man" refused to work "he shall be sent to the next port" and forced to work at sea for three years. To Locke the solution to the problem of relief consisted "in finding work for them." For those under fourteen this consisted of a special obligatory work-school. The placing of children in work-schools was to give more "liberty to work" for the mother and would insure extra income for the family; at the same time, "the children will be kept in much better order . . . and from infancy inured to work . . . of no small consequence to the making of them sober and industrious all their lives after."[13]

In his famous pedagogical work, *On Education*, Locke urged that corporal punishment be spared and that gentle coaxing, "motivation" in the modern sense, be the mode of learning. This, of course, was the mode of education for the bourgeoisie. The poor deserved no such luxury. Boys were to be apprenticed out, if possible. The schools themselves were really profit-making enterprises "for spinning or knitting, or some other part of woolen manufacture, unless in [districts] where the place shall furnish . . . other materials fitter for the employment of such poor children."[14] Another advantage of the obligatory work-schools was their means of inculcating "religion and morality" (as well as the desire to work) into the minds of young children.

Schools for the poor were primarily means of employing them in enterprises at lower than prevailing wages. The purely mental or ideological aspect of these schools was their emphasis upon religion, morality and industriousness. These were the qualities within the working class most appreciated by an employer as well as the state. However, the basics of their education related fundamentally to their role in production. These early work-schools were really semipublic capitalist enterprises dedicated to employing a segment of the poor populations of the nation and of indoctrinating them in the teachings of bourgeois ideology. The logic behind the solution, that the poor were easily categorized into the worthy and nonworthy, did not alter the methods by which the state was to discharge its philanthropic duties. The alternatives for the poor would either be voluntary work, forced work, or charity. This "logic" has to this day survived the vicissitudes of time.

Education for the landed gentleman was intended to develop a sense of individual property rights. How did these rights apply to the poorest of society? No property belonged to them, so no practical value was served by their learning the rights of property. Their individuality appeared to be submerged in the misery of poverty. Yet, while they were not property owners, they were taught that their poverty was of their own doing. Thus, their individuality was derived from being nonproperty owners. Poverty, according to the bourgeoisie, was individual in nature and the bourgeoisie through the state apparatus inculcated strong doses of individualism in the working class.

Individualism, the ideological linchpin of private appropriation of capitalist property, was stressed among the bourgeoisie in a formal and direct way through a child-centered education. For the masses of poor, the poor laws and the work-schools only emphasized over and over that poverty was not social in nature but simply an effect of differing individual levels of industriousness. Thus, the political theories derived from the bourgeoisie in practice placed unequal emphasis upon the mental aspects of education. For the poor, education was best served through a work-school or simply in finding employment. Furthermore, in stressing an individualistic causation of wealth and poverty among the entire people, the tendency would weigh towards the acceptance and continuation of the social order dominated by the bourgeosie. This is how the bourgeoisie, out of self-interest, were to have it.

b. Jean Jacques Rousseau

Rousseau stated that "God makes all things good; man meddles with them and they become evil." The solution was for men to correlate education with the natural qualities of human beings.[15] Thus, the problem emanating from an erroneous approach to the unversal nature of the individual was to be resolved through the natural approach to children and their education. Each child came into the world with a set of natural tendencies, which education should develop rather than stifle. The object of education was to develop the natural man, and by so doing to create the basis for a harmonious society.

The fundamental tenets of the bourgeoisie were the individual's natural right to property and that the principal building block of society was the individual. Throughout Rousseau's major work on education, *Emile*, he stressed the individuality of the natural man. "The natural man lives for himself, he is the unit, the whole, dependent only on himself." Unfortunately, "good social institutions" make man "unnatural," forcing him to "exchange his independence for dependence."[16] The object of education was to develop a consciousness of individualism, and by so doing, to create social institutions in accord with the natural capacities of human beings.

The object of education was to develop wholly those natural tendencies which were in accord with the political and economic theories of the bourgeoisie. The first idea the child must learn is that of property, and this for Rousseau was the development of the natural, universal qualities inherent in each human being. "Therefore, the first idea he needs is not that of liberty but of property, and that he may get this idea he must have something of his own." Following the theory elaborated by Locke in his *Two Treatises* that from the individual's labor flows the right to appropriate the fruits of that labor, Rousseau propsed that the child plant a garden, the products of which belonged to him. "To explain what this word 'belong' means, I show him he has given his time, his labour, and his trouble; his very self to it, that in the ground there is part of himself which he can claim against all the world."[17] Thus the products of his labor, and that of no one else, are privately and therefore naturally appropriated.

The basis of society's continued production rested upon the correct grasp of the rights of property, and society itself rested upon the interworking among the branches of production, or arts:

> The solidarity of the arts consists in the exchange of industry, that of commerce in the exchange of commodities, that of banks in the exchange of money or securities. All these ideas hang together, and their foundation has already been laid in early childhood with the help of the garden. All we have to do is to substitute general ideas for the particular, and to enlarge these ideas . . . so as to make the child understand the game of business.[18]

Later, in the nineteenth century, the conception of the "solidarity of the arts" would evolve under the extreme pressure of an organized labor struggle into the "society as an organism" analogy. The roots of the organism theory had its precursor in the bourgeois conception of production and exchange. Adam Smith expressed the solidarity theme in a somewhat different form. The "invisible hand of God," which naturally regulated a capitalist economy, operated when certain conditions were present, namely, free trade. It is important to keep in mind the emphasis the bourgeoisie placed upon mutual exchange and order within society. The guiding star became, in the role of education, the need to consolidate, organize, and fortify bourgeois society. Methods were, therefore, reflective of the ends.

Rousseau consequently stressed personal experience as the best basis for learning, and the experience of growing a garden and appropriating its products as the best means of inculcating the conception of private property. Notions of private property then become the foundations for the future solidarity of production and exchange. It should be recognized that Rousseau, like Locke, presented his fully developed ideas on education as a means of educating the sons of the bourgeoisie, not those of the peasantry or wage laborers. He advised "child-centered" ideas of education, of sense verification, of personal experience and interaction with the environment. These, however, were but means and ends based upon bourgeois notions of individualism and private property. The bourgeois concept of society as a unit of production and exchange of commodities was the foundation for the education Rousseau proposed. "There can be no society without exchange, no exchange without a common standard of measurement," and these depended upon the natural equality stemming from everyone's right to acquire property. "A child's political knowledge," stated Rousseau, "should be clear and restricted: he should know nothing of government in general beyond what concerns the rights of property."[19]

The formal aspects of learning, that is, the emphasis upon the child, environment, etc., were entirely dependent upon the economic and political foundations of bourgeois society. Without these foundations, child-centered ends had no real content, but became merely incongruous techniques. Education, being social, was for Rousseau, as for Locke, an instrument for the development of bourgeois society. It was an entirely practical application of their political and economic theories. Child-centered techniques and ends stemmed logically from their political doctrines of individualism and private property. The development of each individual bourgeois child to his or her capacity was the fulfillment of the political theories of the bourgeoisie, which in turn reflected the economic doctrine of production for exchange and the social right to private property in production and exchange.

c. *Adam Smith*

The industrial revolution made its appearance first in England in the late eighteenth century. Smith was the first bourgeois economist whose writings developed within a context of developing industrial capitalism. *The Wealth of Nations* was published at a time when the bourgeoisie had gained power, in contrast to the writings of Locke, which appeared when the sway of the bourgeoisie was in its infancy, and those of Rousseau, who wrote in the interests of a class which had not yet gained state power. Consequently, Smith does not direct his educational ideas toward the emerging bourgeoisie, but towards society dominated by capitalist production and bourgeois ideas.

By the middle of the eighteenth century, capitalism in England had created a sizeable working class, as well as a sizeable class of unemployed. In the wake of the demise of feudalism peasants, thrown off the land by the country gentleman farmers, found their way to the cities; these either found employment in the manufacturing establishments or begged. Large populations in the cities lived in dire poverty. In contrast to the optimism of Rousseau for mutual production and exchange, the right of private property in production became the right of a minority under industrial capitalism. Legislative measures such as Locke's poor law had not proved effective in remedying poverty, although they served socially to control the poor. Smith wrote in a period when the problem of poverty was clearly evident and growing.

He was also writing at a time when the class of employed wage laborers was reaching large proportions. Consequently, Smith wrote during a period when class conflicts were daily becoming clearer and sharper. The direction of his educational ideas was aimed at consolidating bourgeois society and indirectly, rather than directly, at advancing the interests of the rising bourgeoisie. By 1763, the year *Wealth of Nations* was published, the bourgeoisie was in firm control. How to conserve that control, given the state of society, became the function of Smith's educational ideas.

The upper classes deserved to be the "well-instructed," but Smith felt that the "common people," i.e., the working people, deserved "the most essential parts of education ... to read, write, and account ... even for those who are bred to the lowest occupation." Semipublic instruction within each parish could bring rudimentary learning within the reach of each individual before entering permanent employment. Smith felt that the state should impose upon every citizen compulsory forms of education, not only to facilitate the performance of an occupation but also to maintain a "martial spirit."[20]

The "security of every society depended more or less upon the martial spirit of the great body of people." Rather than having a standing army to ensure social order, a "martial spirit" could very well achieve the same ends. Through the instruction of the "inferior ranks of people . . . the state . . . derives no inconsiderable advantage. . . . The more they are instructed, the less liable they are to the delusions of enthusiasm and superstition, which, among ignorant nations, frequently occasions the most dreadful disorders. An instructed and intelligent people, besides, are always more decent and orderly than an ignorant and stupid one." Furthermore, the more the lower classes are instructed, the more "their lawful superiors will respect them," and, conversely the more the inferior will respect the superior. Education would, consequently, bring about a mutual admiration and a resultant cohesion between the social classes in society. Moreover, educated lower classes are "more capable of seeing through the interested complaints of faction and sedition . . . less apt to be misled into any wanton or unnecessary opposition to the measures of government." Smith continued:

> In free countries, where the safety of government depends very much upon the favorable judgement which people may form of its conduct, it must surely be of the highest importance that they should not be disposed to judge rashly or capriciously concerning it.[21]

Smith then viewed education from at least two points. First, education is not to be given equally to each member of society: "The common people cannot, in any civilized society to be so well instructed as people of some rank and fortune."[22] Secondly, his idea of education for the lower classes was not to alter the social and economic character of the society, but was to reinforce it. While it would bring the masses a higher cultural level, its purpose was derived from the concrete social and economic problems of an early phase of industrial capitalism. Locke and Rousseau, in general, felt no inclination to educate the "lower orders" (except through work-schools); their principal concern centered about the private education of the bourgeoisie itself.

Smith, however, was faced with the problem wrought by capitalist production and exchange: the emerging proletariat and the unemployed in the cities. His solution coincided with the bourgeoisie's expectations of the state, the protection of property. Smith directed education towards the forming of correct values for the masses as a means of creating social order. Thus, the political function of education was preservation of the existing social and economic system and forms the essence of his educational proposals. Through socializing the working classes in a broader and more academic way, the practical interests of the bourgeoisie were therefore to be enhanced.

2. *Ideology and Social Relations of Production*

The legacy of bourgeois educational theory has remained quite active to the present. It has done so only because the foundation of bourgeois society then, as now, continues to be private ownership of the means of society's production. I will argue that the critical ideas on education put forward by the three theorists discussed are in the main very much the essence of education in capitalist societies today. I also wish to point out that their theories were, at some time or another, principal elements of the domestic policy of bourgeois nations, and that this policy was not a product merely of their individual minds, but also of the concrete conditions of society. These concrete material conditions consisted of the social distribution and use of productive instruments, or property.

The only logical educational policies, given the material conditions, which included the existence of classes composed mainly of capitalists and free wage laborers, were those outlined in this chapter. Briefly, these were: 1) an education that emphasized individualism, a consequence of private property; 2) an education that reflected the social distribution of property, resulting in a qualitatively different education for the bourgeoisie, which emphasized intellectual and mental tasks and used child-centered techniques; for the poor and working class, the emphases were on the physical, nonmental aspects of learning;

3) education was a means of creating order in the society through a political socialization of the working class in the interests of capitalist production; 4) education was a means of protecting and insuring the uninterrupted development of bourgeois society through training the nonpropertied classes as far as necessary in skills relating to productive processes.

In the economic and social development of the United States, the above four points are integral to the operation of the educational system. The general theoretical foundations were provided by the classical bourgeois political economists. The specific adoptions and further elaborations, culminating in mass, free, and compulsory education, were grafted on during the late nineteenth century, and are linked intimately to the monopolistic stage of capitalism. The major ideas of bourgeois education form the foundation of Progressive reform of education and cannot be separated from its further elaboration, because the reality of private ownership of the means of production continued to be the cornerstone of capitalism.

We turn now to the development of Progressivism and to its links to Progressive education.

Chapter Three
MONOPOLY CAPITALISM AND PROGRESSIVE REFORMISM

1. *The Evolution of Capitalism and Nineteenth-Century Educational Reform*

Public education has been radically altered by the historical development of capitalism. Its development in the United States has been structured by needs emanating from the economic organization, with changes in the latter reverberating to affect and shape the schooling enterprise. When capitalism in the United States continued its evolution and began to break up an agrarian-commercial economy and to create the era of industrial capitalism, and then monopoly capitalism, the internal structure of society also underwent substantial changes. At the roots of this revolution were changes in the methods of production. The economic base of society moved from one of small independent manufacturers, from a commercial trading society based largely on independent farming enterprises to a society organized upon highly mechanized monopolistic mass production necessitating a huge urban proletariat. The change from a rural, primarily agrarian society to an urban-industrial capitalist society can be truly described as radical. Culture, family structure, distribution of property, class divisions, demographic distribution, and system of education underwent profound alterations. The pattern of life characteristic of the old agrarian past was suddenly jolted, dismantled, and in its wake a "reformed" society was created with a new institutional organization and ideological core to provide for the successful operation of the monopoly-capitalist order.

When we consider the changes which occurred as the result of the transition from agrarian-commercial capitalism to industrial capitalism alone, a number of repercussions become evident. Urbanization became increasingly characteristic of the new society. The industrial capitalist society could no longer base itself upon the social or political structures of the past. Rural agrarian society had vastly different demands and its own unique institutions, which served to support that particular form of society. No extensive bureaucracy was necessary, no techniques of mass education, no professional organizations, no cult of efficiency. These did not exist, because they were not necessary for the successful and smooth operation of a commercial, agrarian social order.

Once, however, the industrial laissez-faire era began, the nascent reform movement was shaping itself into what was later to be a major force in American history. Unmistakable, although faint, images of Progressive theories of social reform were evident in 1850, and they were formed in direct relationship to changes in the methods of production, that is, to industrial capitalism. Much in the tradition of classical bourgeois political theorists, the promoters of early school reform agreed that schools were to create the correct social basis for continued capitalist progress and improved social harmony. For example, Horace Mann of Massachusetts, the pioneer advocate of free and universal public education, was really a spokesman for social reform through education so that schools would be "the means of instilling in the population the qualities necessary for success in industrial society."[1] The substance of the ideas on school reform generated by contemporaries of Mann were quite similar to the ideas adhered to by the many social reformers of the late nineteenth century. Whether the reforms were in the area of education or welfare, the general motives were in essence identical. The early educational reforms of Massachusetts demonstrate the thread linking the larger picture of nineteenth-century reform with its roots in the rise of capitalism itself. Economic changes, as they matured, also matured perspectives toward society and its reform.

Mann can only be understood through the context in which he lived. First, Massachusetts was undergoing rapid industrialization and some towns were mushrooming overnight. Lawrence, Massachusetts, for example, became an industrial city in two decades. "In 1846 Lawrence was a strip of land beside the Merrimac River; by 1865 Lawrence was a booming factory town."[2] Not merely the tremendous growth, but the class tensions and antagonisms inherent within industrial capitalism, became threats to social stability. For the first time in the history of Lawrence, a strike occurred in 1860, organized by former independent tradesmen and unskilled factory operators lumped together through the mechanized factory system. In New England and the Middle-Atlantic states similar conditions were being created where industry had settled and urbanization, urban problems, and class warfare emerged.

Secondly, immigration began to affect the crisis of the class struggles in the city, and another element—ethnic and religious rivalry—was injected into class antagonisms. In Massachusetts in the 1860s, the Irish became the object of epithets, for not only were the Irish "foreign," they were also the poorest, living in slums, and working in occupations with the lowest social valuation. The social differentiation molded by the factory system became closely related to ethnic differentiation within society.

Thirdly, the total character of urban secular life appeared to school reformers to lack the proper refinements that were to them a part of an idealized past. The potential of the "mob" now seemed all too present in the proletarian quarters, and the reformers perceived the working class to be a cancer upon society that necessitated adequate control lest it destroy civilization.[3]

The breakdown of the old agrarian economy and the development of industrial urban cities created a number of critical social problems necessitating state action. The early educational reformers working within this context defined the school as the instrument both for the creation of proper social conditions for industrial growth and for the control of urban social problems, which were essentially manifested in class warfare.

Spokesmen for education reform in Massachusetts, contemporaries of Mann, addressed themselves directly to these questions in their writings regarding school reform. Consider this 1861 statement by a Massachusetts teacher:

> That the habit of prompt action in the performance of the duty required of the boy, by the teacher at school becomes in the man of business confirmed; thus system and order characterize the employment of the day laborer. He must begin each half day with as much promptness as he drops his tools at the close of it; and he must meet every appointment and order during the hours of the day with no less precision. It is in this way that regularity and economy of time have become characteristic of our community as appears in the

running "on time" of long trains on our great network of railways; the strict regulations of all large manufacturing establishments; as well as the daily arrangement of our school duties. . . . Thus, what has been instilled in the mind of the pupil, as the principle, becomes thoroughly recognized by the man as of the first importance in the transaction of business.[4]

The following statement made by a member of the Massachusetts Board of Education underscored the theme of class unity and is similar to Adam Smith's pleadings for a spirit of unity among members of society:

The children of the rich and the poor, of the honored and the unknown, meet together on common ground. Their pursuits, their aims and aspirations are one. No distinctions find place, but such as talent and industry and good conduct create. In the competitions, the defeats and the successes of the schoolroom they meet each other as they are to meet in the broader fields of life before them, they are "taught to distinguish between the essential and factitious. . . . Thus, a vast and mutual benefit is the result. Thus, and only thus, can the rising generation be best prepared for the duties and responsibilities of citizenship in a free commonwealth. No foundation will be laid in our social life for the brazen walls of caste; and our political life, which is but the outgrowth of the social, will pulsate in harmony with it, and so be kept true to the grand ideals of the fathers and founders of the republic.[5]

I have suggested three parallel motives which undergirded midcentury educational reform. The first was directed toward creating the necessary social conditions for the frictionless operation of industrial production. The second was aimed at encouraging the competitive struggle among unequal individuals culminating in that same inequality, and third, to curb, in the meanwhile, the conflict between labor and capital. The three tendencies became interwoven, although competition was emphasized over cooperation.

The Massachusetts reform movement, generated as it was by industrial capitalism, must be analyzed in part in relationship to the substantive underlying contradictions within capitalism. Beneath the struggle between capital and labor was the increasing concentration of ownership of productive instruments (machinery, land, and banking), in the hands of fewer and fewer individuals. Meanwhile, artisans, machinists, farmers, and small businessmen, who had formerly owned instruments of production, become fewer and fewer. But the working class, those with no relationship to the machinery with which they produced except that they operated it and were paid a wage for doing so, became larger and larger.

Class antagonisms reflected private ownership of the means of production and social production. By the late nineteenth century, masses of workers employed in the expanding industrial establishments owned by a small capitalist class became enemies in countless strikes in many cities. This antagonism could only have occurred because the productive machinery was owned individually by a class of capitalists. Simultaneously, production itself, the operation of the machinery, was carried out socially through hired wage labor. This unequal distribution of property and therefore of labor formed a basis for a social division of labor and reflected itself in slums, tenements, urban squalor, low wages, union organizing, and strikes, as well as in Fifth Avenue apartments, luxuriously upholstered corporation offices, Newport yachts, and European villas. This contradiction in the social world was rooted in the economic sphere.

When the Progressive reform movement achieved national prominence, it had become in reality the maturing, the uniting, of a reform movement born in the struggle between the preindustrial capitalist and industrial capitalist epochs. By the late nineteenth century, the forces of industrialization were still struggling with the vestiges of an idyllic past but had triumphed in the form of monopoly capitalism. We shall see that this triumph was clearly evident and complete in the system of education.

Without the great conflict between masses of workers and their employers, without the great social problems that stemmed from the capitalist mode of production, there would have been little need for progressive reform. Beginning in the 1830s, the gigantic economic upheaval in methods of production impelling the social and political reorganization of society created the conditions for the nascent reform movement.

Under conditions of capitalist relations of production (wage labor), the technological advances in production have historically created an increasingly socialized, albeit specialized, division of labor. The drive for profits has moved capitalism from a form of production characterized by the small shop, with a correspondingly low level of technology, to a situation where many workers, sometimes thousands, produce a single commodity through a series of specialized operations demanded by complex technology.

Several general consequences of technological changes under conditions of capitalist production can be posited: 1) The cost of technology, under constant pressure to change and improve, steadily rises. This has historically narrowed the existing opportunities for the acquisition of productive property for increasingly larger proportions of the population. 2) Advanced levels of technology under capitalist relations of production have created a basis for the socialization of the productive process characteristic of modern capitalism. Thus factories are historically differentiated from previous forms of capitalist production by the use of socialized, as contrasted with individual and small-shop forms of production. 3) Production becomes increasingly centralized and concentrated in urban centers. The immense size of new machinery, its dependence upon sources of raw materials, machinery, parts, energy, labor, food supply, transportation, and other factors necessary for production determine its urban placement, and its effect in shaping urban centers. In the nineteenth and twentieth centuries this situation further differentiated the rural from the urban precisely because of uneven levels of technology.

In 1895 C.D. Wright, United States Commissioner of Labor, carefully observed the march of technological changes and noted the following:

> Perhaps the most striking illustration of the influence of inventions is to be found in the manufacture of boots and shoes.... This industry was formerly carried on in little shops, in which rarely more than four, worked upon the bench, upon stock received from the manufacturer, cut out and ready to be put together. These little shops are closed; the great shoe factory has taken their place, and in it is to be seen the perfect adaptation of the manufacture of goods by successive, harmonious processes. To all industries where such successive, harmonious processes can be applied ... the factory system of labor has been adapted. In all textile manufacturers, this has been the case, while outside the textile trades the expansion of the new system has been rapid, until the statistics of industry ... comprehend to a large degree the statistics of ... the factory system.[6]

The rapid change from an agrarian to a monopoly-capitalist society caused the greatest potential for socialist revolution that the nation had yet faced. The nation of small farmers, artisans, merchants, and professionals swiftly became a nation of propertyless workers, of a growing middle class of intellectuals, technicians, and managers and a diminishing class of owners of industrial and financial capital. The nation had passed from an economy where small producers and owners played an important role to the very antithesis of the classical bourgeois ideal: the subordination of individual entrepreneurship to the requirements of monopolies.

The conflicting interests of monopolies (both industrial and financial), individual entrepreneurs (or the smaller businessmen and the farmer), and the working class in the latter quarter of the nineteenth century are all reflected. Out of this complex historical confrontation, monopoly capitalism emerged victorious, and the stronger for it. The evolutionary process begun by industrialization was not reversed by the antagonisms capital had engendered; it may have been slowed here and there, but it moved forward nonetheless. In its forward movement, old ideals, social institutions, political organization, came under relentless scrutiny, if not attack. The cultural norms of the past, the political ideology of laissez faire, the individualism of classical capitalism, the social structures and functions of preindustrial and premonopoly society were subordinated to a different social, economic, and political situation. Conditions demanded an entirely new society in which capitalism had come under the power of monopolies. The demands were accommodations to the altered mode of capitalist production.

2. *Monopoly and the Intensification of Class Conflict*

Since the latter nineteenth century the economy, and thus society, of "the United States has been characterized by the domination of a relatively few giants"[7] and the intensification of class conflict. A consequence of the heightened conflict between wage labor and capital was the massive political reform movement known as Progressivism.[8] The principal impetus toward Progressivism centered about certain interrelated social conditions which had been not nearly so highly developed in the competitive period. First, the size of the industrial working class under monopoly capitalism became enormous. Between 1860 and 1900 it had grown four times, from one and one-third millions to five and one-third millions. Secondly, the urban conditions under which the workers lived and worked were increasingly difficult, causing large-scale discontent. Low wages, poor living conditions, and long hours of work were the workers' lot as the United States rapidly became the industrial and financial center of the world. Third, and most important, the strength of anticapitalist feelings and class organizational activity among the workers, very weak in the 1840s and 1850s, became very pronounced in the monopoly period. Conflicts between capital and labor grew in number and intensity. Philip Foner notes that only 168 strikes occurred in the United States between the year 1833 and 1837. Using those four years as a point of reference, we can safely assume that in the decade of the 1830s fewer than one thousand strikes occurred. By the 1880s the number of strikes had risen phenomenally.[9] Between 1880 and 1890 over 20,000 strikes and lockouts involving tens of thousands of workers took place. There was a definite qualitative change in the relationship between capital and labor in the fifty years following the 1830s.

Foner also shows that a distinct change in the composition of labor organizations occurred between the early and later periods of capitalism. In the early phase, the 1830s and 1840s, scattered local unions were dominated by declining artisans, who were losing their economic function as industrialization proceeded. In the 1880s labor organizers were no longer semi-independent tradesmen, but skilled and unskilled wage laborers. The early unions reflected the localized interests of a declining class of producers, whereas the later union organizations were national in scope and reflected the socialization of labor under monopoly capitalism.

Concurrent with monopoly in the economy and the socialization of production were increasingly severe economic depressions. This combination proved explosive. The first great industrial conflict in U.S. history, the Great Railroad Strike, started during the depression of 1877. The strike resulted in the paralysis of two-thirds of the nation's railroad mileage. Such national paralysis was inconceivable during the competitive stage when production was small and scattered. Strikes under competitive capitalism usually affected only small portions of any branch of production. However, under monopoly a strike against one giant affects a large portion of production in that branch. One result of pools, trusts, mergers, and other forms of monopoly is the enforcement of common wage rates and conditions of work among several giants. In railroads (that branch of production in which monopoly first manifests itself) the concentration of capital and socialization of labor and the consequent common forms of exploitation led directly to the first national strike in the nation's history.[10]

Paralyzing and bloody strikes occurred repeatedly after 1877. The struggle between capital and labor threatened the capitalist social order. It was literally a life-and-death war. In the railroad uprisings of 1877 "more than a hundred workmen were killed and several hundred badly wounded."[11] Twenty of these were killed and twenty-nine were wounded in Pittsburgh when the Philadelphia militia fired wildly into a large crowd of strikers and supporters. The *New York Herald*'s July 22 edition wrote of this carnage:

> Old men and boys attracted to the [scene] ... lay writhing in the agonies of death, while numbers of children were killed

outright. Yellowside, the neighborhood of the scene of the conflict, was actually dotted with the dead and dying, while weeping women, cursing loudly and deeply the instruments which made them widows, were clinging to the bleeding corpses.[12]

Again in 1877 nineteen so-called "Molly Maguires," Irish coal miners, were hanged for taking part in a union strike. In Chicago in 1897 the infamous Haymarket incident resulted in the hanging of four union leaders. In Colorado during 1903-1904 there were miners' strikes: 42 dead, 112 wounded, 1,345 arrested, 773 deported from the state. At Northern Idaho in 1892 (a depression year) again miners went on strike: 1,200 held without charge for six months in concentration camps. "Many died while their families starved and only twelve were charged with any crime."[13] During the same depression at Pullman, Illinois, attempts to organize a union and strike resulted in the deaths of thirty, injury to nearly one hundred. In that same year at Carnegie's Homestead Steel Works 40 strikers were killed and 300 injured, many seriously.[14] Seventy-three children were crushed to death when a company hireling yelled, "Fire!" into a Christmas party sponsored by the Western Federation of Miners in Michigan's copper country. In 1914 at Ludlow, Colorado, during a strike against Rockefeller's Colorado Fuel and Iron Company, thirteen children were killed by machine-gun fire on Easter Sunday; later one woman and five men were killed in the same strike. Struggles between the two antagonistic classes rose and fell leaving behind a history predicated upon private ownership of the means of production and socialized production.

Labor historian Sidney Lens writes of these labor struggles:

> in the quarter of a century of enormous economic growth from 1881 and 1905, there were 38,303 strikes and lockouts, involving seven and a half million workers, Few, of course, were as blood-soaked as the 1877 Railroad Men's War, but that they were not effete is indicated by an *Outlook* magazine study in 1904 of the previous thirty-three months. During that time, *Outlook* revealed, 198 picketers or sympathizers had been killed; 1,966 wounded; 6,114 arrested. The number of deaths in this relatively short span was about half of those on the battlefield during the entire Spanish-American war; the number of wounded slightly higher than American wounded in that war.[15]

The struggles were reactions of the steadily enlarging working class to low wages, bad working conditions, and equally bad living conditions, safety and health hazards, and yellow-dog contracts, in short to the policies of the owners of means of production and employers of wage labor. In 1886, according to the Federal Labor Commissioner, C.D. Wright, the average weekly wage for workers "ranged from $7.50 to $8.00, while carpenters in 1883 averaged $1.45 a day." The average work day, in some industries, according to contemporary studies was between fourteen and eighteen hours. In New York City, bakers toiled eighteen hours daily; a work week of "one hundred and twenty hours a week and ninety to one hundred hours weekly was not uncommon."[16] In 1910, 20% of the work force were women; their average wage for a week's work: six dollars. Approximately, seventy-five percent of male workers "earned less than $15.00 weekly." Meanwhile, a report of the Commission of Industrial Relations issued in 1914 stated that "approximately 35,000 persons were killed last year in American industry and at least one half of these deaths were preventable."[17] Thousands more were injured, many permanently crippled.

The organization on the part of labor precipitated the reaction of capital. The many casualties were in fact victims of capitalist reactionary policy. Mine owners in the East and West declared all union activity illegal and supported by the federal government, organized state and local militia along with Pinkertons and vigilante groups and fought determinedly against strikers and their sympathizers. One organization formed of small and middle-sized capitalists, the National Association of Manufacturers, founded in 1895, slugged it out with labor. It adopted a "Declaration of Labor Principles," which proclaimed the right of an employer to hire workers "at wages mutually satisfactory, without interference or dictation on the part of individuals or organizations not directly parties to such contracts." The declaration contended that unions knew "only one law, and that is the law of physical force. . . . Its history is stained with blood and ruin."[18]

The last two decades of the nineteenth century were bloody decades, and the capitalists' survival required force. The ideology of the workers could not be stomached by the "lawful and orderly" classes of society. It was not until the American Federation of Labor openly espoused purely economic goals at its founding in 1886 that labor in an organized fashion supported the capitalist system. In the latter third of the nineteenth century "the two dominant labor organizations, the National Labor Union and the Knights of Labor, called for the replacement of the capitalist system by an economy owned and operated by the people."[19] Socialism had a strong following among the workers, and it was no accident that the socialist labor leader Eugene Debs polled nearly a million votes in the presidential election of 1912. Herbert Croly wrote in 1909 that the "discontented poor are beginning to charge their poverty to an unjust political and economic organization, and reforming agitators do not hesitate to support them in their contention."[20] In 1902 the Western Federation of Miners, 25,000 strong, declared in their resolution "for a policy of independent political action and do advise and recommend the adoption of the platform of the Socialist Party by the locals of the Federation."[21] Harry Barnard wrote in his biography of John P. Altgeld that a development among labor in the latter part of the nineteenth century "was the remarkable hold that socialism had. Never before, nor since, has this doctrine of a New Society had so many converts among the laboring masses, both native and foreign born."[22]

The reaction was violent. In 1885 the *New York Tribune* wrote of unions: "These brutal creatures can understand no other reasoning than that of force and enough of it to be remembered among them for generations." The *Chicago Times* said of a particular strike: "Hand grenades should be thrown among [them] . . . other strikers could take warning from their fate." The attempts to organize and strike, often no more than a peaceful demonstration protesting bad working conditions, low salaries, and long hours, were met with denunciations and brutal violence.

Capitalists invariably responded to union organizing and striking with enormous force, and for a time this response would succeed. However, like the legendary solitary keeper of a dike riddled with small holes but with only ten fingers, the capitalists could not prevent the water breaking through at several points. Union struggles would flare up, die out, rise again, die out. Violence, the response of the employers and their managers aided by local police, state and federal militia, Pinkertons, and deputized goon squads, never succeeded in abolishing the union movement, although they helped impede its progress.

3. *Progressivism: The Politics of Monopoly Capitalism*

Much as the capitalists heartily declared war, the problem went unresolved. Society could not long endure this violent confrontation. It became evident that the policy of force and disregard for the welfare of workers did nothing but engender greater struggle from the workers. Some capitalists, principally the monopolistic industrialists and financiers with greater capital resources and therefore greater political flexibility, began to see the necessity of altering their policy towards labor, of creating certain changes in order to dissolve the continuous state of warfare between the classes. An "enlightened" policy was first promulgated by the monopoly capitalists who not only were removed from the scenes of battle, but who were also in a financial position to "bargain" with organized labor, perhaps even to use this flexibility to destroy their smaller capitalist opponents.

In a general way, the essence of reform was encapsulated in that ancient analogy popularly used in the late nineteenth and early twentieth centuries comparing society to a biological organism. Such an analogy came into popular usage because it conveyed the fundamental interests of monopoly capitalism: society as an organism was the ideal; the perfect functioning of this organism was the goal which determined the thrust of their work. Just how to bring the various antagonistic elements into a harmonious balance without changing the nature of the organism was the problem that provided the impetus to the theories of Ross, Cooley, Commons, Ely, Addams, Dewey, James, and countless others who followed the reformist path created for them. As long as the necessary ideal was to construct a cooperative society, one based on cooperative ideals rather than on individualistic (i.e., competitive) or socialist goals, no danger to the social order was posed. For it meant only that the class interests of the workers, even unionized workers, were identical to those of the capitalist bourgeoisie, that cooperation rather than competition between the two was necessary for the society as a whole to maintain the continued functioning of the organism. Thus class consciousness or even the recognition that class in fact existed (a fact recognized by laissez-faire classical political economy) was deemed irresponsible and antisocial. The organism would attain stability, indeed would develop, only when cooperative ideals (i.e., monopoly-capitalist ideals) were predominant in the consciousness of the entire population.

The principal danger to the organism was the class-conscious and politically organized working class, but there was also danger from irresponsible and "individualistic" capitalists who completely disregarded the effects of their policies upon the development of working-class struggles. Thus, the major reformers and theorists tended to castigate the irresponsible bourgeoisie as well as the radical of the working class for putting forth the wrong policies. The correct policy (basically a capitalist paternalism) from the bourgeoisie would elicit the correct response from the working class. Nevertheless, this "correct" tactic was urged upon the bourgeoisie by social scientists as well as social reformers, not to change the form of the mode of production (i.e., monopoly capitalism) but to preserve it.

That preservation of the social order not only meant a correct policy from the bourgeoisie but also correct (which meant a corresponding) policy and programs from both the private and public agencies. This study examines the relationship between the need to preserve the social order, expressed by the most influential social scientists and reformers of the period in their theoretical constructs, and the system of public education. The development of social theory was of an eminently practical nature—each social scientist may have acted out of individual interests, but his social outlook was not a product of an independent searching mind or that of a democratic minded middle class. The reform movement exhibited a general unity around key concepts which, I argue, was conditioned by the material, social and economic, conditions of the day. Thus, educational reformers were carried by the social current and their ideals were molded by the prevailing social, economic, and political conditions. Most social theorists recognized the changing conditions, the necessity to meet the challenge of a society in transition, but they also recognized the social tensions and conflicts growing from these changes. Rather than roll back advances in changing production, they attempted to reform, if necessary, both the consciousness of individuals and the antagonistic conditions of society. Rather than conflicting with monopoly capitalism, they were molded by it and in turn strove to mold society to it.

The class struggle, brought to a head because of monopoly capitalism, was the principal target of Progressive reform. To bring the two rival classes into "harmonious balance" meant, or course, that working-class activism would have to conform to the economic exigencies of capitalist production. This meant that activism among the working class would have to give way to purely economic demands within the parameters of the employer's needs and shun political activism. The balance was not the end of the status quo, but its perfection. For the class of capitalist employers, their continued profit-making enterprise would be insured by such a balanced relationship. James Weinstein has effectively presented the role of monopoly capitalists in the struggle for a nonconflicting relationship with the working class out of self-interest, that is, out of total commitment to preserve monopoly capital. Such self-interest generated the founding of organizations such as the National Civic Federation, which brought together capital, labor, and the "public" for the purposes of "mutually" working out problems affecting them as individual groups.

The National Civic Federation, founded in 1905, was a brain child of Charles Perkins of the House of Morgan. The Federation declared its aim to be "bringing together the three great interested forces of capital, labor, and the general public to work out industrial problems through evolutionary rather than revolutionary processes."[23] On the executive committee, among others, sat Andrew Carnegie, representing the "public"(!); Henry Phipps, director of U.S. Steel, representing capital; Samuel Gompers, ever the friend of capital, representing labor. They stood for industrial peace between capital and labor. Smaller capitalists formed the National Association of Manufacturers and declined to join NCF. NAM members were smaller capitalists who were succumbing steadily to the power of monopoly and could not afford to adopt such principles. Its goal was to stamp out the union movement, so it stood clear of NCF aims.

The two organizations, representing the two groupings—monopoly and nonmonopoly capitalists—took identical stands only in particular cases. Even while the NCF proclaimed industrial peace, its representatives waged a relentless struggle against unions in a large number of strikes. Such a policy corresponded to their principles. Bad unions waged strikes; good unions sat down "to talk it over" with capital. So, in the case of striking unions, NCF members often acted in a manner identical to that of their smaller fellow capitalists. The NAM, however, failed to distinguish between good and bad unions; for them, all unions were bad; they would no more sit down to discuss wages with a labor organization than with the devil. A carryover from an earlier era, the nonmonopoly capitalists could not afford to raise wages while raising production and increasing profits so easily as the monopolies could. Organized labor in any form was their enemy simply because they did not have the resources, especially the capital, to deal flexibly with unions. Larger monopolies could take the road of accommodation and reform if it meant a loyal labor force. Their immense size and capitalization, their ability to incorporate labor-saving machinery, left them with room to maneuver with their economic and political rivals, their own employees.

That policy of reform which generated the NCF was tremendously popular among middle-class reformers, especially the intelligentsia. Reform seemed to promise the resolution of the social upheavals which threatened their own privileged position in society. However, the reformism of the monopoly era was reform which in the final analysis was for the benefit of monopoly.[24] The nature of the existing system of production, of its social relations, and of social conflict was the foundation upon which the popular theory of the organic society developed. The theory of the organic society argued in essence for a harmony of interests between labor and capital. That goal was the driving force behind the Progressive Era. To the Progressive reformer, such as Jane Addams, Walter Lippmann, or John R. Commons, the violent reaction to a more or less peaceful union movement could only have led to an escalation of armed struggle and socialistic politics from the workers. The system could be saved, they thought, through better methods than those used by so many employers. Their campaign was a campaign to save capitalism. The leading monopoly capitalists were well aware of this truth; thus a Morgan associate, Willard Straight, could afford to organize and underwrite the principal publication advocating industrial peace, *The New Republic*.

a. The Social Reformers

If we examine the writings of two well-known and influential reformers, Josiah Strong and Jacob Riis, we can clearly discern the relationship between their political viewpoints and their practical value in the continuation of monopoly capitalism. I do this briefly, primarily to show the prevalence of the theme under discussion and its extreme usefulness in resolving the fundamental conflict of the period. Writers are often confused by the "humanitarian" impulse of the liberal reformers of the turn of the century and fail to discern the deeper antagonisms which gave rise to the "organic society" analogy. However much the reformers may have exhibited a social awareness, their ideological outlook was much more in tune with monopoly capitalism than with the class interests of the poor.

JOSIAH STRONG

The religious tenets popular in the early nineteenth century were under sharp attack by the latter part of the century. The battle lines were drawn between a theological fundamentalism based upon strict dogma of God's will with individual salvation on the one hand and on the other a religious institution which placed great emphasis upon social issues and their resolution. The social gospel responded to the important social questions of the era, not through appeals to the Bible or to authority, but to the pragmatic resolution of pressing social problems. Francis G. Peabody, Harvard professor of Christian morals, in 1900 summarized the social gospel creed when he wrote: "the social question of the present age is not a question of mitigating the evils of the existing order, but a question whether the existing order shall last."[25] The solution to the continuation of the existing order, he continued, was not in theology, but in a stable relationship between capital and labor. The proponents of the social gospel chose not to lean back upon a hands-off individualistic attitude of the fundamentalists, but to insist upon an intervention into the social process. Religious historian Sidney E. Mead has noted that the "social gospel" movement was a "widespread sentiment" for "instrumenting planned social and economic controls" and that this entailed "a revolution in thinking and attitudes as well as practice."[26] In effect, then, Mead argues that the social gospel was an important aspect of the Progressive movement.

My findings would not dispute such a view. A comparison of Strong, Riis, Ross, T. Roosevelt, and Dewey reveals this essential unity of political outlook.

Strong was not in the top echelon of theoretical leadership of the Progressive movement. Strong was, however, an important popularizer of the social gospel. His best-selling book, *Our Country*, sold over 500,000 copies in the twenty years after its publication. Richard Hofstadter has remarked that Strong was a more popular figure publicizing overseas expansion than was either Henry Cabot Lodge or Alfred T. Mahan.[27] In any case, Strong was influential, widely read, and popular—an important exponent of the politics generated by monopoly capitalism. It should be noted that John R. Commons, Richard T. Ely, and Josiah Strong were urging nearly identical social reforms for a similar reason: to keep radicalism from spreading among the working people.[28] Strong was a popularizer, and as such played an important role within a larger movement to change attitudes toward social reform. He was, as were Moody, Raushenbush, and Gladden, molding a political idea within a religious expression.

Strong's reforms were aimed not at making the lot of the worker easier, but at making the lot of the worker less conducive to socialist revolution. The end was not the welfare of the worker; the goal was the preservation of private property, of monopoly capitalism, and therefore of a belief in the inevitability of classes.[29] The worker was a worker by virtue of the individual distinctions manifested in a system of equal opportunity. Socioeconomic inequalities were the universal reflection of the inherent inequality in human beings, or of the unequal distribution of "quality" among the population. Thus, any other system that pretended to create equality was by nature unnatural.

Strong was a product of the society in which he lived—more precisely, a product of the social antagonisms of his time, the great class conflicts of the late nineteenth century. An analysis of his two works, *Our Country* and *The Twentieth Century City*, reveals three main themes. First, society faces a major danger from the masses of poor in the form of socialism. Second, the cause of the danger is discontent itself, exacerbated by fixed classes; and third, the solution to both is a Christian social spirit (in effect, cooperation between capital and labor). Short analysis of these main lines of thought is instructive, because it clarifies the fundamental parallels between this social reformer and educational theories to be discussed in chapter 4. I further intend to show that the message put forth in a religious form by Strong had the identical political and social content of the prevailing social theory to be discussed later in this chapter.

Let us consider the first question, that of the major threat to social order. The masses of poor were found in the large industrial cities across the nation. The city itself was not the problem; the crisis was the antagonistic elements found within the city. The city enclosed the conjuncture of several ingredients forming a dangerous compound: "ignorance, vice, and wretchedness combined constitute social dynamite . . . the city slum is the magazine."[30] The "social dynamite" was the masses of workers and unemployed living in the wretched tenement districts of the industrial and commercial centers. In addition, the situation was made more critical by the immigration and settlement of "foreigners"—an element that Strong felt stood outside of the political and social traditions and customs governing acceptable behavior.

Strong's vehement denunciation of immigrants with their "low intelligence," "ignorant habits," and "vice" can only be understood in relation to his fear of the working class rising in revolt. One scholar has written that in "the last quarter of the nineteenth century immigrants and their American-born children accounted for two-thirds or more of the population of the cities in the industrial center of the economy."[31] Thus, the working class, the inhabitants of the slum, were to a very significant extent comprised of the foreign-born and their children.

The city contained the potential for anarchy, mobs, and revolution; the point had been reached where the city had become a menace to the nation. Not only was the "compound" a threat, wrote Strong alarmingly, the powder had already been ignited on several occasions:

> Most of our great cities have at some time been in the hands of a mob. In the summer of 1892, within a few days of each other, New York, Pennsylvania, and Tennessee ordered out their militia, and Idaho called on United States troops to suppress labor riots. . . . That is not self-government but government by force.[32]

The cause for alarm was found in the cities, thought Strong; however, the cause of the "social dynamite" was not in the presence of a working class, but in the "mental make-up" of the antagonistic elements. The existence of a working class was a necessary effect of industrialization and, as societies modernized, the productive organization of society became more complex. This complexity was reflected in the social structure, but by itself is not the source of the problem.

In fact, the divisions of labor bound individuals together more closely.

> Modern social conditions have been produced by modern industrial conditions. As industry becomes more highly organized and the division of labor more complete, the interdependence of men becomes more entire, and the oneness of the life of society grows more real and obvious. Society is beginning to arrive at self-consciousness . . . it is beginning to recognize itself as an organism . . . whose interests are one.[33]

If the problem was not the division of society into capitalist employer and worker, what then was the problem? The greed of individual capitalists needed to be transformed into the concern of the capitalist for his employees in the form of fair wages and "fair" return on investments; this concern for the employee would elicit a concern of the employee for the employer; low wages created discontent, fixed classes and no hope for escaping upward. These conditions made fertile ground for socialist agitation and propaganda. The latter in turn made the slum a "social dynamite." The fundamental problem was that the principal division of labor manifested itself in class antipathies, and that the two antagonistic forces often stood like "two hostile armies" facing each other.[34] This situation was brought about by a lack of a correct policy towards employees by capitalists, caused, in turn, by the greed of individual capitalists. Strong was quite critical of capitalists who were not concerned with the social effects of their endeavors. These mindless souls would carry the nation into the great conflagration unless restrained by higher principles.

It is important to note that for Strong the root of the problem was not capitalism, the division of labor, private property, or even monopolies. The cause was to be found in "bad" capitalists and "bad" unions. Through reform the division of labor could finally operate interdependently as one organism. Certain conditions, however, had to be present. For example, classes were inevitable; that some were wealthy and others poor was "natural." It is only when "fixed" classes were present that the division of labor was prevented from operating interdependently. "Bad" capitalists paid low wages, paid wages far below the normal needs of the worker. The result was that there was no hope for a better future, no hope to move into a higher social position.

"Property," wrote Strong, "is one of the cardinal facts of our civilization."[35] It was a two-edged sword which needed to be used with great care—principally, "in the way that will best honor God."[36] That some will have much money, and others have very little did not disturb him: "It is the duty of some men to make a great deal of money. God has given to them the money-making talent; and it is wrong to bury that talent."[37]

Thus, the unequal distribution of wealth was a product of the varying capacities of individuals, and when classes were merely reflections of an open competitive struggle, a natural social order would result. "Everyone," claimed Strong, "was (or should be) free to enter the lists of the aristocracy."[38] However, such a state of society was achieved only when the consciousness of the individual was bound to the existing nature of the social organism. This required consciousness was a new social spirit in which it was believed "that God's will is done as perfectly as it is in heaven; one in which absolute obedience is rendered to every law of our being."[39] That spirit was the acceptance by each individual that the possession of wealth by some and the poverty of others was the effect of wholly individual differences, that persons rose or fell depending upon their personal virtues. The social organism needed a spirit transcending the "graduations of wealth" and based upon Christian teachings:

> the awakening of social conscience needs to be educated and the teachings of Jesus contain precisely the fundamental principles necessary for its instruction. The multiplied and complex relations of the new civilization have greatly increased and complicated our social obligations . . . this new social spirit, and this new social ideal all belong to the great social organism which is now becoming conscious of itself.[40]

Within the division of labor, how might the new social spirit manifest itself? Strong summarized his solution to the problem of socialism in the cities:

> Instances . . . within the writer's personal knowledge of the Golden Rule printed in large letters on the office walls and made the working rule of the business; of workmen sending a committee to their employer and asking that their wages might be cut down sufficiently to increase his profits to a given figure; of capitalists whose great object would seem to be not to accumulate money but to increase the intelligence, morality and physical well-being of their employees. The businesses referred to are eminently prosperous, and are not troubled with strikes and lock-outs.[41]

There was in Strong's perception no need for classes to act on behalf of their interests. The solution rested principally in changing the individualistic consciousness of capitalists and the antagonistic consciousness of the workers. The missing link, thought Strong, was a consciousness corresponding to the singularity of the social organism.

Unless the "dangerous elements of our civilization," exclaimed Strong, "are Christianized, free institutions would be destroyed" (i.e., classes, wealth, private ownership of the means of production)[42] and socialism would triumph. Christianity was merely the *form* in which his apologia and ultimate solution for the survival of capitalism presented itself. We shall see that his conclusions did not differ in essence from those of the secular social sciences and paralleled substantively the ideas of the well-known social reformer, Jacob Riis.

JACOB RIIS

Riis' most famous contribution to the reform literature was *How the Other Half Lives* (1890). It followed the general pattern of the Progressive social reformers, arguing that changes in the environment must be effected or else a social revolution would erupt. Riis' book falls into a tendency which also characterized John R. Commons' *Social Reform and the Church* (1895), as well as the alarming expressions of Josiah Strong.

Riis, like many Progressives, was an active reformer and participated in the National Civic Federation, as well as the National Child Labor Committee. Both organizations were controlled by leading monopoly capitalists. The support, writes Jeremy Felt, for the NCLC came principally from a group of large capitalists.[43] Such figures as Jacob Schiff of the Kuhn-Loeb Investment Banking were, among other big capitalists, on the NCLC's membership list.

One cannot assume that because Riis participated in two organizations supporting legislation in the interests of monopoly that he therefore supported monopoly. One must look, however, at the reforms which he proposed, and at the social relations which he idealized. Here we see that Strong and Riis were in agreement as to the solution to the labor-capital question.

Riis, like Strong, was critical of capitalists but not of capitalism, and also felt that the slum was the locus of the main social and political problems facing the United States. Similarly to Strong, Riis thought that its cause could be found in (1) the degenerate poor (as opposed to the worthy poor), and (2) the greedy capitalists (as opposed to "good" capitalists) and (3) the conflict between capital and labor.

"The danger to society," however, did not arise from the tenements in themselves or from the degenerate poor, but from "ill-spent wealth that reared them."[44] Greedy capitalists expecting a profit far out of line with their investment cared not one bit for the comfort and well-being of the inhabitants. The result was that a well-meaning portion of the working population was forced to live under conditions as if they were animals. These tenements in turn become "nurseries of crime,"[45] seeds of disease and contagion, and a hotbed of labor agitation. The "mob," as contemporaries so often referred to labor during their struggles with capital, was considered by Riis to be a product of low wages, of child labor, of hunger, of "little ones crying for bread around the cold and cheerless hearth," and of crazed individuals seeking revenge against those who enjoyed wealth.[46]

The problem then was the greedy capitalists who invested in substandard slum dwellings and who paid wages below subsistence levels. The effects in turn bred the social evils that plagued the United States: tenements, which in turn bred crime, disease, as well as the sharp battles for higher wages, which often erupted into community-wide struggles, which made a mockery of the political principles of the democracy. Riis' arguments paralleled Strong's on this fundamental point: "the slum was the magazine"; and discontent bred the potential for violence from the "mob." The mob, as they defined it, was any kind of defiant action taken by groups of individuals against the state in any form, i.e., local police, state government, etc. Labor struggles by definition became mobs if they clashed with local, state, or national authorities, and as we know, these sorts of "mobs" were the most visible and active in the late nineteenth century. When these reformers spoke of anarchy, they of course spoke of political action taken by the poor, and this meant the factory workers and their supporters.

In concluding *How the Other Half Lives*, Riis wrote vividly and melodramatically of the danger from below, of that "sea of a mighty population" restive in their bleak tenements. He offered this analogy, which undoubtedly was aimed at disturbing the "gilded" set:

> during the fierce storms of winter it happened that this sea, now so calm, rose in rage and beat down, broke over the bluff, sweeping all before it. No barrier built by human hands had power to stay it then. The sea of mighty population held in galling fetters, heaves uneasily in the tenements. Once already our city . . . has felt the swell of its resistless flood. If it rises once more, no human power may avail to check it.[47]

Riis had a particular distaste for tenements, blaming them for the major social ills facing society. However, his solutions to the problem did not stop at the tenement, but were composed of an enlarged social and economic picture, specifically, workers and employers. First, in considering the tenement as a problem stemming from selfish greed, Riis proposed that "capital that wrought the evil must itself undo it."[48] Riis felt that the working masses deserved decent housing and on this point he was adamant. He was also equally adamant in maintaining that capitalism could make a good investment in "decent housing."

Riis proposed slum regulations which would make the tenement safer, sanitary, more salutary, and less crowded. These regulations were not intended to do away with working-class quarters, but to eliminate the more aggravating conditions creating the discontent. Note, however, that Riis did not propose better housing, or even jobs, for the unemployed. "The poorest," wrote Riis, "are shiftless, destructive, and stupid."[49] These were the degenerates who committed the street crimes, the murders, thefts, and mayhem upon an innocent public. In this instance, the "drunk-tank," a county or state penal system, would provite the necessary solution. "Ill-applied charity" only made this situation of drifters more hopeless.[50] For these no slum reform would prove beneficial, and one gathers from Riis that only the complete outlawing of saloons and liquor would save these unfortunates. On the other hand, the deserving poor required more than negative legislation: they required housing which insured a stable family; a home, thought Riis, was the best insurance against revolt. "Rome perished," he wrote, "when most of her people became . . . homeless."[51] The situation demanded a wise "philanthropic" investment policy and sound municipal tenement regulation; thus slum reform could be effected and dissolve much of the discontent.

But Riis could not stop there, for he knew that the "restless sea" did not confine itself to the communities in which it lived. Most often the antagonism between the "mob" and "decent society" took place outside of the slum, in the factories and work places. What then could one propose? What reforms could one effect? Here Riis was quite clear: only a policy of cooperation rather than competition between capital and labor could overcome the anarchistic potential from the working class. However, the bargain struck could not affect the social order, could not change the distribution of property to any significant extent. This policy proposed by Riis would strengthen capital by making its control over the means of production safe from the forceful sallies of activist labor unions. He described this encounter between labor and capital which took place during the depression of 1893, and offered it as the ideal relationship between capitalist and worker:

> a deputation of workmen, with serious looks on their faces, filed into Colonel Kelbourne's office . . . and this was their errand . . . : "We know that times are bad. We know that your warehouses are filling up with goods you cannot sell . . . and that you cannot get your pay for the goods you have sold. And yet you keep us at work. We do not know what your circumstances are, but you have stood by us and we have come

to stand by you. . . . We have had good pay; we have been able to save up some money, and here it is; it is all yours, if you need it in the business."[52]

In the establishment managed by the Colonel "no disagreement of any kind has ever arisen;" this, of course, was to the benefit of the owner of the establishment. It also meant that the system of capitalist production and distribution of property would not be altered. Reforming the slums and changing the consciousness of workers towards their employers had important corollaries. First, reform of the slums stood within the purview of sound investment policy. These owners of tenement property should expect to receive "rents . . . as low as consistent with the idea of a business investment that must return a reasonable interest to be successful."[53] Model tenements, however, paid well enough if the owner would be content with "as high as seven percent on his investment."[54] Anything above a reasonable return consistent with the political goals of reform did nothing to resolve the crisis of the slum. Riis argued that money could still be made, only less of it, but that the end result, social stability, far outweighed the lesser profits.

Second, cooperation between capital and labor was also a sound business policy. Giving a worker a "living wage" along with a decent home was thought to be the sweet guarantee for the continued functioning of capitalism. These proposals were in essence political exigencies that at their heart were in the interests of the capitalist economy. "If capital sought but its just reward, it would find it compatible with giving labor its full share," wrote Riis. Furthermore, labor should think of its rights as identical with those of the employer:

If labor thought of the rights of the employer with its own; if the fight were ever for the good of the race as it was meant to be; if the union label always guaranteed honest work, a living wage, no sweatshop of child labor, a clean shop and a fair observance of the factory laws, its cause would be irresistible.[55]

Without having once mentioned the term "organism," Riis nevertheless reflected the same essential ideas about society and social problems articulated by Josiah Strong. The cooperation of the various sections, or divisions, of the social organism was both the abstract ideal and the medium through which the social order was to be stabilized. This is the fundamental point of both of these social reformers, products of the "Progressive Period."

Industrialization (and by this reformers meant technological advancement) had created a division of labor that weighed heavily upon the shoulders of society. However, this division of labor was not the problem; the problem was in its "irrational" functioning. On the other hand, the proper functioning rested upon reform: that is, a correct domestic policy from the capitalists, and as we shall see in the case of E.A. Ross, a correct foreign imperialist policy. It was incumbent upon them that they make the poor less discontented, or else the discontented eventually would forcibly trade places with the wealthy. This latter situation could be averted through a reform program. But such a reform program would only strengthen the existing division of labor. It was a reform based upon capitalist self-interest and necessitated making the lot of the poor less wretched, on the basis of which a consciousness of cooperation of workers with capital could be created. It was only through an amelioration of the slum situation that the consciousness-changing would proceed.

Both of the major divisions in the productive process, the capitalists and workers, were asked to compromise, and join "organically." The employers were asked to become truly interested in the welfare of their employees; and the employees were asked to return the favor and become truly interested in the welfare of the employer. Thus, the interests of both were joined, and the distinctions only formal. The social division of labor would become a harmonious interworking of its separate, unequal, and formerly contending parts.

The capitalist stood to make a profit of reform. He stood to benefit from the stabilization of a hazardous social situation; his business could expect a cooperative work force, loyal to the employer, shunning strikes, accepting the ups and downs in the economy and subsequent measures such as layoffs, speed-ups, wage-cuts as wholly legitimate and just economic policy towards employees. One necessary change for eliciting the correct consciousness was to create wholly new ideological categories. Society would no longer function on the basis of conflict but of cooperative effort. Employers "would become a conservative element in society" if they were to adopt a more conciliatory attitude towards their laborers, wrote Richard T. Ely. He added a corollary: "Workingmen too must remember ... to cultivate a more conciliatory tone in all their relations." These principles, he (like most Progressives) argued, provided the "remedy against the evils of socialism, nihilism and anarchism."[56]

b. The Social Sciences

Late nineteenth century social-science theory, forerunner of modern social-science theory, was also subordinated to the exigencies of monopoly capitalism. Not only the middle-class social reformers but virtually all of the famous social scientists were ideologically in tune with monopoly. An examination of social-science theory, educational theory, and the key ideas of social reformers shows striking parallels in a substantial number of areas. The several well-known Progressives analyzed in this chapter bowed before monopoly, before the existing socioeconomic relationships between classes, before private property, and to the primacy of cooperative individualism and the necessity to incorporate consistent social change based upon monopoly production into institutional structures. The changing productive techniques, bureaucratic necessities, methods of distribution, and especially social relations were reflected in the theories of the social sciences, in the writings of social reformers, and in the goals of the Progressive educators.

An examination of the relationship between the popular theories of the sciences and monopoly capitalism in the late nineteenth century should help in clarifying the nature of Progressive education. We shall see that the forces which shaped the theories of the social sciences of the period also shaped the theory of Progressive education. Let us examine the famous Progressive sociologist Edward Alsworth Ross.

EDWARD A. ROSS

Edward Alsworth Ross studied economics under Richard T. Ely at Johns Hopkins and early in his career became enmeshed with sociology. In the middle 1890s he was one of only three professors of sociology in the United States. During his career Ross was an enormously popular figure in his field. He authored twenty-four books (sales totaled over 300,000 copies) and hundreds of articles. He was elected president of the American Sociological Association in 1914 and again in 1915. He eventually retired in 1937 after serving as chairman of the Sociology department for eight years at the University of Wisconsin. Ross has not the stature of a Weber, or a Parsons, but he was an important thinker and popularizer of the social theory being developed by himself, along with Albion Small, Franklin Gidding, and Charles H. Cooley.[57] Upon his death, a summary of Ross's achievements was published in the *American Sociological Review*; it read, in part, "Sociological pioneer and internationally recognized contributor of fundamental principles of sociological theory, the greatest and most adroit popularizer of American sociology to date . . . that is Ross."[58]

Edward A. Ross represented much of the thinking of the leadership, both academic and political, of the day. Theodore Roosevelt knew Ross personally and had written the introduction to Ross's *Sin and Society*.[59] Justice Oliver Wendell Holmes had introduced Roosevelt to Ross's writings and had once written of Ross that "he [had] sympathetically read all the academician's works." For our purposes Ross's ideas, motives, and goals are important because they are examples of the manner in which contemporary scholars acted and thought in a monopoly capitalist society.

One of Ross's famous works, *Social Control: A Survey of the Foundations for Order*, first published in 1901, contains many clues for our understanding of the formation of Ross's ideas, especially of his ideas on the role of education in a progressive society.[60] In it he explains that he does not propose to eradicate social and economic inequality but to create an orderly society from an unequal one through the effects of a consciously applied social control. Ross derived his theory directly from the conditions of contemporary American society as well as from the historical legacy of bourgeois ideology. Historically, he argued, the necessity for forms of artificial social control appeared as soon as inequalities appear: between leaders and the led, between those who do manual work and those who do mental work, between wealthy and poor, learned and unlearned, etc. Natural social control spontaneously governs when inequalities are absent, when everyone labors side by side; in short, when the division of labor is absent. Once the unequal division of labor appeared, spontaneous order waned, and the need to create the bases for social order also appeared. The very essence of his scholarship was the need for social cooperation, especially the formation of unique institutions and social conditions which insured an organic, unified, and self-directed society. Ross's conception of social cooperation was neither unique nor original and paralleled several of his contemporaries. Emile Durkheim, Josiah Strong, Albion Small, Charles Horton Cooley and John Dewey held views essentially similar to Ross's ideas of early twentieth-century society. This social division of labor created the basis for "corporate organic solidarity" in the terminology of Durkheim, the "Christian social spirit" of Strong, of the "organic unity" of Small—and of "social control" for Ross. In each, the division through which people entered into relationships for production was fundamental to the operation of society; without constant interaction, mutual cooperation and solidarity, society ceased. The prominent social psychologist and Progressive at the University of Michigan, Charles Horton Cooley, followed a similar theoretical path. He contended that "the greater the complexity and interdependence of the social order, the greater the need of soundness in all parts." Therefore unreliable individuals were a "public nuisance." As societies evolved into more complex forms, the greater the "unification of aim, specialization of activities in view of a common purpose [and] a growing interdependence among the parts of society."[61] Such social theory was not unique to a handful of social scientists. Albion Small, writing in the early twentieth century, stated that "few sociologists would find occasion for dissent" from such a sociological conceptualization.⁶² According to this theory the social division of labor placed each individual into a particular role; that role of specialization was the cell within the division in the operation of the entire social body. Each division composed of individuals must have a proper social outlook for that division to function within the totality of divisions. This outlook was the corporate-consciousness and made the corporate, or organic, society possible.⁶³

Ross wrote that the more complex the division of labor, "the denser the traffic, . . . the higher the grade of order," was to be expected.⁶⁴ As society grew more complex, it required the "nice adjustment of multifarious activities according to some prearranged plan"⁶⁵ The force of social survival required that individuals submit to the necessity of social cooperation rather than expressing unbridled individualism. Ross, like Cooley, assumed that each individual had a self-interest which must be constantly kept in check by the social interest.⁶⁴ The social interest was the higher, "loftier" level of interaction within which order becomes a reality, harmony, a way of life. Society constantly watched against freewheeling individuals bending the impulsive to the social will. Once individuals became socialized to the common interests, order became a reality and disorder would be defeated. Ross argued that the individual, in order to contribute to social cooperation, had to submit to the plan through which the social division of labor could function. Those who branched out, for whatever reasons, from the "prearranged plan" did so because of a particular noncooperative "mental make-up." The psychological state of the myriad of cells within each·division had to conform to the plan, otherwise collisions within the social order would occur. Thus, mankind evolved to higher planes of being through more intricate and complicated achievements in social order. Such order was achieved only when social cooperation was the basis for society, and social cooperation became a reality only when individuals recognized that order was the most important goal and condition of society.

The division of labor was a succinct expression of the ordering of labor into special units for the purpose of production and distribution. Many areas of production, especially monopoly production, depended upon highly specialized, though not necessarily skilled, labor. Often large production units depended upon large numbers of smaller units. Ross saw professionals, housewives, investors, workers, farmers as having a particular task which, when carried out in a cooperative manner, insured the operation of the total division of labor.⁶⁷ However, the really crucial element in the division of labor consisted of the wage workers. These were placed in a strategic locale that made it imperative that efforts to develop the cooperative principle be emphasized among them. Later, we shall see how Ross proposed that education be geared accordingly.

Ross argued that inequality was an inevitable condition of higher social organization. A benign competition assured the selecting of the more intelligent individuals to the differing classes of social structure. Those better able to lead, think, invent, promote production, govern, i.e., the more intelligent, "bubbled" to the top; the inferiors formed the masses in varying graduation. However, it was a cooperative struggle through which social development took place. Order within this struggle was achieved when each individual recognized the justice of such a process and limited his or her individualism accordingly. The order within the social body was a result of the correspondence of the thought processes of all the members of society as to what the means and ends of the society were.

Explicit in Ross's idealistic theory of social order was the contention that it was the consciousness of class divisions that was "dysfunctional" and that class cooperation was necessary to overcome the stress of the unequal social structure. Ross wrote that a hierarchical social class structure "is still more a test of orderliness, inasmuch as in the sharing of unlike burdens and the division of unequal benefits men are apt to run afoul of one another."[68]

The problem became one of assimilating the masses or poor and the working class to an ideology consonant with the interests of capitalist production and distribution in particular and to social stability in general. Ross thought it a delusion "to think that order is part of one's inherited genes." He added that "it is rather the exercise of proper social control."[69] The correct method of creating social order, in his opinion, was for the social organism to exercise restraint and place limitations upon the individual members of the group. The state then would inculcate the correct values, which would bind the citizenry together. Ross, in much the same fashion as Albion Small, described the role of public education as a necessary foundation for orderly progress.[70] The "suggestibility of youth makes it imperative," wrote Ross, "to base social order on a system of education. Children would be trained for self-control and the habit of obedience to an external law . . . given by good school discipline."[71] Ross did not exactly know "just what shape this new education will take," but, like Dewey, thought it would be a practical education, "realistic, with its starting point the facts of personal and social life."[72] A "realistic" education was one which functioned within the parameters of the existing social organization; education conceived as such would instruct each class to respect the other. In the fashion of the welfare state, upper classes would be given an understanding of their responsibility for the welfare of the lower class; the latter, in turn, would honor its debt to the upper class and cooperate for the best interests of society as a whole.[73]

Like Josiah Strong and Jacob Riis, Ross deplored an idle and parasitic upper class as much as an uncooperative, class-conscious and politically active working class. He felt that if the propertied classes refrained from the excesses that marked the European feudal nobility, the class action of the lower classes could be prevented.[74] Ross's principal interest was a theory of social stability in which class conflict was prevented from developing through a correct method of rule by the propertied class. Such policies as would insure "upward mobility" for a select few could serve as an escape valve for excess pressure. "For the poor do not generate a militant ethos of their own if their elite are able to escape upward," said Ross.[75] For such a safety valve to function, colonies must be founded and the government should actively intervene to foster "industry and commerce."[76] Like most progressive reformers, Ross was urging a level of state intervention in the social and economic process at odds with the prevalent theory and practice of the capitalist state. So much did Progressives differ with existing theory and practice that throughout the Progressive period the need for state intervention had to be constantly reiterated. Progressives were not creating a straw man. They were in opposition to the traditional laissez-faire view of the proper role of the state. Progressivism, therefore, can be distinguished by its open theoretical declaration for a consistent state intervention. This was a sharp turn away from classical social and political theory.[77] Ross's theories were practical only through the rejection of the laissez-faire state. The "policy for a government that feels the deck leaping beneath its feet" was colonial expansion, state intervention in the economy, and a "realistic" educational system.[78] Unless these policies were effected, exclaimed Ross, a "class spirit will rend society in twain" and the "weakening of social control and a shifting toward disorder" would be the result.[79]

The link that connected the social scientist Ross with the Progressive Teddy Roosevelt was their ideological similarity. Roosevelt wrote the introduction to Ross's work, *Sin and Society*, and identified closely with the scholar's ideas. Both believed that the essential unity of society was based on individuals, not classes; they also shared belief in the danger of class consciousness, in the necessity for monopoly, and in the division between "good" and "bad" monopolies as well as "good" and "bad" unions. A speech delivered by Roosevelt in 1903 contains parallels with the basic ideas of Ross. In it Roosevelt spoke of the necessity for recognizing the "community of interest among our people." He continued:

> The welfare of each of us is dependent fundamentally upon the welfare of all of us, and therefore in public life that man is the best representative of each of us who seeks to do good to all; in other words, whose endeavor it is, not to represent any special class and promote merely that class' special interest, but to represent all true, and honest men of all sections and all classes and to work for their interests for our common country.[80]

The language has noticeably changed but the substance of their thought continued unaltered. The politician Roosevelt adapted the language of the academic to the everyday language of the ordinary citizen. Society, exclaimed Roosevelt, has a common set of interests binding classes together, and political programs must focus on those ends. Citizens, rich and poor alike, work together to achieve common ends. In the same speech he thundered:

> Men sincerely interested in the due protection of property, and men sincerely interested in seeing that the just rights of labor are guaranteed, should alike remember not only that in the long run neither the capitalist nor the wage worker can be helped in healthy fashion save by helping the other; but also that to require either side to obey the law and do its full duty toward the community is emphatically to that side's real interest.[81]

The self-interests of the men of wealth imposed upon them the responsibility for creating a proper climate for mutual cooperation between capital and labor. This was argued by Ross as well as Roosevelt (and, as we shall see, by Dewey). The "very rich man" who violated laws while conducting business, said Roosevelt, "increased the difficulty of the task of upholding order when the disorder is a menace to men of property." Furthermore, if the public became aware that the wealthy condoned illegal activity, "the community is apt to assume the dangerous and unwholesome attitude of condoning crimes of violence committed against the interests of men of property."[82] Property, as it was then distributed, must be protected, but each individual who together with other individuals composed society must first be bound by "proper ideals." In an address before the NEA in 1905, Roosevelt urged teachers and educators "throughout the land" to remedy this state of "social dynamite" existing wherever labor and capital had confronted each other "uncooperatively."[83]

3. Capitalism and Progressive Reformism / 83

Roosevelt, as well as Ross, was quite aware of the changing social relations being affected by monopoly capitalism, and he perceived especially the evolution of class antagonisms. Ross's scholarship and Roosevelt's politics were dedicated to the preservation of the still-developing society in which they lived through a method of domination which served the interests of the capitalist class. Neither Roosevelt nor Ross were at odds with the distribution of property and the consequent division of society into classes. Moreover, they were dedicated to preserving this kind of social stratification protected through a proper social restraint based upon an ideology in consonance with monopoly capitalism.

Molding the psychology of the mass of individuals to the cooperative principle was a particularly important task for the functioning and survival of the division of labor. That goal was to be developed by correct methods of rule by the state. The state institution which was given a weighty responsibility in this task was the educational system. Ideological training was crucial for the owners of the means of production. The very survival of monopoly capitalism depended upon a wage-laborer who placed the cooperative principle above individual or class interests. In the final analysis, "cooperation" was a principle expressly in the interests of monopoly capitalist production. Within this sphere of interest, public education was destined to play a principal role.

Chapter Four
JOHN DEWEY, THEORETICIAN OF PROGRESSIVE EDUCATION

Dewey has been the subject of much discussion, especially among critical historians. Some, such as the radical revisionist Clarence Karier, feel that Dewey was one more Progressive who put in his time for the benefit of the corporate society.[1] Karier, who is very critical of Dewey, feels that Dewey represented the ideals of the middle class. Karier's interpretation sees no fundamental relationship between Progressivism and capitalism, much less monopoly capitalism. While Karier is generally correct in his description of Dewey's liberalism (and liberalism in general), he has not given an adequate explanation for the rise of Progressivism. Karier employs a pluralist methodology and, therefore, contends that elites formulated educational policy. Dewey is consequently described as a member of a middle-class elitist movement to dominate society. Others have argued that Dewey differed substantially from the main flow of Progressive thought. For example, Martin Carnoy writes that Dewey

> called for a change in the organization of work from an orientation to the needs of the economy—that is, the production of more goods—to the needs of the individual or society. . . . Dewey wanted the school to provide a period for the child in which he could live and learn without economic pressure, carrying out activities for their intrinsic value . . . internalizing the joy of intellectual experience.[2]

For Carnoy, Dewey remained apart from "educators who worked to make the capitalist and economic and social system . . . function." One assumes then that Dewey pressed for an educational system that functioned in the interests of the people it allegedly served, rather than for the capitalist system. Samuel Bowles and Herbert Gintis claim in their recent study that Dewey had one foot in each camp. On the one hand, Dewey seemed "to have been aware of these constraints (the capitalist economy) and true to his pragmatism, to have operated consciously within them."[3] On the other hand, they assert that Dewey remained independent of the "in-house" reformers: "The practice of the reform movement was clearly out of step with the democratic and open education advocated by John Dewey,"[4] and in the same essay they contend that "Dewey's overall framework seems eminently correct."[5]

Based upon the evidence discussed below, Dewey represented the theoretical epitome of Progressive thought, and thus cannot be ideologically nor theoretically separated from Progressivism in general. The parallels are much too clear, although apparent ambiguity in Dewey's writings may leave room for misinterpretation. The evidence points in the direction of Dewey, the Progressive, and as we shall see, the apologist, not of middle-class elites as Karier erroneously contends, nor of democracy as Bowles and Gintis argue, but of the ideology corresponding to monopoly capitalism.

Much the same as Emile Durkheim, Dewey thought that the psychologist and social scientist were indispensable for the full and sound development of education. Although better known as a sociologist, Durkheim held the chair of "Science of Education" at the Sorbonne, allotting two-thirds of his teaching to pedagogy. There are distinctive parallels between Dewey and the educator-social-scientist Durkheim which merit some thought. First, both felt that the interests of various strata and classes were bound into a single corporate structure. This unity was the ultimate expression of civilization. Second, the aim of society was to secure this unity of thought and being. Third, in relation to education as a means of attaining this unity, the psychologist and social scientist were indispensable "experts" guiding the educational enterprise. Dewey wrote that psychologists "gave added insight into individual structure and laws of growth."[6] The internal mysteries of human thought processes could be unraveled by an expert in that area. Teachers needed to know how to approach the learner from the vantage point of general laws of learning and behavior. The task could be made both simpler and more effective. The correct method of teaching was an important part, but only one part, of the socialization program.

The social scientists, on the other hand, according to Dewey, added "to our knowledge of the right organization of individuals."[7] This statement is vitally important because it tells us that Dewey concluded that the social scientist using scientific methods (i.e., social-science methodology) could provide the "scientific resources . . . for the purposes of education."[8] When Dewey spoke of a scientific education, he was directly referring to the contribution of social science as well as of psychology to the efforts of educators. A scientific education was one which took into consideration the latest developments in areas that were particularly relevant to constantly evolving modern conditions. The means, or methods, would be developed with the aid of the insight of the psychologist; the goals would be established by the social scientist.

1. Instinct Theory and Dewey's Educational Psychology

Like the social scientist Ross, Dewey's philosophical and educational work had as its principal end the unification of society. In discussing Dewey's educational theories, it is extremely important to examine first the psychological principles of William James, and then to see the manner in which Dewey incorporated these principles into his education theory.

James began his major work, *Principles of Psychology*, with a discussion of the physiological functions of the nervous system. His purpose in doing so was to argue that thought and movement were responses initially conditioned within the organism and not by an external stimulus. The human organism, according to James, was fully capable of filtering external effects into internally structured thought. In effect the nervous structures were the principal conditioning agents functioning independently of external stimulus. James contended that "All nervous centres have . . . one essential function, that of 'intelligent action.' They feel, prefer one thing to another, and have 'ends.' "[9] Reality found its point of departure not in the external material sensation, but in the person; "The foundation and origin of all reality," wrote James, "is thus subjective, is ourselves."[10]

These structures were set at birth and could be modified only within their natural limits. According to James, heredity plays a key role in determining human behavior. In defense of James's theories, Dewey wrote: "The idea of heredity has made familiar the notion that the equipment of the individual, mental as well as physical, is an inheritance from the race: a capital inherited by the individual from the past and held in trust by him for the future."[11] Thus, at birth, the human organism is characterized, and its life significantly determined, by "natural tendencies which we know as . . . instincts."[12]

Instincts were those faculties "of acting [which] produce certain ends, without foresight . . . and without previous education."[13] Dewey found that "every interest grows out of some instinct or some habit that in turn is finally based upon an original instinct."[14] Furthermore, "every instinct is an impulse."[15] Without instinct there would be no human action or emotion; all behavior had its origin in an instinct. External stimuli function only in relationship to a nervous system which is preorganized in such a way to respond to corresponding stimuli. Dewey, for example, remarked that the "organism acts in accordance with its own structure."[16] Without instinct there is no effective stimulus. All action, whether cerebral or physical, originates in instinct. Instinctive behavior, however, is modified by experience; original instincts are externally conditioned by environment, repetition, education, and by their variation in each individual. Two elements thus combine to form human conduct: instincts and the conditioning of those instincts through experience.

Nevertheless, the range of human behavior is based upon a prearranged instinctual structure. James's list of traits included: imitation, rivalry, pugnacity, acquisitiveness, greediness, and sociability. Instincts found their expression and modification within society. Once an instinct is manifested, it becomes a "conscious end," ceases to be blind and is subject to intellectual hesitation and choice and social modification. Instincts, therefore, do not exist in random fashion, manifesting themselves here and then there without a pattern. Instincts are fashioned into habits. "Instincts," wrote James, "are implanted for the sake of giving rise to habits."[17] Habits, in turn, are the forces which prevent society from shattering into atomistic parts: "Habit is thus the enormous flywheel of society, its most precious conservative agent. It alone keeps us all within the bounds of ordinance, and saves the children of fortune from the envious uprisings of the poor."[18] Habits are ordered expressions of instincts. The social organism is glued together by habits which function to maintain the organism. Those habits which would create disequilibrium would not be allowed to integrate themselves into that gigantic interaction and combination of habits known as society. For example, "The impulse to own is usually checked by a variety of considerations; and only passes over into action under circumstances legitimized by habit and common consent, an additional example of the way in which one instinctive tendency may be inhabited by others."[19] Thus society watches over itself in such a fashion that particular instincts are developed into habits, others remain at the instinctual level. Furthermore, habits are the principal force in structuring society into distinct socioeconomic categories. "Habit," James had written, "alone prevents the hardest and most repulsive walks of life from being deserted by those brought up to tread therein. It keeps the fisherman and the deckhand at sea through the winter; it holds the miner in the darkness. . . . It keeps different social strata from mixing."[20] Dewey had written a similar statement on habits: "Habits become negative limits because they are at first positive agencies . . . the sailor is intellectually at home in the sea, the hunter in the forest, the painter in his studio, the man of science in his laboratory."[21] Thus the division of labor in society is a set of habits which find their origins in instincts.

James placed his arguments for the new psychology alongside attacks upon the Lockean conceptions of the mind. "The associationist psychology," said James, "denies that there is any blind premature instinct to appropriate."[22] James correctly identified the distinction between his psychology and the psychology of classical bourgeois thinkers. Locke and Rousseau, for example, never considered property to be the consequence of instincts; their position was that the child needed to learn to appropriate property. Education did not center on instincts, but upon the need to teach new ideas, based upon natural laws which would develop into new forms of behavior. James, however, denied that the conception of property was learned. Humans were born with an instinct to acquire property, to envy it, and to appropriate it whenever possible:

> The beginnings of acquisitiveness are seen in the impulse which very young children display, to snatch at, or beg for, any object which pleases their attentions. Later when they begin to speak, among the first words they emphasize are "me" and "mine." Their earliest quarrels . . . are about questions of ownership.[23]

Each individual, born equipped with instincts, manifested those instincts in unique ways. Instincts, consequently, had a general and a particular aspect. Such phenomena as war and private property were instinctual, and therefore were destined to survive through the ages. Their particular manifestation was that each individual expressed a unique version of those instincts. It would follow then that "the instincts of construction and production," which Dewey considered the most important instincts, were characterized by a variation in manifestation.[24] Differing capacities impelled some towards mental tasks, others toward manual tasks. Some were prone towards leadership, others to become followers.[25] Instinct theory, an important component of James's psychology, was incorporated into Dewey's theory of education.

Dewey's general aim in education was twofold: to expel the old, traditional education (which enjoyed predominance) and to impose the psychological approach. The old educational scheme, based upon discredited Lockean conceptions, was at cross-purposes with the necessary ideological reformations. The old system employed a methodology which implicitly accepted a deterministic conception of subject-object relations. "The traditional scheme," fretted Dewey, "is one of imposition from . . . outside."[26] Education in the traditional method was the transmission of knowledge (the discredited clusters of sensations) "worked out in the past." Thus schools were bridges where summed-up knowledge was passed along to youth and in turn applied and further developed. In this very general sketch the images of Locke are clear: the child's faculties are "filled," and knowledge, in turn, is further developed. The child therefore was not trained to rely upon a subjective method of analyzing the world; mechanical external forces were still dominant in the development of the individual and of society.

The task at hand, explained Dewey, "means the necessity of the introduction of a new order of conception leading to new modes or practices."[27] The battle lines were drawn between those who believed that education was a process of interrelations between the individual and environment, and those who held that it was "formation from without."[28] The rejection of the traditional method presented the educator with the problem of filling that void. This categorical rejection created the necessity to develop an education based upon wholly new psychological principles.[29] It was urgent and pressing, added Dewey, that education be based upon a psychology of experience.[30] If such were not successfully completed, the principles of the traditional system would continue to dominate. Changing conditions dictated a radical change in education. Only through such change would the school complement society.

Dewey tested James's psychology in his laboratory school at the University of Chicago. It was, he said, the application of the "principles of mental acitivity and processes of growth made known by modern psychology."[31] Dewey credited William James for bequeathing the psychological principles upon which the school functioned. Dewey once wrote that James's psychology was "the 'spiritual progenitor' of his own work in philosophy and education."[32] The general purpose of Dewey's educational theory was one with the psychology of James, the social science of Ross, and the politics of Roosevelt: the "end in view [of education] is the development of a spirit of social cooperation and community life, discipline must grow out of and be relative to such an aim."[33] The new education emphasized "whatever binds people together in cooperative human pursuits."[34] The foundation of that educational purpose was a psychology of instincts and habits; and upon that basis Dewey created his structure of educational theory. Dewey's purpose, at the most general level, was an education which provided the child "with the instruments of effective self-direction." Such an education, Dewey concluded, was the "deepest and best guarantee of a larger society which is worthy, lovely, and harmonious."[35]

The reader should easily see the relationships between James's psychology and Dewey's version of Progressive education. That relationship stands out boldly when focusing upon the emphasis Dewey placed upon habits, reflecting an allegiance to James's instinct theory. Dewey's educational theory made James much more a part of the everyday life of the common citizen than James did on his own. Dewey believed that instincts "belong to [man] by structure." He had written that each impulse is an instinct, and each idea had behind it some impulse. Mankind was a structured system of instincts (impulses), ideas, and beliefs (habits). This was the basis for human behavior (in its relationship to environment). Dewey argued that the old educational scheme subjected the individual to laissez-faire individualism and so, "Habits were divided against one another." The "remedy lies," he continued, "in the development of a new morale which can be attained only as released impulses are intelligently employed to form harmonious habits adapted to one another in a new situation."[36] James emphasized habits as a necessary "flywheel," the conservative force; habits were necessary for the maintenance of the social organism. More important than mere habits were correct habits which functioned harmoniously between the past and present experience. In Progressive communities the:

> endeavor [is] to shape the experiences of the young so that instead of reproducing current habits, better habits shall be formed, and thus the future adult society be an improvement on their own.[37]

Dewey considered the fundamental task of the teacher "to see to it that the greatest number of ideas . . . become . . . mature forces in the guidance of conduct."[38] The link between instincts and habits was made through Dewey's confusing term *growth*. *Growth* meant the child's constant unfolding of instincts and their structure into habits. The child's *growth* depended upon the sensitivity of the teacher in detecting the appearance of budding instincts, taking hold of them and shaping them into constructive habits. The problem for the educator was in forming instincts into habits which were socially desirable. As a child develops, particular instincts manifest themselves on a continual basis: instincts appear "at a certain age and then fade away," wrote James.[39] Now, in order for an instinct to become a habit it must be stimulated, "objects adequate to arouse it" must confront it. The theory of *growth* was founded upon the principle which James formulated in his *Principles of Psychology:*

> In all pedagogy the great thing is to strike the iron while hot, and to seize the wane of the pupil's interest in each successive subject before its ebb has come, so that knowledge may be got and a habit or skill acquired—a headway of interest, in short, secured on which afterwards the individual may float.[40]

Dewey, in popularizing that principle, retained its essence: "it is the teacher's business to know what powers are striving for utterance at a given period in the child's development, and what sorts of activity will bring these to helpful expression, in order then to supply the requisite stimuli and needed materials."[41] The importance of Dewey's *growth* concept is apparent only when it is recognized that inherited instincts structured and determined behavior. When Dewey urged that education focus upon "the full development of the child's powers,"[42] he was admitting the inevitable relationship between schooling and inherited determinants of learning. The full meaning of education (as defined by Dewey) included "all the influences that go to form the attitudes and dispositions . . . which constitute dominant habits of mind and character."[43]

Society was shaped by innumerable individuals guided by instinct. The question of *growth* was the correlation of instinctual structures with their exprsssion as social, political, and economic structures. The child-centered education of Rousseau, which emphasized objective learning, was replaced by the instinct-centered education emphasized by the subjective Pragmatists. "The child's own instincts and powers," exclaimed Dewey, "furnish the material and give the starting point for all education."[44] Instincts, in order to be nurtured, must be met by a purposeful stimulus—a stimulus which carried beyond the classroom: Dewey contended that "instincts and tendencies" were meaningless unless translated "into their social equivalents" and carried "back into a social past and [we] see them as the inheritance of previous race activities."[45] Instincts found their correlate in the existing structure of society, in industrialization, and in its massive development as well as in the distribution of property, in poverty and wealth, in the power of the few and the powerlessness of the many.

Modern education, argued Dewey, must correspond to the real

basis for social organization. Failure to do that had created social instability in the past; traditional schooling emphasized competitiveness rather than cooperation, an emphasis derived from classical liberalism. "At present," lamented Dewey, "the impulses which lie at the basis of the industrial system are either practically neglected or positively distorted during the school period. Until the instincts of construction and production are systematically laid hold of in the years of childhood . . . until they are trained in social directions . . . we certainly are in no sense to locate the source of our economic evils, much less to deal with them effectively."[46]

The gap between school and society emanated from the failure to correlate structure with structure: instincts with the products of instincts. The object of Progressive education was to "eliminate obvious social ills through starting the young on paths which shall not produce these ills."[47] We shall see that by organizing education in such a way, the existing social relations were apotheosized in the classroom.

Dewey felt that James's psychology must not only govern the method of instruction, it also must be the content of instruction. It was not sufficient to create a structure of schooling in which the teacher knew what was in process of completion. The student must also be taught a method of comprehending reality and of acting in accordance with the pedagogical principles governing the teacher. Dewey rejected external force as the principal method of restraining the individual. Habits contributed to maintaining a cooperative society only as long as they were "internally directed:"

> When external control is rejcted, the problem becomes that of finding the factors of control that are inherent within experience. When external authority is rejected, it does not follow that all authority should be rejected, but rather that there is need to search for a more effective source of authority.[48]

On the one hand, this task generated the teaching of a social consciousness, one which negated the force of class. Consequently, an inwardly conscious individualism, which negated the centrifugal force of classes but also contributed to creating a quiescent society, was required. The discipline of the classroom, according to Dewey, must have as its ends "the development of a spirit of social cooperation."[49] Furthermore, to complement the social spirit, the reality of existing social relations must also be stressed:

> Upon the playground, in game and sport, social organization takes place spontaneously and inevitably. There is something to do, some activity to be carried on, requiring natural divisions

of labor, selection of leaders and followers, mutual cooperation and emulation.[50]

On the other hand, the child must act independently of the teacher at some point without abandoning the principles of instincts and habits. At the age of eight or nine the child is made aware of the method utilized by the teacher in order to apply it on his own. This change in emphasis moved from teacher to child: "Bring the child to recognize the necessity of similar development within himself—the need for securing, for himself, practical and intellectual control of such methods of work and inquiry as will enable him to realize results for himself."[51] In the development of habits, that habit which would be secured would be the method of judging action by the practical consequences of such action for the maintenance of the organic unity of society.

There were differences among children in the manifestation of instinct, but these differences were not barriers to social cooperation. They are elements which are worked into the reality with which schools and teachers must work. In order for individual differences to be orchestrated into social orderliness, the logic and naturalness of a cooperarive individualism must be taught:

> The world in which most of us live is a world in which everyone has a calling and occupation, something to do. Some are managers and other subordinates. But the great thing for one as for the other is that each shall have had the education which enables him to see within his daily work all there is in it of large and human significance.[52]

According to Dewey, "There are few individuals who have the native capacity . . . required to invent the stationary steam engine."[53] Nevertheless, a lessened capacity was sufficient to utilize "embodiments of intelligence, once they are a part of the organized means of associated living."[54] Unless steps were taken, warned Dewey, for the less intelligent "to share [note: not to formulate] the potentially available social intelligence [i.e., social-science theory], it would be a hopeless task to talk of social cooperation."[55]

2. Society as Organism: Social Harmony in Dewey's Educational Purpose

A central contention of this study is that the most important contribution put forward by contemporary social scientists was the necessity for a "social" consciousness, of the organic unity of all individuals into a "community of interests."

The school, in Dewey's educational scheme, was the only fundamental agency "capable of fostering among very diverse elements . . .

a spirit of unity and brotherhood so that a sense of common interests and aims has prevailed over the strong forces working to divide our people into classes."[56]

Dewey did not articulate a social-science theory as fully as Ross, but he did repeat the same concepts in his educational writings: "I believe," he said, "that society is an organic union of individuals."[57] Furthermore, the child by virtue "of the social situation" in which all children found themselves, must be "stimulated to act as a member of a unity . . . to conceive of himself from the standpoint of the welfare of the group to which he belongs."[58] This followed from the conception that all societies must of necessity be harmonious machines "humming" in perfect interaction, or else face decline.

Dewey wrote that societies were composed of "relations of individuals to one another" and precisely nothing more than that. Thus, relations between individuals "compose human society," and this included:

> the give and take of participation, of a sharing that increases, that expands and deepens, the capacity and significance of the interacting factors. Conformity is a name for the absence of vital interplay. . . . But an institution that is other than the structure of human contact and intercourse is a fossil of some past society; organization, as in any living organism, is the cooperative consensus of multitudes of cells, each living in exchange with others.[59]

However, Dewey could not escape the existing divisions of society for purposes of production. Without the explicitness of Ross, he nonetheless operated from that inescapable fact. In his opinion production was a particular relationship between individuals, and it was social and not economic in nature. To attempt to change society upon the basis of class interests was in error, because this was not the basis upon which society existed. People randomly came together and separated themselves out for purposes of production, but they nevertheless constituted a social body, a cluster of individuals, not of classes, and this cluster or community constituted a social organism. All societies were social entities, capitalist as well as primitive societies. The social had to be predominant over the individual, region, class, ethnicity, or occupation. Supposedly, the acceptance of "class" as a political entity meant conflict, and for this Dewey had no stomach. Dewey separated the existing economy from "universal" attributes found in all societies. Teachers must never teach from the principle of class interest, but from the principle of universal social cooperation:

> It is possible to be alert and active in the struggle for social

reorganization and yet recognize that it is *social* reorganization that is required, and that it must be undertaken in the social, rather than a class interest.[60]

Given the nature of societies everywhere, the true objective of the social organism was to seek the greatest possible harmonious interaction of individuals. Like the social scientists, Dewey knew objectively that monopoly capitalism had substantially altered social relations:

> Perhaps the constantly increasing role of corporations in our economic life gives a clue to a fitting name. The word may be used in a wider sense than is conveyed by its technical legal meaning. We may then say that the United States has steadily moved from an earlier pioneer individualism to a condition of dominant corporateness. The influence business corporations exercize in determining present industrial and economic activities is both a cause and a symbol of the tendency to combination in all phases of life.[61]

Within these changes the attitude of the people must be altered accordingly:

> When the corporateness becomes internal, when, that is, it is realized in thought and purpose, it will become qualitative. In this change, law will be realized not as a rule arbitrarily imposed from without but as the relations which hold individuals together. The balance of the individual and the social will be organic.[62]

If the unity could be achieved through internal, self-directed means rather than external sanction, i.e., force, the possibility of effective organic unison would be greatly advanced. However, the necessity for an internalized ethic sprang from the concrete conditions of social interaction. The problem then was in balancing individualism with the indispensable monopolization of modern industrial capitalism. The corporate society was not the patterning of society after corporations, however, but the determination of institutional structures and their functions by the social relations within monopoly capitalist production.

How similar was the thinking of Progressives concerning the identity of interests in the division of labor. This cornerstone of "Progressive" thought is found prominently displayed by Dewey's didactic work on the new individualism of the monopoly era entitled, *Individualism: Old and New*. The public welfare was the highest welfare, wrote Dewey, and the public, therefore, should incorporate a new corporate spirit, the spirit of cooperation between capital and labor:

It would be in accord with the spirit of American life if the movement were undertaken by voluntary agreement and endeavor rather than by government coercion. . . . A coordinating and directive council in which captains of industry and finance would meet with representatives of labor and public officials to plan the regulation of industrial activity.[63]

Dewey hoped for a voluntary coordinating council, but what he ignored was that, as long as labor remained propertyless and property remained in the hands of capitalists, the meeting was a meeting of unequals and as such could only, under conditions outlined by Dewey, act as a conservative force in retaining the existing distribution of property. The final outcome was the cooperative effort of unequals resulting in the preservation and continuation of that inequality.

Regardless of the theoretical similarity, Dewey was much more practical than Ross in actually conceiving of school "methods and content," even to the point of developing his own laboratory school at the University of Chicago. Whereas Ross was not sure just what "shape this new education will take," Dewey was one of many who took part in molding that education, giving it shape as well as content.

The need for the Progressive content in education corresponded to the reality of ongoing monopolization, social change and labor struggles, and was, therefore, necessary for the orderly functioning of that society. Of this Dewey wrote:

Modern conditions of production and exchange of commodities have made the world one to a degree never approximated before. . . . Consequently, there is a demand which never existed before that all the terms of school instruction shall be seen and appreciated in their bearing upon the network of social activities which bind people together.[64]

Dewey's concern here was the adjustment of education to correspond with contemporary economic forms, and to prepare the citizenry to act within the structure of society without causing instability. Ross proposed a belief structure that unified rather than divided. Dewey saw social order as a pragmatic necessity. Progressive educators placed that necessity well within the goal orientation of the educational enterprise. If such was needed for the smooth operation of society, then education should incorporate it. Dewey insisted:

The interest of the teachers is not centered on the welfare of any one industry, but on the welfare of the young people of the community. If the material prosperity of a community is almost entirely due to one or two industries, obviously the welfare of the individuals of the community is very closely connected with these industries. Then the educational purpose is training the children to the most intelligent use of their own capabilities and of their industries as the material for the strictly utilitarian part of their training. The problem of general public school education is not to train workers for a trade, but to make use of the whole environment of the child in order to supply motive and meaning to work.[65]

A critical reading reveals Dewey at his pragmatic best, tightrope walking his way between individualism and social cooperation: the welfare of the individual is supreme, yet it cannot be separated from the welfare of a single capitalist enterprise. In the final analysis, it was monopoly capitalism which created the unique conditions upon which his ideas on education and individualism were based. For example, Dewey spoke at length of the necessity to incorporate the larger aspects of social interaction of the "interdependence" binding the "activity of every farmer, manufacturer, laborer, and merchant, in every part of the civilized globe."[66] Within each particular phase of production, each worker, in order that he or she may work with a consciousness of the social interdependence binding production, should know the fundamentals of those particular and general productive processes.[67]

The substance of the effort at providing this general knowledge to workers was principally to orient them towards a greater feeling of "social interdependence." "Industrial . . . processes," Dewey said, "depend today upon knowledge of facts and laws of natural and social science in much greater degree than ever before."[68] Consequently, the adjustment of individuals to the necessity of harmonious social relationships (the organic society) depended upon their understanding of the productive processes, in their particular place of work, and, in general, in the interdependence of society's and the world's production. Dewey could only conclude that the "real question is one of reorganization of all education to meet the changed conditions of life . . . accompanying the revolution in industry."[69]

Progressive education, in general, and Dewey, in particular, upheld the proposition that education "gives an equal chance to everyone because it will base itself on the world in which children live."[70] Dewey accepted the mode of production as given, and although at odds with the more negative aspects of the environment, agreed basically with the economic and political foundations of the society. Given this, Dewey's task consisted of fitting the child to the parameters of that real, living environment. Dewey feared a school which did not grow with the "new elements and needs of society."[71] Therefore, Dewey asked that "each one of our schools [be] an embryonic community . . . active with types of occupations that reflect the life of the larger society. . . . When the school introduces and trains each child of society into membership within such a little community, saturating him with the spirit of service, and providing him with instruments of effective self-direction, we shall have the deepest and best guarantee of a larger society which is worthy, lovely, and harmonious."[72] Progressive education, in practice, harmonized the individual with the social changes caused by the changing methods of production. Dewey expressed the idea completely when he wrote: "The teacher then becomes the one who sees that the pupils get proper material and that they use it in ways that are true; that is, in ways that represent relations and conditions that actually exist outside the classroom."[73] Those "relations and conditions" existing in the social environment were inevitable social situations which one did not attack, but rather worked with. The causes of poverty, slums, or racism were not "windmills" to be attacked by a Progressive pragmatism, which understood that to attack the roots of such conditions would have meant conflict with their own privileged position and that of the powerful industrialists and financiers. Dewey proposed a liberal ideology, but one welded to monopoly capitalism. Never ideologically opposed to the existing social order, never at odds with the existing social structure, Dewey perceived with insight necessity for radical departures in education as a means of socializing youth.[74] If he fought any major battles, it was with those who were wedded to educational tradition. Traditionalists, Dewey said, held a conception "which no longer fits the facts of every-man-for-himself society which ceased to exist a hundred years ago."[75]

Like most Progressives, Dewey felt the premonopoly laissez-faire individualism was posing conflicts within the existing social relations under monopoly over production. Dewey clearly defined the basis of the new individualism.

> The problem of constructing a new individuality consonant with the objective conditions under which we live is the deepest problem of our times. . . . The problem is . . . essentially that of creation of a new individualism as significant for modern conditions as the old individualism at its best was for its day and place. The first step in further definition of this problem is realization of the collective age which we have already entered. When that is apprehended, the issue will define itself as utilization of the realities of a corporate civilization to validate and embody the distinctive moral element in the American version of individualism.[76]

Schools therefore were to inculcate an appreciation of social cooperation rather than competitiveness (which characterized the educational reforms of Massachusetts under Horace Mann). Social unity was the goal which allowed each individual to rise to his or her capabilities within the parameters of capitalism. The restrained cooperative individualism of the monopoly era was one which Progressive education was to nurture through instruction which "vitally and sincerely" interested the students, and which informed them "of the social and scientific bearing of the calling they were to enter."[77] Progressive educational reforms thus preserved the ideal of the individual who was able to realize his or her potential but was able to submerge his individualism within the higher ideal of the social "good." The logical consequence of this socializing and conservative functioning of the schools was the constant reinforcement of the social relations of capitalist production. The social relations of production are the relationship and distinction between (1) the owners of the means of production who directly or indirectly purchase the labor-power, of (2) propertyless laborers whose survival depends upon marketing their labor-power. The realization of the labor-power in actual production and circulation and the importance of putting workers to work is the pivot of capitalist production upon which Progressive reformers, either consciously or unconsciously, elaborated their theories. If we lose sight of this very real concrete condition, both the theories of Ross and of Dewey lose their fundamental relationship to monopoly capitalism in general. It was capitalist production itself which created the intense class conflicts which the theorists perceived most clearly and towards which they consciously directed their practical theories; however, it was the relations of production (and, therefore, production) which were consciously being supported through the emphasis upon the organic society, in general, and as the content and purpose of Progressive education, in particular (and eventually the entire IQ testing and tracking system). Their theories justified the increased state intervention required by the changed social order of monopoly capitalism; this was reflected not only in the content of educational theory but in the fact of the increased social control inherent in the institutionalization of mass public education.

3. Relations of Production and Dewey's Educational Scheme

Within just such a theoretical framework, the social good was an orderly society, organic with a common consciousness and common goals. Nevertheless, the real living environment was not common to all; some were rich, others poor; some owned the factories, others worked in them. In practice, Progressive education corresponded to the reality of classes in society, regardless of its stated commitment to an equal education for all. Dewey found vocational training for "colored" workers and "foreign district" schools and Americanization programs quite consonant with the Progressive movement.[78] Furthermore, he thought that vocational training in the poorer communities enabled "the child to pick up the thread of life in his own community by giving him an understanding of the elements of the occupations that supply man's daily needs."[79] And, if the "practical world is the real world," why prepare the son of an unskilled worker for a professional calling? Dewey felt that the school should work closely with local industrial occupations, in contrast to what he perceived to be a tendency towards separating school and community: "one of the chief evils of the present state of affairs is the accidental and unintelligent way in which workers, especially of the youthful age, find their jobs." He asked that schools integrate the vocational with the academic (such as occurred in the Gary, Indiana, schools): "after a careful survey of its own actual local conditions and needs . . . both the industrial and the educational situation in each of the larger towns should be studied."[80] Dewey's example of integration of school with community was Public School No. 26 "located in the poor, crowded, colored district of Indianapolis." Dewey's comments in his *School and Society* indicate his perspective on vocational education for poor communities:

> It was decided to use the [school] buildings for social and industrial purposes. One of them was fitted up by the pupils and neighbors interested as a manual training building. In this there was a carpenter shop, a sewing room, and a room for the class in shoemaking. Each grade devotes a regular number of hours a week to handwork, and has an opportunity to join other industrial classes after school.[81]

In School No. 26, girls were trained in clothing, millinery, crocheting, and cooking. "The girls not only learn to cook real meals, but they learn how to serve them, and then how to take care of the demonstration house." Dewey recommended that such schools "be started in all our great cities" in districts "where the children come from homes with limited resources and meager surroundings."[82] Pragmatically, Progressive education was "to meet the needs of the neighborhood" and as such coordinated the content of education for that practical consideration by placing heavy emphasis on vocational education in working-class and poor neighborhood schools.

The existing division of labor demanded a particular educational process that prepared unequals for inequality. For the working class, two elements combined to form their education: on the one hand, vocational education, and on the other, a method of despotic domination characteristic of factories. Dewey made the despotism of the factory a reality in the classroom: "The simple facts of the case are that in the great majority of human beings the distinctively intellectual interests are not dominant." Consequently, he stated, "some are managers and others are subordinates." In the classroom this demanded a method whereby all "activity to be carried on" would be divided into "natural divisions of labor, selection of leaders and followers."[83] By so doing, schools inculcated in the working class a consciousness which would predispose them to engage cooperatively in production.

Dewey, like Ross, had a strong dislike for aristocratic privileges and fixed classes; education was the means of "leveling" society through making mobility possible but not inevitable from lower to high classes. The ideal of socioeconomic mobility in the thinking of Progressive social scientists was expressed through an abiding faith in the power of the individual to better himself or herself. Education was to provide the bulk of that opportunity for individualism to continue its historical journey.[84] However, that providing of equal opportunity was not and could not be practiced, although individualism was nurtured nevertheless. Since Dewey never proposed the elimination of social classes, it was logical that vocational training be fostered in schools where such training would prepare students without altering the distribution of property or negatively affecting capitalist production.

Dewey reacted to criticism that he focused on a narrow vocational education fitting individuals to slots, and angrily retorted that his conception of vocational education was a training which had as its principal interest the furthering "of such intelligent initiative, ingenuity and executive capacity as shall make workers, as far as may be, the masters of their own industrial fate."[85]

The qualifying phrase "as far as may be" is the key to understanding exactly how ambiguously Dewey developed his thinking, but at the same time how well he remained a Progressive at heart. How far could the regime be transformed, when "social" rather than class action was fundamental to his thesis on social change? The preservation of the status quo directly resulted from the "as far as may be" approach to industrial training—for as Dewey had written, society was an organic union of individuals. Dewey claimed at one time to be a socialist and even joined the Socialist Party, but his conception of socialism included state regulation of the economy in the interests of monopoly capitalism. He considered such loyal federal agencies as the Interstate Commerce Commission, the Federal Reserve Board, and the Farm Relief Board as examples of "socialistic undertakings on a large scale."[86] Private ownership of the means of production, of banking and financial empires, did not move Dewey towards advocating socialization of ownership, which, of course, forms the economic foundation of socialism. Dewey moved obviously towards state capitalism, one in which "governmental agencies" would regulate the same enterprises in the "public" interest.

In this manner, Dewey assumed, capitalism could be "transformed without the civil war which Soviet Russia experienced."[87] Neither the end nor the means were defined precisely, but he thought that it was to be a "kind of socialism" and of the "public" rather than the "capitalist" type (public in the sense which referred to an organic society). Did Dewey genuinely expect a "gentlemanly" transition to socialism? Not to socialism in the Marxist sense. Dewey was a staunch opponent of communism, upheld corporate individualism, the role of corporations, and therefore private property and the division between mental and physical labor. His real hope was that the present social order could achieve a harmonious state, but he never challenged the tenets of capitalist production. This is precisely how Dewey and his educational thought must be understood. He often employed the term "socialism," but, if one reads within the context of his educational and philosophical theory, it would seem that he envisioned an "organic" society when he spoke of the necessity "for some kind of socialism."[88]

Dewey's educational goals corresponded to Ross's functionalist theories in the effort at creating the skills in workers that operated within the limits of the "practical" world of monopoly production. This, however, was not the essence nor the extent of Progressive education. If social unity under a common ideology was to be realized, then the state must be able to command the respect and allegiance of its citizenry. Progressives concurred. Americanization programs were "Progressive," because they tended to bring the immigrant into cultural and political harmony with fundamental institutions and values. A commentary of Dewey's on a patriotic festival at a public school in Chicago's "foreign district" is illuminating:

> The patriotic value of such exercises is greater than the daily flag salute, or patriotic poem, for the children understand what they are supposed to be enthusiastic about, as they see

before them the things which naturally arouse patriotic emotions.[89]

Dewey also expressed an imperialist nationalism which coincided with his scientific approach towards society. He wrote warmly when patriotism and imperialism were taught through the "learning by doing method." The United States takeover of Panama, the forced treaty granting exclusive jurisdiction over the Canal Zone, and the military value of the Canal to the United States' imperialist ambitions were facts not unknown to Dewey. Moreover, he was quite willing to base an example of Progressive methodology upon the necessity of the Canal to United States interests.[90] The teaching of the practicality of imperialism was, for Dewey, not the issue. The issue was whether one successfully connected the individual in a conscious and scientific manner to the existing social order.

We must see all sides of this Progressive. He was at all times proposing an educational enterprise whose ideological content was consonant with the determining economic structure and the social and political relationships inherent in that structure.

Schooling under any mode of production governed by private property has as its principal task an ideological socialization which attempts to undermine the contradictions between classes. In the era of monopoly capitalism such a task required that the ideology reflect class cooperation rather than competition. In this manner the form of the contradiction between labor and capital was ostensibly challenged. In addition, the division of labor required that the schools train youth as far as necessary in varying aspects of production through vocational coursework. This, however, meant that the relations of production would necessarily be strengthened through the schools.

Chapter Five

THE RISE OF INTELLIGENCE TESTING*

A discussion of Progressive educational theory would be incomplete without a discussion of the methodology incorporated into the classroom. Teaching methods are means through which ends are attained. There is an integral relationship between the two. If the principle of education is the organic unity of the division of labor, then the means employed will necessarily be the pathway towards that goal. The most fundamental method incorporated into education in the early twentieth century was intelligence testing. In this chapter I shall focus upon the material basis for the rise of intelligence testing. Current critiques of intelligence testing usually ignore the connection of intelligence testing to the rise of monopoly capitalism. These critiques, while they generate deserved criticism of these pseudoscientific devices, fail to understand completely the purpose of testing. There are many routes which can be taken to destroy the credibility of IQ tests. The most popular has been to confront testing on its own ground: that is, to show that as a quantification system, these tests do not stand up to rigorous scientific

---

*Sections of this chapter have appeared in *The United States Educational System: Marxist Approaches*, ed. Marvin J. Berlowitz and Frank E. Chapman (Minneapolis: Marxist Educational Press, 1980), and in *The Insurgent Sociologist*, Fall, 1977.

analysis. The tests, therefore, do not measure scientifically what they pretend to measure. This is the approach taken by Leon J. Kamin, and by Samuel Bowles and Herbert Gintis.[1] I shall argue that one should not confine oneself to discussing the scientific merits of testing, but go one step further and look at the historical development as well as the material foundation of the use of the concept of intelligence. It is here that the key to understanding the use of testing in the classroom is found.

Several criticisms of testing have emphasized the sorting effect that tests promote, the close relationship between social class and IQ. Again, this does not subject the concept of intelligence, to sufficient critique, only its manifestations. This approach, often presented in conjunction with the statistical approach, defines testing as a method of allocating unequal education; Noam Chomsky, Leon J. Kamin, and Clarence Karier have reached this conclusion.[2] While the argument adequately describes apparent effects of these tests, it does not delve below the manifestation. Testing and the concept of intelligence itself are historical categories that can only be understood through analyzing their material historical development. In this way, we can judge their function and scientific merit in contemporary society.

1. *Classical Psychology vs. the "New" Psychology*

In the late nineteenth century the idea that individuals differed in their levels of intelligence, and that this intellectual difference was the basis for socioeconomic differentiation, was a comparatively new concept. In the eighteenth and in most of the nineteenth centuries it was thought that humans were endowed by nature with similar, if not identical, powers of the mind. Nature endowed each human with more or less equal mental organs; their use and application depended upon the "will" of the individual. Thus, self-willed qualities of industriousness and frugality were means through which social differences were finally obtained. It was not the brain or intelligence per se that figured principally into the social order. John Locke conceived of the mind as a *tabula rasa* upon which the social experiences of the individual were impressed. The concept of the mind as a blank space conceded the general equality of the mind but not the equality of the experiences. Locke could then argue that education, or the totality of learning experiences, was of fundamental importance in the determination of the social being of the individual.[3]

Faculty psychology was the theoretical summary of classical bourgeois ideas of the nature of the mind. Here it was claimed that all mental perceptions were due to impressions caused externally. Hobbes formulated the idea of faculties, or functions, and his formulation assumed the equal capacity of the various human functions.[4] Human faculties, he wrote, are divided into two main categories: 1) bodily or physical functions such as nutrition and reproduction, and 2) the mental, or mind, functions such as cognition and motivation. According to Hobbes cognition is a function enabling any individual to acquire knowledge entirely through the senses; this ability to "sense" the world is not inherited; all that has been inherited is the capacity, or faculty, i.e., the sensory power. Relation to the external world depended upon the accurate reflection of external reality upon the senses. It is, however, extremely important to point out that the senses themselves—and he spoke of humans in general—were regarded as innately equal. Faculty psychology then assumed a more or less equal mind, or sensory organ, from which laws of the mental process could be deduced through scientific study.

Psychology, as a discipline, gained a following in the advanced (or advancing) capitalist countries in the nineteenth century and until the twentieth century, adhered to the Hobbesian conception of the universal equality of sense organs. One common measure of comparing the thinking of children was age. Rather than saying that so-and-so acted as if she had an IQ of 65, one would say she acted like a four-year-old. Age, however, was a very general approach to understanding behavior and of little use in experiments comparing "intelligence," since age could only be useful in comparing more or less innately equal individuals.

Psychology in the midnineteenth century studied individuals as if they were of equal mental capacity. The principal objectives of early psychological studies branched into two areas. Some experiments involved general laws of behavior, applicable to all humans. Thus, for example, Wundt's famous psychological laboratory in Leipzig studied reaction time, sensory stimulation, and other psychological phenomena in order to discern general human behavioral characteristics. It was assumed that all humans were endowed with equal behavioral manifestations so that experimental studies of broad numbers could indicate general laws. Laboratories were established to discover what all (i.e., normal) humans were capable of experiencing.[5]

The second branch experimented with extreme mental disorders. Students of psychology who studied psychological problems before the rise of the concept of intelligence concentrated upon extremes rather than problem cases within the "normal" population. Medical doctors working in psychology tended to study extreme forms of mental disorders, searching for cures, and they were obsessed more with mental abnormalities of the extreme type than with the "average" person. There was a decided emphasis upon searching for causes of abnormality and studying the behavioral characteristics of extreme mental illness. A logical extension from this was to embrace the doctrine of individual mental differences among the entire population. In this way the practices of those engaged in studying behavioral phenomena moved from a focus on extreme mental problems and general laws of human behavior to a focus on general laws of human behavior stressing individual differences.[6]

Gradually, the idea of innate equality gave way to the idea of innate differences. The pioneering studies carried out by Galton at midcentury on mental inheritance were still not of sufficient precision for arguing that intelligence was the dividing line between individuals.[7] The outlines of an inherited intellectual continuum such as that proposed by Terman emerged in Galton's work. However, no such concept of "intelligence" had yet been proposed by the midnineteenth century. Apologists for laissez faire such as Galton and Spencer noted that individuals were selected in or out by a natural selection process which had as much to do with mental ability as it had with general industriousness of individuals. Nevertheless, attention was beginning to be focused on potential differences of the mind. Galton is certainly a precursor, but in 1869, when his famous book *Hereditary Genius* appeared, Lockean notions still honeycombed his presentation.

The breakdown of faculty psychology occurred by degrees, reaching a final disintegration about the turn of the century. Initial assaults upon the doctrine of innate equality were ambiguous, but in the direction of change. Galton, for example, used some of the concepts of classical psychology but also incorporated new content; he therefore focused on individual mental differences to a much greater degree but could still remark that "the capacity for labor" was also a fundamental quality of individual differences:

> The particular meaning in which I employ the word ability, does not restrict my argument from a wider application— that the concrete triple event of ability combined with zeal and with capacity for hard labor, is inherited, much more will there be justification for believing that any one of its three elements, whether it be ability, zeal, or capacity for labour, is similarly a gift of inheritance.[8]

Galton had presumed a fluid social structure in which individuals rose and fell in social standing. Something reminiscent of Ben Franklin's homilies can be detected in the arguments Galton presented in *Hereditary Genius*. He claimed that "social hindrances" could not impede men of high ability from becoming eminent; on the other hand, those incompetents born into "social advantage" would never reach eminence.[9] The one important concept injected into bourgeois ideology by Galton was that of a continuum of natural abilty inherited from high to low. What Galton did not develop in 1869, the date when *Hereditary Genius* appeared, was that social classes were a reflection of the process of inherited intelligence. That conceptualization would be developed in the future, and would accompany the unveiling of the intelligence test.

Over a period of time the concept of intelligence would develop. However, early students of individual psychological differences would be some time in concocting a coherent theory of innate intelligence. James McKeen Cattell, one of the leaders of mental testing in the United States, had studied under Wundt in Leipzig but had broken with his mentor over the question of individual differences. Cattell claimed that individuals differed in such behavior as reaction time and that psychological studies should concentrate on those differences rather than on the similarity of reactions, sensory perceptions and similar phenomena. Wundt disliked his student's innovation but nonetheless allowed Cattell to write a doctoral dissertation on individual differences in sense perceptions. This individual break in continuity between classical and neoclassical notions of the mind was a prelude to several decades of similar assaults on the Lockean conceptions of the mind.[10]

Behind the final conceptualization of intelligence stood a number of necessary postulates. Pragmatism evolved from practical needs to solve the problem of social disorganization and consequently its exponents openly attacked the materialist conceptions of cognition which characterized classical liberal philosophy. Wundt's studies of reflex were examples of the psychology against which James and Dewey waged constant battle.[11] James's psychology opposed sensory experiments, because the latter posited equal relationships between subjects and objects. Wundt expected a stimulus to elicit a corresponding response. James contended that no such relationship can ever be observed, for a stimulus creates a particular response only through the individual's particular structure. "These reaction-time experiments" warned James, "are then in no sense measurements of the swiftness of thought."[12] Reaction varies with the individual, with age, fatigue, stimulants and so on. Reaction-time experiments conceived of consciousness "as a purely cognitive form of being," and for James this earned it the epithet a "thoroughly antipsychologist" school.[13]

The senses created the vision of reality, selecting this or that object, elements of objects, and combinations of objects to form an individualized world. James's psychology recognized the primacy of the subject in ordering reality; Wundt's psychology (and the psychology of classical liberalism) focused upon the relationship between object (stimulus) and subject (response) and ultimately admitted an important role for the material stiumulus. For James, a stimulus can never be measured, for its is always different things for different people. There was "no proof that the same bodily sensation is ever got by twice."[14] In the final analysis, "Every thought we have of a given fact is . . . unique, and only bears a resemblance . . . with our other thoughts of the same fact."[15] The fact that "no two ideas are ever exactly the same," wrote James, made it impossible to follow the Lockean school.[16]

The "mind chooses to suit itself," according to James, "but it does so not on the basis of external 'laws,' or forces; the only actual determinants of behavior are immediate practical consequences. The mind chooses a course of action suited to its 'private interest.' "[17] Thus, all action is based upon an immediate "sizing-up" of the consequences of a number of possible choices for action. Dewey expressed this point very well when he said: "We always live at the time we live and not at some other time, and only by extracting at each present time the full meaning of each present experience are we prepared for doing the same thing in the future."[18] If a person successfully chooses correct, or practical, behavior—then we can say that the person has acted "intelligently." The senses reason, "break up the totality of the phenomenon reasoned about in parts," said James, and then pick "from among these the particular one which . . . may lead to the proper conclusion."[19] Not all were endowed with equal capacities for intelligent action. A man of genius "is he who will always stick in his bill at the right point, and bring it out with the right element—'reason' if the emergency be theoretical, 'means' if it be practical—transfixed upon it."[20]

James distinguished at least two levels of reasoned thought:

> one where similarity merely operates to call up cognate thoughts, and another further stage, where the bond of identity between the cognate thoughts is noticed; so minds of genius may be divided into two main sorts, those who notice the bond and those who merely obey it. The first are called abstract reasoners . . . men of science and philosophers—the analysts . . . men of intuition. These judge rightly.[21]

Pragmatists were explicit on a hierarchy of intelligence; James wrote:

> In all ages the man whose determinations are swayed by reference to the most distant ends has been held to possess the highest intelligence, the tramp who lives from hour to

hour; the bohemian whose engagements are from day to day; the bachelor who builds but for a single life; the father who acts for another generation; the patriot who thinks for a whole community and many generations; and finally, the philosopher and saint whose cares are for humanity and for eternity— these range themselves in an unbroken hierarchy, wherein each successive grade results from an increased manifestation of the special form of action by which the cerebral centres are distinguished from all below them."[22]

Thus, concrete social relationships were arranged according to intelligence—from the tramp to the philosopher. Pragmatism was the systematic laying of the foundation for the use of intelligence testing: the reality of society is a reality which can be measured only through the subjective quality of intelligence. Finally, this psychology denied the possibility of altering a set of instinctive structures; one was either born with a certain capacity for intelligence or not. Society was predetermined, just as individuals could not escape their stamp of intelligence given at birth.

Society, being a sum total of accumulated intelligence, arranged itself according to the continuum of intelligence. For some, as Dewey said, there is a distinctive intellectual superiority; there were to be the leaders. Those with lesser capacities for intelligent action were the followers. Dewey concluded that the "simple facts of the case are that in the great majority of human beings the distinctively intellectual interest is not dominant."[23] These natural dimensions were reflected in the world of production: "Some are managers and others are subordinates."[24]

Pragmatism served to prepare the way for the fuller development of intelligence testing. Its first task was to depose systematically classical psychology; the second task was to present a coherent theory of consciousness. In so doing, the conceptualization of intelligence testing was inevitable. Upon this foundation, the pioneers of testing, Terman, Thorndike, and Goddard (and more recently Jensen, Herrnstein, and Shockley) constructed their intelligence theories.[25]

The pragmatic concept of intelligence implied several important "hidden" aspects. First, it implied the existence of only a small number of gifted, or highly intelligent, individuals in society and a large number of average citizens. Second, it implied that leadership, political or economic, should be in the hands of a small number of people, the intellectual elite. Third, it underscored the logic of "experts" in every branch of organized economics or political activity and separated the masses of people from the leadership. The logic of this concept led directly to legitimizing the process of reducing popular participation in government, to the further centralization of power, and to the domination of a small elite over the majority. Lastly, intelligence advanced the separation of theory and practice, a separation between experts and followers. Experts were fundamentally theoreticians who guided the practical activity of the citizenry. Those who participated physically, for example, in the production of automobiles, had no relationship to the final product other than through their manual labor. On the other hand, theoreticians—engineers, managers, executives—had no other relationship to the final product than the planning which directed physical production. In politics and economics, conceptualization of intelligence reflected an authoritarian social relationship between an elite and masses of average or below-average individuals. In essence, this social relationship evolved directly from the process of monopolization of the means of production. In the application of intelligence testing, the "hidden curriculum" taught the inevitability of an elite dominating the masses. It made palatable the centralization of all power, political and economic; ultimately, it made despotism into a natural human relationship. Testing fostered a quiescent population, uninformed both in politics and in economics. These were matters for the elite. Such was the logic and consequence of intelligence testing, a tool to harmonize a society bristling with antagonisms. Through the repeated use of testing, "intelligence" became a "natural" habit.

By the early 1890s in the United States, a pragmatist school of psychology stressing purely intellectual ability formed. A separation appeared between the "sensory" or faculty approach, and the neoclassical school of psychology, which not only stressed individual differences but also something to be later called "intelligence," or purely innate intellectual processes. Franz Boas in 1891 studied memory and the "intellectual acuteness" of 1,500 school children. J.A. Gilbert in New Haven, 1893, searching for a composite index of "general ability" of 1,200 school children, diagnosed the results of several mental tests. By 1891 Hugo Munsterberg was applying mental tests, not the kind of sensory measures characteristic of Wundt and even Cattell. Munsterberg's tests consisted of fourteen different tasks such as addition and recall as well as identifying colors, designs, and lengths. The objective of such new concepts was the investigation of variations in individual responses, responses which were considered by the researcher to be of an intellectual rather than sensory nature.[26]

It was Binet, Henry, and Simon who together carried out the final advance in the development of intelligence as a concept.[27] Here it was not a case of immediate discovery, but of a gradual development. Binet's earlier writings remained somewhat enmeshed in faculty psychology. Initially, the purpose of his tests were to weed out the feebleminded from the educational system and were not meant to gauge a full range of mental abilities. One task alone guided his work: identification of the feebleminded. The educational process of the state was to be thus left unhampered by "laggards." The radical departure that gave Binet his fame was his use of a number of concepts eventually latched onto by intelligence-test pioneers. First, he used multiple tests reflecting a composite picture of the individual and based them on a scale. Children were judged upon a score formulated in comparison with the responses of "normal" children. Secondly, Binet based the norm on "normal" children whose sensory organs were acknowledged to be more or less equal. It was the feebleminded whom he judged to be abnormal. The "early" Binet was not yet prepared to accept the later notions of intelligence. When two investigators using Binet's tests found that children of the bourgeoisie scored higher, Binet could dismiss their conclusion, claiming that environmental conditions as well as superior educational experiences were the basis for the discrepancy.

The testing movement was initially bound to classical ideas of the mind as a sense organ but the outlines of the new formulation were beginning to develop. Binet decided to establish a scale of "intelligence" and in 1905, for the first time, he introduced an instrument for the measurement of pure, or natural, intelligence. In a short time that scale would be used for specific reasons other than seeking out the feebleminded from the public schools or identifying morons in asylums. Intelligence testing had moved away from a close association with extreme mental disorder to a much wider social application. It is this particular social application which concerns us—for the concepts contained within the instrument of the mental test, individual differences and intelligence, would have decided effects when applied to the entire society.

Binet, too, changed his point of view of testing, from a gauge for the detection of feeblemindedness to a measurement of the mental level of "normal" children. Moving from an interest in a common standard for discerning the feebleminded, he eventually proposed a common measure for assessing the intelligence of children for pedagogical purposes. Binet prepared the general framework for modern testing practices by stating:

> We ought not to expect that all children of a given age should be of the same intellectual level. This is very evident. All are not equally intelligent; and if all were able to reply in the same manner to any one test, it would simply prove that the test was poorly made, and subject to some error, for example,

to suggestion. Let us reckon then that in a group of children of the same age some are necessarily behind in intelligence, others in advance, others regular. What we have a right to demand is that there should be a balance between those who are behind and those who are in advance.[28]

Binet soon arrived at the conclusion that "natural intelligence" was the object of the measuring device. The intelligence of children was for Binet an independent faculty, "independent not only of instruction" but also of the ability of students to retain or learn. Binet sought to measure the uncultured, natural intellectual capacity of individuals. What was this "natural faculty?" Of what did it consist? As Binet described it: "Intelligence marks itself by the best possible adaptation of the individual to his environment."[29] This definition left much room for misinterpretation, but in the context of his writing it meant only one thing: to the extent that the individual conformed to the roles expected of him, he was intelligent. More succinctly: how well does one cope? Or how well does the individual function within the given social order?

Both in England and in France, investigators reported differences in intelligence between socioeconomic classes. When the initial conclusions indicating class differentials in intelligence were sent to him, Binet vacillated on the question of nature or nurture. He quickly suggested individualized instruction as one possible cause of the superior intelligence of the rich. Later, he began to consider the validity of these conclusions. During the last phase of his work, Binet, moved by the conclusions of various investigators who reported differences in intelligence between socioeconomic classes, urged psychologists to begin to make comparative studies of groups. Rather than continue in the development of the measuring instrument, Binet urged comparative analysis of the results, comparing the results of the poor and the rich. Binet had assumed, long before he had begun the development of his tests, that the poor were inferior to the rich, but he had never intended his tests as devices for comparing classes, only individuals.

As a possible answer to the question of social-class intelligence, Binet suggested that psychologists make a "comprehensive study of (the tests') significance, a calculation of their results."[30] This meant, for example, that tests of suggestibility would be grouped "to make a classification."[31] The question uppermost in the mind of Binet was the use of the experimental method as a means of concluding what were until then principally impressionistic conclusions to data derived for other reasons. He would, therefore, reprove an English researcher for "having confused . . . the averages of [children of different social classes] which thus lost some of their significance"—i.e., alleged social-class differences in intelligence.[32] The problem for the scientifically-minded Binet was to retain the full significance of the group averages.

Certain numbers of any given group were inferior, others normal, others superior. Binet clearly posited this assessment after many years of investigation. He also presented a completely new vision of the basis for the social order: rather than property and its distribution, Binet offered intelligence as the essential element in social intercourse:

> Of what use is a measure of intelligence? Without doubt one could conceive many possible applications of the process, in dreaming of a future where the social sphere would be better organized than ours; where everyone would work according to his known aptitudes in such a way that no particle of psychic force shall be lost for society. That would be the ideal city.[33]

Clearly, Binet expressed a model for the functioning of society identical to that of the Progressive social scientists to whom the crucial problem was the "right organization of individuals." Intelligence testing contributed to the very same goal that motivated Progressive scholars and reformers.

Binet served the state quite well in France, pointing out the value of mental tests for more effective military recruitment. Like his counterparts in Progressive education, Binet urged slower students to study nonacademic courses:

> Certain children, to whom the ordinary work of the class is distasteful make compensations in manual work, sewing, designing . . . little girls, weak in orthography, are strong in sewing and capable of instruction concerning housekeeping; and, all things considered, this is more important for their future.[34]

The tests as applied in the United States would be in step with Binet at this point. It was at this juncture that intelligence testing in the U.S. became more than the business of a group of psychological innovators. Its social function now became quite clear. When Binet's scale was brought to the United States, its immediate consequence was the identification of social problems with intelligence, and correlation with Mendelian principles of inheritance. Henry H. Goddard's famous book, *The Kallikak Family* (1914), indicted the poor for being mentally deficient and conjured up lurid scenes from the netherworld of the slums. His conclusions were drawn from the application of Binet's test to inmates of a mental institution in New Jersey. By then, faculty psychology had been totally discredited among the leading schools of psychology; its place was assumed by pragmatism, which stressed individual differences of mental abilities and implicitly accepted a range of individual intelligence in any given population. How did this fundamental alteration in the scientific understanding of the nature of the mind occur? Again, one must look at the changes in social relations effected by monopoly capitalism.

2. The Concept of Intelligence as an Ideological Construct

The transition from premonopoly forms of capitalism to monopoly capitalism is the base upon which both the scientific conception of the nature of the mind and the ideological rationales for capitalism evolved. Although the intense contradiction between capital and labor under monopoly was the main force in propelling "intelligence" to the ideological front, other aspects of the social relations of production were also important. The classical bourgeois notion of the material equality of the human organism found its basis in the distribution of property and in the social relations of production. For example, in 1776 at the time of the American Revolution, 80% of adult white males owned some form of productive property—principally land for yeoman farming. More importantly, it was not uncommon for these property owners to engage directly in production. Benjamin Franklin not only owned a print shop, but also engaged directly, alongside his apprentices, in the production of a commodity. In other words, Franklin, as was common in premonopoly bourgeois society, soiled his hands through directly engaging in production on his property. Had bourgeois ideology of wealth been based upon any other foundation than industriousness, thrift, or frugality (i.e., labor), individuals such as Franklin and countless property owners would have found it difficult to establish the logic of their relationship to property. As long as society was based upon small-scale commodity production, and as long as the mass of people simultaneously owned instruments of production and carried on production with them, ideological equality of mental being was indispensable. Under such conditions, faculty psychology was the logical reflection of the development of the productive forces of society. Each individual was considered free to acquire property and that which prevented a person from doing so was not some innate quality, but the lack of a strong will to succeed, or zeal, as Galton declared. The Lockean perspective on the nature of the individual mind corresponded to the ideological underpinnings of the existence of inequality in the distribution of property. Those who had no property or less than others were thought to be less industrious, or thrifty, but not less endowed by nature with "brain-power." This same rationale continued under industrial capitalism because it was still valid for many owners of capitalist enterprises, although, as we saw in the case of Galton, it necessarily began to weaken with the development of a propertyless working class. Employers often worked in their shops, sometimes alongside their employees, or else managed the plant directly and knew the various processes of production. This form of relations of production was continually eroded through an increasing level of technology and concentration of ownership. Eventually, as production became socialized but ownership concentrated, that is, as greater concentration of production occurred, there was a constantly increasing separation between owner and direct producer, or laborer. This final stage in the development of capitalist production destroyed the basis for both faculty psychology and the use of "industriousness," "zeal," and "thrift" as the ideological foundation for inequality. Classical bourgeois ideology buckled under the weight of monopoly capitalism as faculty psychology no longer corresponded to the relations of production. From faculty psychology the transition was made to a neoclassical psychology which explicitly posited a theory of innate intelligence.

Under monopoly capitalism, intelligence became a principal criterion for explaining socioeconomic inequality, supplanting the older bourgeois "industriousness and frugality" in importance. True, the inequitable social order was to a significant extent still explained by the industriousness of certain individuals. Nevertheless, intelligence, unadulterated by notions of labor, rapidly became the principal rationale for the social structure. Intelligence as a fundamental criterion was necessary, because an increasingly larger portion of the population was directly involved solely in production and circulation, while a much smaller portion directed either through management or direct ownership. Monopoly capitalism then revealed a clear division between mental and physical labor. By the late nineteenth century in the United States, the vast majority of the population earned a living through manual labor. Monopoly capital necessitated a rationale different from the old competitiveness reflected in the "industriousness" of the agrarian-commercial economy. Intelligence, or mental work—this entailed management, direction, planning, supervision—was the most obvious and significant differentiation of function in the division of labor. No longer could one claim that hard work alone resulted in wealth. In early nineteenth-century America, the majority of white males owned some instruments of production and labored with these instruments, especially artisans' or mechanics' tools, or land, and hard work could in fact result in greater wealth. Under monopoly capitalism, industriousness or hard work alone could not explain the differences in wealth: on the contrary, those who worked directly in production without owning the instruments of production became the outcasts, were the poor tenement dwellers and, as we have seen, the principal opponents of capitalism.

Intelligence was fashioned into the ideological framework of capitalism at a particular time when the old rationales no longer corresponded with the social relations in the process of production. We have seen how intelligence needed to be quantified and measured in order to be applied socially and how quantification made intelligence into an effective rationale within the socialization process involving every child under sixteen. IQ tests were the concrete results of the new ideological weapon corresponding to monopoly capitalism. Intelligence testing was the materialization of theory; it was "intelligence" (as a rationalization) in practice. Its principal aspect as an educational device was that of an ideological tool.

3. The Materialization of "Intelligence" in Testing Instruments

If the theory of education was guided by the need to develop the organic society with liberal theory now asserting that intelligence divided individuals from one another, testing could be brought into education as a perfect instrument for more effectively socializing children.

The political outlook among those social scientists involved in intelligence testing viewed the propertied classes as the more naturally gifted of society, whose social position was attributed directly to superior intellectual qualities. The image of the paternal state is unmistakably reflected in this statement by Progressive Edward L. Thorndike:

> It is the great good fortune of mankind that there is a substantial correlation between intelligence and morality, including good will toward one's fellows. Consequently, our superiors in ability are on the average our benefactors, and it is often safer to trust our interests to them than to ourselves. No group of men can be expected to act one hundred per cent in the interest of mankind, but this group of the ablest men will come nearest to the ideal.[35]

Thorndike's model for ability grouping was a rational ordering of society into harmonious elements, each with mutual obligations, rights, and duties. Thus, if it could be established that by nature an unequal social structure was not only inevitable but necessary for the elementary operation of society, then the fundamental duty of each individual in society was to promote the common welfare of that social order. The grouping of likes and unlikes, of superiors and inferiors, ordered society in such a way that those so classified would consciously accept the results of the scientific tests. If the masses accepted the decisions of the social engineers, and if the groups were placed in proper relationship one to another, and if these tasks, mutual obligations, etc. were learned, all that was then needed was to put the great machine into motion. The expected conclusion would be a precise, smooth-running social order.

The guiding principle in Thorndike's theories was the distribution of property, which he attributed to the distribution of intelligence in the population.[36] Property was the reflection of innate abilities—those who had acquired it had generally done so through the powers of their intelligence. Thorndike thought that society was operating in accord with natural law when an individual with the intelligence of a banker became an owner of a bank. In the ferment of the social order, the naturally gifted apportioned property to themselves in a wholesome and legal manner through their efforts. To limit the rights of individuals to appropriate private property of any sort would create discord, since the limitations themselves limited the expression and development of natural individual abilities and intelligence. Retracing Rousseau, Thorndike wrote that the frustration of individual talents not only led to unwholesome and unnatural social relationships, but it also prevented the further development of the total wealth of the society.[37] The intellectual powers of a few to develop resources, production, science, etc. added to the total social wealth. Through limiting the right of the chairman of the board of a giant corporation to acquire unlimited capital, one impinged upon the motive to create more total capital. Thorndike thus objected to "schemes" for equal social distribution of wealth, claiming that the wealth available was made possible by the intelligence of the few, who were rewarded with extra portions of the existing wealth of a society.

The fundamental hypothesis which guided Thorndike was that capitalism was the best of all possible systems.[38] The smoother it functioned, the better for all. Thorndike was purposely seeking the means through which that system would truly operate as a system. He assumed that human nature up to that time had operated quite unconsciously in the development of capitalism and that its further rational development depended upon the conscious acquiescence to the "realities" of human nature. The rational system of capitalism became even more rational when its internal dynamics, i.e., the laws of its development, become binding for all. The web which should connect the society into a whole was the conscious acceptance of the natural forces causing social development on the part of all individuals at whatever social levels they find themselves. Thus, civil society must correspond to natural forces, which in effect meant the scientific integration of innate abilities, or intelligence, with the economic system of capitalism. The freedom of the intellectually gifted to appropriate private property had accounted for the success of capitalsim up to that time; its further development would be the conscious ordering of that combination, making its operation efficient, functioning in a clockwork fashion.

In order to socialize children into accepting intelligence as the basis for natural divisions within societies (hence, classes), some method was needed to impress upon the nonpropertied and propertied classes the seriousness and legitimacy of intelligence. The administration of intelligence tests in the schools could impress upon all the awesomeness of IQ. The practical value was that objective tests "measuring" intelligence appeared to be the decisive and nonsubjective factor in the educational process. Intelligence testing explicitly defined success or failure, not on one's socioeconomic background, the amount of property one owned, or upon schooling, but rather upon an innate instinctual factor; the class structure, however, was conveniently reflected in the scores, so nothing was to be altered in a social or economic sense.

Built into the class system are particular types of social patterns in attitudes, language, customs, past educational opportunities, etc., which generally correlate with class. The tests employed these variables as keys or measures, quantifying them in such a way that in a random sampling of the population there would be a close correlation between socioeconomic class and test score. Using socialization as the foundation—and to the extent that tests "measured"—tests reflected what one had learned within the limitations of one's class background. Tests measured one class against another, measured the privileges of the educated classes against the class that historically, under capitalism, has been excluded from receiving formal education.

As such, the tests were useful for giving the impression to students—or at least to condition their thinking—that scientific and objective instruments should be used to determine whether one should become a menial worker, a skilled, or professional employee. The inclination on the part of those administering and those taking the tests was to accept *all* test results as legitimate. The facts were assembled in such a way that it was still the individual who was important, not one who rose or fell according to hard work, but one either destined for success or failure according to innate mental instincts.

Within the schools, IQ tests were one fundamental method by which unequal education could be made legitimate under the pressures of mass education. Further, IQ tests had the appearance of providing a non-class-biased technical allocator of education. In this capacity, no one could argue that "class education" or unequal education was being forced on anyone. Indeed, it was not manifestly forced on anyone except through the covert content of the IQ tests and unequal schooling depending upon neighborhood.

A great amount of writing was expended in demonstrating the practicality in slotting children for differing levels of curriculum. It is true that tests slotted individuals, but not to be members of the working class or of the bourgeoisie. This was already determined. The outcome was rather to insure that nothing was altered through the process of education. The general correspondence between test scores and class was predetermined and insured little possibility for "mobility" from one non-property-owning class to the higher salaried professional and small property-owning middle class. The greatest impediment to "social advance" was, however, the close correspondence between class and the curriculum in local schools. Unequal education was much more effective if given through the local schools, with their varying levels of curriculum, than through an IQ test sorting out the class structure. No such socioeconomic integration has necessitated a thorough ranking system, because the geographical segregation of classes has been one factor that schools have taken advantage of in providing unequal education. IQ testing has done a great deal to reinforce this segregation both in the conscious and geogrphical sense as well as in reinforcing the provisions of the organic society.

Testing also makes it possible for some exceptional individuals to score higher than normal for their socioeconomic class. As Ross said, the "elite must escape upwards," the "elite" as reflected in an IQ score were to be given special consideration and conditioning, usually a preparation for a nonmanual, or even professional training. That this happened (although seldom) only reinforced the strength of an ideology stressing intelligence as the basis for social status. The effect depended upon the opposite: working-class children assumed working-class jobs after a long educational process delayed their entry into the labor market. The exception, however, became a part of the glorified mythology overshadowing the everyday experiences of the masses of youth in schools.

Since not everyone had equal abilities, all children would be urged to reach the limits of their natural abilities. They could now be told that hard work was no stigma as long as one worked to his or her capacity. This meant, however, that children of working-class parents, scoring working-class scores on IQ tests, and knowing their level of intelligence, if socialized well, would work diligently to fulfill the criteria for success. They would seek those tasks in production reserved for those who owned no property and would become "achievers" in an occupation equal to their mental (i.e., class) level.

4. Racism and the Concept of Intelligence

Between 1890 and 1930, over one hundred social intelligence studies of Blacks, Asians, Africans, Latin Americans, and Europeans were published in various professional and scholarly journals. They formed a mass of "scientific" evidence on racial differences. In theory and methods the various studies were parallel. One can interchange subjects without changing the essence of the studies: whether of Mexicans, Indians, "half-breeds," Blacks or Italians, the studies were seemingly uniformly conceived and written. Their conclusions did vary, but only according to average IQ or behavioral trait under study. Thus, a range rather than identical IQs or traits were found. However, on one factor alone the investigators were united: the racial inferiority of poor white, Southern European, and "non-white" nationalities and races, i.e., the working class, was quite real.

Scholars such as E.A. Ross, Lewis Terman, E.L. Thorndike, and Robert Yerkes, who had formed part of the vanguard of Progressivism, also were quite active in promoting scientific racism. Each of these supported and was active in campaigns for the forced sterilization of "social deviants." Their activities in eugenics constituted one aspect of the resolution to the threat to the social order. Since, they claimed, the nature of the social order was a sum total of inherited characteristics, a quick solution would be a form of birth control through forced sterilization. By 1907 fifteen states had passed sterilization laws, and by 1928 at least 8,500 people were sterilized through the enforcement of these laws. This was one extreme aspect of scientific racism; the more popular form, one which appears most often in the literature, was the simple identification of culturally and physically distinct peoples as biologically (instinctively) inferior. This positive identification was supported through the findings of hundreds of research studies into the intelligence of racial and national minorities.[39]

Scientific racism functioned quite well within the general goal of the organic society. Racism was an ideological explanation for the social structure; it did not affect the distribution of property, but it did rationalize that distribution. Progressivism renounced classes as a socioeconomic concept, yet poverty and wealth remained. How was this contradiction to be explained, yet maintained? One answer rested with the nature of the individual, but not a random selection of individuals. Scientific racism, a variant of James's pragmatic psychology, postulated that the social structure was determined by the inherited nature of racial or national groups. This inherited characteristic was simply intelligence.

Racism distinguished between segments of the working class on a biological basis. Within the division of labor, the category of workers was seen as composed of unequals, ranked in a hierarchical order. The organic ideal of society might appear difficult to reach if one group (capital) looked upon segments of the labor force as genetically inferior. That would logically have been the case, except that the "inferiors" were to be socialized to believe in their inferiority.

Explaining the social order by intelligence and genes could simultaneously dissolve social discontent by socializing the racial minority and poor white groups to accept their inferiority as natural. Furthermore, by artifically separating workers from each other outwardly on the basis of culture, race, or nationality, the working class would be segmented within itself. The first effect would be to place the explanation for the distribution of wealth upon the intelligence of racial groups. The second effect was to prevent the development of a class consciousness within the working class.

The organic society was the ideal; how one reached that state of interaction of the division of labor, i.e., *production*, depended on any number of particular situations. Racism has often been used by employers as a divisive tactic in controlling labor struggles. At other times, it undoubtedly has been reflected in antagonistic relationships between workers of one racial or national group and employers, or their representatives in the place of work.

For the capitalist, the principal good that can result from racism is development of racism among workers. Every antagonism between members of the working class results in a corresponding loss of unity within that class. Thus, the advantage to the capitalist of racism among workers is clear—as long as workers struggle against each other, they will have little time (and little unity) to stand up to their employer. The development of race consciousness among the working class has had a function in the process of production.

Initially, racism was only a subsidiary aspect of the testing movement and was not generic to intelligence testing itself. The most important function of testing was to provide an ideology within the educational institution for purposes of training. The argument that Mexicans, Blacks, or Orientals as a group were less intelligent did not need that argument for the tests to continue reporting that Mexicans were less "intelligent." The testing instrument was not intended to select races to be one thing or another; its fundamental purpose was the realization of a stable society, and as such it would relegate working-class children to commensurate socialization and skill training. Thus, scientific racism and intelligence testing served complementary goals and, when scientific racism appeared to have lost its appeal and to have collapsed under the blows of liberal scholars during the 1930s, intelligence testing continued to serve an identical function: sifting out the "likes and unlikes" in the process of education.

In their incorporation of racism into "respectable" scholarship, the academics made race respectable as an explanation for the existence of the chaos they saw at the bottom. In their quest for relevancy, they accepted racism and, in their academic manner, went about formulating racist theories dedicated to the preservation of capitalism. The result was that, as the university became increasingly important as a shaper of public policy, the conclusions of academic research took on the stamp of legitimacy within educational practices. Research through the university and the Progressive education movement were very closely related phenomena, for its was the university which simultaneously (1) produced racist research, and (2) provided much of the context for progressive expression and reform in educational practices. In major universities throughout the nation, the notion that the scholar's role was part of a process of social intervention and not only abstractly intellectual meant vast changes in the role of the university in the modern era.

One might claim that it was solely on the basis of race, physical characteristics (e.g., color of skin), or culture (and, therefore, language, dress, customs, etc.) that these men and women carried out their investigations. On closer scrutiny one can see that these investigators never assumed equality among peoples, since their pragmatic ideology postulated inequality and, furthermore, the subjects were socially not the equals of the "scientists," nor of the propertied classes. The scholars investigating racial differences were products of an unequal society, a society that distributed property in terms of classes. How could they infer inferiority among the wealthy, or superiority among the poor, or even equality between them? The social scientists of the Progressive Era generally assumed that one's objective socioeconomic condition was the result of innate and not social causes. Like James and Dewey they accepted the contradiction between poverty and wealth in that the structure of society was viewed as a permanent, unalterable object which had as its basis the genetic inheritance of peoples. In seeking explanations of the social and economic organization, they were also apologists for that organization in arguing that the poor were poor for reasons not rooted in the manner in which society was organized. Society, for them, was structured upon individual and inherent human factors. Thus, the social structure of society was conveniently explained on the basis of the subjective nature of each individual. This conclusion based upon pragmatism formed the foundation for the scientific racism of the twentieth century.

Theories of racial differences ran the gamut from the "hardnosed" racism of Madison Grant to the "softer" versions of Otto Klineberg, who thought that racial differences in intelligence and behavior were possible but needed to be verified. By the 1920s, one could pick and choose from a wide variety of tests, methods, and conclusions. The importance of these theories is that they have become so much a part of the philosophies and programs of public and private social agencies across the United States. Many of these scientists proposed that society base its well-being upon the "scientific theories" of racial differences and that through such an approach the social problems of society would be greatly reduced, if not solved. The classical bourgeois ideology no longer was viable: Lewis Terman vehemently concluded that the United States must reform its Lockean philosophy of innate equality among people, that it was mere sentimentalism which served only to endanger the progress of civilization and therefore of the "white race."[40]

Not surprisingly, through the efforts of the academic world, these theories have become commonly held ideas. It must, however, be borne in mind that they were always based upon the existing social order and that they served to reinforce the continuance of that social order. A racial theory of society was useful only when it served the need for the continuation of the social order, although the existence of these racial theories of intelligence has been rationalized on the basis of pseudoscientific theories, a priori assumptions and race prejudice.

5. *The Role of Intelligence Testing in the Schools*

Locke could argue that one's "station" defined the type of education one was to receive, but he also argued that industriousness was the basis for the distribution of property. In the late nineteenth century, under the extreme pressure from the working class, to argue that one's class defined his or her education became politically dangerous talk. Locke and Smith intended an unequal education for an unequal society. Political conditions of the time made the task of distributing unequal education relatively easy. One task of IQ tests was to make it appear that equal educational opportunity was given, but unequal education dispensed, not on the basis of class, but on the basis of innate ability. In practice, Locke's old dictum that not all classes were deserving of the same quality of education was practiced covertly under the mantle of science.

Herbert Spencer and his disciples of laissez faire defined education in Lockean terms, but Spencerian arguments succumbed to the political necessity for reform. However, the essence of Locke remained: class still defined the education one received and it was not the educational system which was to sort classes. The type of education to be given depended upon one's socioeconomic class. The need to impart differing levels of education derived from the reality that classes had certain relationships to each other stemming from production. The need to make education appear "equal," while basing inequality in education upon the intelligence of students, derived from the political crisis of monopoly capitalism. Education, however, faced the practical reality of having to allocate learning and preparation for tasks unequally. The specific content and method of education derived from monopoly capitalism; the need to impart it on a mass basis stemmed from mechanization. The practical use of intelligence testing became operational only through the necessity for mass compulsory education.

Chapter Six
MASS EDUCATION AND THE FORCES OF PRODUCTION

A combination of forces stirred by capitalism provided the basis for extending the length of the average child's school experience and extending the participation of children in schools on an increasing scale. These results in general stemmed from mechanization, which reached its height under monopolies. Again, several effects stemming from monopoly production can be discerned: 1) child labor became increasingly superfluous, hazardous, and uneconomical; 2) direct participation of bankers and industrialists in reform movements effectively agitated for compulsory education and child-labor legislation; 3) labor unions viewed child labor as cheap labor and agitated for its abolition through legislation. This combination of factors (although the superfluousness of children in production was primary) pulled working-class children out of production and into the educational system.

1. Technological Change and Child Labor

During the early phase of mass education, very few working-class children went beyond the primary grades. Still fewer graduated from secondary schools. Michael Katz's investigations reveal that the working class of Beverly, Massachusetts, voted in 1860 to discontinue the local high school, since the school was of little use to the working class.[1] Few children of workers could afford not to work, yet workers' taxes supported to a significant extent the town's school. Those who could attend were of the middle and upper property-owning classes. The high school could scarcely be said to have served the working classes, although it did provide the skills and learning for the middle and upper propertied classes. Yet the crux of the issue is why the working class participated at a relatively young age in production rather than attend school.

The early Massachusetts schools increasingly served the interests of the middle and upper classes: that is, there was a steady decline of working-class children through the grades with a simultaneous proportional increase in the percentage of nonworking class children. Why did children of the working class increasingly participate in production rather than in schools? Part of the answer was very much like the answer of today's dropout eager for a job: "There's no money in going to school at a time when money is needed." More importantly, because of the low level of technology, production was labor intensive rather than capital intensive. Thus there was a need for all available hands, children as well as men and women. Lack of working-class attendance in the school, on the other hand, had no social or economic consequences. The fact that schools, as one proceeded through the grades, found fewer and fewer working-class children was particularly unsettling to employers. If these children had not been needed to supplement their parents' income, they probably would have remained in school.

This situation of working-class children tending to participate in production was a salient aspect of industrial capitalism. Industrial capitalism pulled men, women, and children into production; the rise of education was a response to the need for skills and ideological training in an industrial society. Yet, working-class children seldom went beyond the early grades—if they went to school at all. Why was this the case when the stated policy of superintendents of schools was for free schooling for all—primary and secondary? Again, it was because all available hands—men, women, and children—were needed in production. The ideal was one thing, but the reality sided with the needs of employers. As long as production could not part with adults or children, there would be a minimal school attendance from the working classes. This situation was, however, temporary.

Over a period of several decades, child labor gradually became superfluous to production. Capitalism gradually incorporated technological innovations which on the one hand made giant production units inevitable and more profitable, and on the other gradually moved children and (to a degree) women out of production. The larger productive establishments generally had high levels of technology; this factor dictated a greater emphasis on efficiency and on older and more mature workers, while lessening the amount of labor needed per unit of production.

It was as a direct consequence of increasing technological change that effective mass compulsory education became so necessary. First, a means was required of keeping children and teenagers off of the "unemployed lists." Second, industrial capitalism had already made the state the principal socializing agent in society. The combination of an absence of a sufficient socialization process and the force of unemployment and underemployment among children gave to the educational institutions the responsibility for caring for children for an extended length of time. The content of that education was to be provided by the class contradictions tearing at the heart of monopoly capitalism. It was production, in its social as well as its economic sense, which provided the purpose and scale of education to be given to increasing numbers of children in the late nineteenth and early twentieth centuries.

Prior to mass education (in the style of the twentieth century) workers needed no educational system to "train" them for factory jobs. Sons and daughters of the declining rural areas furnished excellent operatives for the textile mills of Waltham and Lowell without the necessity (or privilege) of an education. In the later stages of industrial development young children were employed in a number of occupations—in glass-making, textile, coal mining, and service industries, to name but a few—without first having gone through a period of preparation. Workers were available, not because schools created a particular class of individuals destined to become workers, but because a particular distribution of property forced the propertyless majority to sell their labor power in order to survive. This act of selling their labor power was an effect of the concentration of the means of production in the hands of a minority—a condition that was indispensable for the full development of capitalism.

The entry of children into the labor market became increasingly delayed as technological advances in production appeared. Large numbers of children in the larger industrial and commercial cities became street-rovers without supervision or schooling. Increased emphasis upon "scientific management" on the part of large production enterprises and especially of monopolistic concerns resulted in reluctance to hire children and youth. The experience of management over many years had shown them the advantages of mature workers over the easily distracted, less reliable, and in the long run more costly, child and young workers. Moreover, labor unions and anti-child-labor groups had pressed for many years for stringent laws against child labor as one form of cheap labor. Still, the principal factor in the large increase in unemployed children and youth was the change in the needs of highly mechanized enterprises, which were decreasingly labor intensive as mechanization proceeded, and of management increasingly conscious of productive and reliable labor represented by mature young or older adults. The several conditions pushed children out of the labor market and into the schools.

2. Monopoly Capital and Agitation for Mass Compulsory Education

The relationship between monopoly capital and mass education can be very clearly seen in the movement, or agitation, for child-labor restriction. Although compulsory-education laws appeared as early as 1852, in practice these laws were anything but effective. It was not until the post-World War II era that mass compulsory education became a national reality. However, the first tendency to inaugurate real mass compulsory laws appeared at the turn of the century. The history of this movement demonstrates the strong ties that monopoly had with Progressivism.

Massachusetts passed the first compulsory-schooling law in 1852, and in 1874 New York State passed a law patterned after that of Massachusetts. Provisions of the New York law "required children between the ages of eight to fourteen to attend fourteen weeks a year of which at least eight must be consecutive."[2] The New York law remained unenforced throughout its duration, as did the revisions of the compulsory-school law passed between 1894 and 1896. The revisions required that all children from eight to twelve years old attend class full time for the duration of the school year; those between twelve and fourteen were required to attend school at least eighty days a year. The latter, if not employed, had to be in school.[3] As in the case of the 1874 law, the later revisions, while stringent in appearance, were similarly unenforced. At least two reasons accounted for this: one appeared to be overcrowded schools. Even without a concerted effort to bring more children into schools, more and more were being enrolled. It also appears that a determined effort on the part of some employers destroyed any enforcement. The result was that children attended school in increasing numbers, not because of adequate enforcement of existing educational laws, but probably because they were unemployed and had no other recourse. Eventually, the haphazard manner in which children were placed in schools gave way to the controlled and conscious measures of the state directing children into schools without allowing "experiments" in employment to occur. By this time adequate enforcement had become economically desirable and, therefore, possible.

It is at this juncture, the turn of the century, that anti-child-labor agitation appeared. Nearly a century after the appearance of child labor in industry, the first truly organized anti-child-labor groups were formed. The most prominent, the National Child Labor Committee, was founded in 1904; the National Civic Federation also had its commission on child labor, and it appeared shortly after the NCLC. The two groups were rivals and originally had distinct approaches toward solving child-labor problems. The NCF proposed uniform state compulsory-education laws and uniform child-labor laws in the states. It hoped to enact common laws on the state level rather than through federal regulations. The NCLC, on the other hand, rather than rely on educational codes in the states, emphasized federal regulation of the minimum age at which an employee may be hired. These differences disappeared in 1915, when the policy of the NCF was accepted by the NCLC, and the groups had similar membership as well as ultimate goals.

Both groups were composed of labor, the "public," and capitalists. The NCLC, for example, had such members as John H. Rhoades, president of the Greenwich Savings Bank; V.E. Macy, member of the Title Guarantee and Trust Company; Paul Warburg, member of Kuhn Loeb Investment Banking; William H. Baldwin, president of the Long Island Railroad, and Jacob Schiff of Kuhn Loeb. Labor was represented by Lyman Abbot and Samuel B. Donnelly, the latter representing the Central Federated Union of New York. The reformers Florence Kelley and Jacob Riis were also members. The NCF membership was similar in social composition. Jeremy Felt, who extensively researched the NCLC's history, writes:

> Since the small group of upper-class businessmen supporting the committee (NCLC) did not depend upon cheap labor, its regulation was something they could sponsor. Indeed, the abolition of child labor could be viewed as a means of driving out marginal manufacturers and tenement operators, hence increasing the consolidation and efficiency of business.[4]

That child-labor reformers were conscious of aiding monopoly is not explicit, but what is clear is that child labor was disappearing among those larger capitalists who represented their interests through both the NCF and NCLC. The NCF's Child Labor Commission chairman was a wealthy southern cotton-mill owner credited with operating a "model" mill. No children were hired, nor needed, in his establishment, and he could consequently afford to push child-labor reforms. One muckraking NCLC publication authored by Edwin Markham,

Benjamin B. Lindsay, and George Creel praised those industrialists who employed labor-saving devices that reduced reliance on child labor. They wrote:

> The horror of this whole glassworks tragedy becomes increasingly poignant when it is robbed of all color of necessity. No less an authority than the National Glass Budget points out that "the introduction of automatic devices has changed the modern factory requirements to such an extent that the glass factory which today requires the work of a small boy is operated in the crudest, the most primitive and most expensive and antiquated manner."[5]

In 1905 Commissioner of Labor Sherman reported that the employment of children under fourteen in the larger factories was rare and occurred mostly in tenement shops and smaller manufacturing establishments and in agriculture.[6] By 1915 the NCLC, rather than pushing to regulate the hiring of children, followed the policy of the NCF, which was emphasizing laws to keep children in school until their sixteenth birthday. The large and growing population of children in schools at the turn of the century appeared not because of compulsory school-attendance laws, but because the labor of children became increasingly unnecessary in large-scale production. Furthermore, because of the uneven development of large-scale production, child labor persisted, not in spite of the compulsory-education laws, but because local enforcement of state laws generally corresponded to local labor needs. Thus, in urban areas compulsory education was enforced, whereas in rural areas the tendency was for compulsory education to remain an ideal.

3. Education in Labor-Intensive and Capital-Intensive Forms of Production

Educational programs are efficient to the extent that they correspond to the forces of production. For example, the educational experiences of laborers in rural areas were substantially different from those in urban areas. In rural areas the tendency was for a near total absence of educational opportunities for working-class or farm-worker and tenant-farming children; in urban areas there were far greater opportunities for participating in schooling. This difference was not one of cultural lag or of a greater sophistication of educators in urban areas. For the absence of schooling in rural areas was predicated upon the organization of labor, which in turn was based upon the level of technology employed in production. Production in much of the agricultural enterprises incorporated low levels of mechanization; this in turn necessitated a particular form of labor organization. The low level of technology that characterized (and to an extent still characterizes) agriculture required a greater amount of human labor than mechanized industry.

Growers often sought a particular *kind* of labor force which would correspond to the productive level of technology. For example, in the cotton-growing industry, growers sought and contracted with whole families. This was also largely true of vegetable farming as well as fruit and nut ranching. The more labor intensive production becomes, the larger the workforce necessary to effect production. The relative skills necessary are so low that children become eligible for employment. Since a large labor force was mandatory (especially during harvests), hiring of children became quite common. Wages were exceedingly low, forcing all family members into production merely for the sake of survival. The low wages were based partly upon a plentiful supply of labor which could be tapped when needs were felt but principally upon striving for maximum profits. Farming was simply not profitable without cheap labor. Few other occupations attracted agricultural workers, especially in the Southwest and South, and agribusiness needed labor only seasonally. Child labor in agriculture was dictated by the technological forces, by the kinds and amount of labor skills needed in production, and by exceedingly low wages.

In 1941 a federal-government study of the socioeconomic conditions of agricultural workers found that in Hidalgo County, Texas, the median income of 342 rural families was $350; the estimated minimum for a family of four at that time was $480. That median income of $350, however, was not based upon earnings of a single parent but also included children. There were 998 children between the ages of 6 and 18 in the 342 families. One-quarter of those aged six to nine and eighty percent of the ten to fourteen group were regularly seeking employment. The study found that "the younger children worked only in cotton picking in the summer and fall months, the older boys and girls generally worked in the fields throughout the year or whenever work was available, even in periods when school was in session."[7] The majority of family members were wage earners. "Nearly three-fifths of the 2,258 family members in the study had worked for hire during the year."[8] Even with several family members working, the combined wages were exceedingly low. In one family three boys worked to support three brothers, their mother, and grandmother. During a representative week, their "combined weekly earnings totaled $9.08." The pay per hour of work was seven cents.[9] The low wages could only be compensated for through the employment of as many family members as could be mustered. This incorporation of children into production was not inefficient, as would have been the case in highly mechanized industries, but was welcomed and promoted by growers. One manager of the largest packing shed in the Rio Grande Valley stated that "children are taken to the fields even while still in diapers. Those from ten years of age up work very well. The younger ones, however, are not efficient."[10] The older they got, the more efficient they became; however, the younger they were, the cheaper the labor. Combining these factors suited the needs of growers quite well.

These conditions of production could scarcely allow mass education. As long as production needed every available laborer—men, women, and children—mass education would be an impossibility. The system of education worked hand-in-hand with agribusiness in disregarding the schooling laws by refusing to admit agricultural workers' children, or in not providing sufficient facilities for their education. On the other hand, the poverty of workers prevented them from enrolling their children in schools; as one parent stated: "I can't keep both my children in school every day, because if their father works alone, he can make only $4 a week, while if the boys work with him, they can earn $6 or $7."[11]

The schools did not step outside of the local labor needs. Working within the limits of the forces of production, agricultural workers' children attended schools irregularly, if at all, and rarely graduated from the eighth grade. The reasons were simple. In the first place, families were so poor that children were needed as wage earners for survival. Second, schools discouraged workers' children from attending, thereby complying with growers' needs. Compulsory-attendance laws were simply not enforced in agricultural areas such as Hidalgo County, and other children were refused admittance on flimsy grounds. In Hidalgo County it was not uncommon for children to be denied admittance "because of the overcrowded conditions," and in some instances because of a "ruling that children might enter after the first three months of the school term only if they presented a transfer certificate establishing school attendance elsewhere during these months." The compulsory school-attendance law had so many loopholes that actual enforcement of the seven to sixteen age limit was never realized. Hidalgo County school principal stated that in his district of 2,600 eligible children, only 1,600 had been enrolled. No effort was ever made to secure enrollment of those absent.[12]

Those children who managed to enter at the first grade rarely made it to the eighth. The material privations were too great to overcome.

They needed to eat much more than they needed to read, for learning to read took time and their immediate need was survival. The irregular attendance resulting from the picking and migration season forced children into lagging behind. The tendency was for children of agricultural workers to cluster disproportionately in the lower grades. It was very unusual for a laborer's child in Hidalgo County to attend school consistently through to the eighth grade. According to the federal study mentioned earlier, of the 998 children investigated, 798 had a record of grade progress. Of these, 591 were reported behind, 290 were normal, and seven were advanced; 480 were behind one to two years, 101 were from three to five years behind.

In five Hidalgo County schools designated as "Latin-American"—most agricultural workers were Mexican—by school authorities, a definite pattern of heavy enrollment in the early grades and light enrollment in the later grades was evident. (See Table.)[13]

School grade	School A	B	C	D	E
First	358	487	354	156	114
Second	121	196	102	54	19
Third	123	225	75	79	20
Fourth	102	209	67	39	22
Fifth	87	no 5th grade	49	70	33

As the school years passed, fewer of the children remained in school. Children filtered into production not because of any lack of "cultural" propensity to educate themselves, but out of the serious needs for a minimal standard of living. As long as production found the little ones "efficient," their education would be of secondary importance.

In the urban areas a far different educational program was effected, although in many ways the content was the same. Many states had put into effect mass educational programs whose content corresponded to monopoly capitalism. The ability of local districts to evade compulsory-attendance laws (as late as 1940) was designed to meet the needs of technologically backward capitalism found in particular regions.

The content of education, whether in Hidalgo County or in Los Angeles, had a similarity of purpose as early as the 1920s. Perhaps the biggest difference was not one of content, but one of attendance (and even in attendance a certain content is implicit). What the children of Hidalgo County did not receive in the schools in "fair" proportion would be handed out to the children of urban areas in "fairer" proportions. One exception must be made in the case of San Antonio, Texas, in the late 1930s. The principal industrial employment in San Antonio was the pecan-shelling industry. During the depression, the several leading companies demechanized their production in order to help lower production costs—which could only have been possible through securing a plentiful supply of cheap hand-labor. Hand-labor could only be less expensive than machinery at an average pay rate of five cents per hour. Under such low wages a family could not be supported. The 1938 study by Selden C. Menefee and Oren C. Cassmore revealed that, in order to insure a minimum existence, an employee of the pecan-shelling industry often brought along relatives. It was not uncommon for some employers to seek out married men with families in the hope of attracting a larger supply of cheap labor. Obviously, children in such a situation would not have much time for schooling. Menefee and Cassmore reported that:

> the proportion of youth attending school at various ages is much lower in San Antonio than in the state as a whole, or in other Texas cities. This is largely because of the inability of the pecan-shellers and the agricultural workers who form the poorest strata of the population to keep their children in school.[14]

When machinery was introduced, as a result of the New Deal's Fair Labor Act (which placed the minimum wage at twenty-five cents per hour, and thereby imposed upon the industry the necessity of mechanizing to *cut* costs) employment was cut drastically from 12,000 to about 3,000. The minimum wage had the effect of shutting down the smaller companies which did not have the capital to invest in machinery, but in the larger concerns mechanization could lower the costs per worker in relation to previous output; in this process competition from smaller concerns was undermined. Greater productivity at lower costs, however, also meant much lower levels of employment. Most affected would be the children. Their level of employment would be lowered, perhaps cut altogether. No figures are available for the postdepression period, but the trend could only have been in the direction of greater school attendance for farmworkers' children.

The clear tendency of the working population to settle in urban areas meant that a sizeable proportion of school-age children was available for schooling. There are exceptions, such as the rural South, but in urban centers where technology was most advanced, unemployable children would be placed into public schooling in greater proportions than their rural employable brothers and sisters.

Unemployed children in the streets presented many problems for society at large. No means were employed to teach them rudiments of ideology, i.e., political socialization—for in fact they did not have the benefit of the socialization afforded through participating in production. It was quite apparent that the process of developing loyal citizens in this trying period was left to chance. Given the very serious labor problems then existing, this was too liberal a course for the welfare of the nation. Schools then were to play two simultaneous roles: on the one hand, creating a consciousness of the organic society; on the other, keeping children "employed" in schools, preparing them to such a high ideological and general skill level that they could participate in production at some point in the future.

That child labor was becoming increasingly unnecessary in production as mechanization advanced is clear. Through the force of technological advancement, increasing numbers of workers became superfluous to production. This was so especially in the larger production units and was most visible in monopolistic production. Children had been a useful sector of the working class as cheap labor during the rise of industrial capitalism. Gradually, under the impact of technology, which included scientific management conceptualized as Taylorization, children became increasingly unprofitable for establishments bent on efficiency. Children were prone to accidents on the high-speed machines, were easily distracted, especially after long hours of work, needed constant supervision because of their lack of maturity, and in the long run simply increased costs in comparison to mature adults. If cost per unit of production were less for an adult worker than for a child or youngster at a machine, the logical conclusion would be to establish a higher and uniform age for hiring. But this could be the case only as long as the labor supply was not affected.

With each depression, modernization moved forward in the form of new technology employed to get the economy "on its feet again." At each economic crisis, a sudden increase in school enrollment occurred, children tended to move into the school during periods of crisis, and at an increasing rate until finally an educational crisis of nearly unmanageable proportions occurred. Florence Kelley estimated that the average school teacher at the turn of the century in New York City taught 70 children. Schools became a "natural" protector of the child when no employment could be managed. Even at this stage, the tendencies had not yet solidified themselves. There was a high dropout rate for children in the primary grades, but there was also a steadily growing rate of retention. Children tended to stay in school longer, but also tended to drop out as the school years rolled by. Yet, gradually children were added to the registers, not primarily through the effect of compulsory-schooling laws (for these were rarely enforced), but through the aid of mechanization in a constantly expanding economy.

The United States experienced the years of greatest economic growth in the post-Civil War period, but it also brought with it a tremendous need for labor in sufficient amounts to match the available investment capital. Domestic workers were too few to match capital and, therefore, immigrants filled that need in levels far beyond the expectations of capitalists. After millions had settled in the innumerable working-class tenements, continued mechanization gradually began to render immigration of industrial labor unnecessary; that situation resulted in the series of restrictions on immigration resulting in the infamous 1924 Immigration Act. The very same conditions which imposed the necessity for immigration restrictions imposed the necessity for compulsory education for every child.

The flow of children into the educational system, in the first stages of industrialization, was organized in such a way that the educational programs corresponded to production needs. This in effect meant little education for the working class beyond the primary grades. This same principle in the era of monopoly could not be justified, nor could it be put into practice. Premonopoly forms of education had restricted secondary and college education to classes owning considerable property. Monopoly capitalism opened the doors of education to wider numbers: however, it definitely was not for the sake of an abstract educational ideal or on behalf of the interests of the majority of individuals affected.

Conclusion
A MARXIST-LENINIST ANALYSIS OF MODERN EDUCATION

The most important element of social theory deriving directly from monopoly capitalism was the functionalist theory of the cooperative (or organic) society, which forms the essence of Progressive thought. The reformism of the Progressive era emanated from within the contradictions of capitalism at a monopoly stage of development. Highly socialized production was the source of the profits for the monopolies. Without a cooperative working class, monopolies faced serious consequences. A working class which would be active politically in seeking its own interests would not be a working class in the interests of capitalism. The emphasis upon the "organic" society repeated endlessly by Progressives was an emphasis which the leading monopolists sponsored. The National Civic Foundation, tool of the House of Morgan, represented the practical application of the theory of cooperation rather than competition between classes. It was the large monopolists who alone could afford to be "lenient" with labor and to maneuver politically in order to curry favor with the public and labor. The nonmonopolists without the requisite capital or flexibility struggled against all labor unions regardless of their politics, while monopolists could use "reason" as well as shows of force to bring labor into line. Monopolists could afford to live with labor unions, and did so, but could do so only so long as labor viewed capital not as its enemy, but as part of one large organic whole made up of individuals. The motivation to progressive reform was essentially political: a major goal was to "defuse" a potentially hazardous situation in the form of a politically active working class. The end was to be the harmonious relationship between classes. One means for accomplishing this was the educational system. The theory of the "organic society" as put forward by many Progressives was the ultimate political ploy utilized by monopoly capitalism for its own ends and was the fundamental content of Progressive education.

The goal of the propertied classes was a harmonious relationship among classes. This simple end formed the essence of Progressive scholarship and reform. Such figures as the sociologist Edward A. Ross, the reformer Jacob Riis, the financier George W. Perkins, the politician Teddy Roosevelt, and the philosopher-educator John Dewey each in his own fashion actively labored for the achievement of the organic union of individuals in society. Their activity could only have had meaning because of the appearance of monopoly production. The essence of Progressive education was the essence of Progressivism in general. The conditions motivating the development of the broad social theory which encompassed Progressive educational theory also motivated the means. Consequently, we can see intelligence testing, curriculum differentiation, and tracking within the general framework of a truly mass compulsory education.

Concomitant with the new individualism and in correspondence with it, the IQ-testing movement also had its origin within the development of monopoly capitalism. Intelligence, as an ideological and "scientific" psychological concept pioneered by James and Dewey, became a principal criterion for explaining classes, wealth, and poverty under monopoly, supplanting in large part the classical bourgeois materialist philosophy. The claim that industriousness or frugality inevitably led to wealth could no longer be sustained. In the competitive stage of capitalism, many citizens were yeoman farmers, artisans, or merchants—property owners who used their property to produce commodities. For them, hard work or abstemious living could conceivably bring an increase in wealth. However, monopoly capitalism eroded that classical principle. In the large forms of production characteristic of monopoly, hard work would not lead to the acquisition of productive property (as wealth was understood in the nineteenth century). Those who labored the hardest were destined to remain the least wealthy, were expected to become unpropertied tenement dwellers.

The idea of intelligence, therefore, was placed in the forefront of the ideological framework of capitalism at that particular time when the old individualism based upon industriousness, frugality, and competitiveness did not mesh with the social relations of production and its political consequences. Intelligence, however, needed to be quantified and measured in order to be an effective rationale within the socialization process. Intelligence testing was the materialization of pragmatic theory, "intelligence" in material form. Dewey had written that, while the social scientist tailored the general purpose of education, the psychologist would develop the method. That purpose was the organic society. One such method of achieving the organic society was through habituating children to the ready acceptance of the concept of intelligence. In order to socialize children into accepting the status quo, the nurturing of a belief in intelligence as the basis for the social organization was a primary step upon the road to a harmonious society. Intelligence, not property or even labor, eventually became accepted as the naturally ordained social differentiator. Merely by administering tests, educators could fix the awesomeness of the notion of intelligence in the minds of impressionable youngsters. Intelligence testing explicitly defined success or failure, not on the basis of capitalism (of course), or on one's socioeconomic background, but on "innate instinctual structure." Tests "scientifically" reflected the amount of "brains" one had and therefore held the power to predict where individuals would eventually stand as adults in society. This illusory inherent power would implicitly lead one to believe that intelligence, not the social distribution of property under capitalism, was responsible for success or failure. While laissez-faire individualism was stifled, the individualism of the monopoly era was promoted, with the purpose of conditioning the consciousness of people to accepting proper "roles" in the division of labor.

Once the desired effect took hold, once children became conscious that innate intellectual differences were the basis for their individuality, differences in wealth (the distribution of property corresponding to the division of labor) could then be justified through intelligence. Psychologists such as Thorndike and Terman recognized that this educational effect could serve capitalist production through contributing to the strengthening of the existing division of labor. Its foremost purpose was in the realm of ideology—for if the working class and its allies had doubts concerning capitalism, the bourgeoisie would rebound with a systematic defense of its own.

Hugo Munsterberg, Harvard professor of psychology, one of the pioneers of intelligence testing along with Binet and Simon, based the use of psychology (i.e., testing) in education upon the need for an "organic society." He wrote in 1909:

> We have brought the work of education under one formula. This is not meant to indicate that education should be uniform. Everybody ought to be made willing and able to realize ideal values, but everybody is called to do it in his own way.... The child who comes from the slums, the child who never saw a green meadow, and the child who never saw a paved street, cannot be educated after a uniform pattern. The education of the boy cannot be the education of the girl, the education of the intelligent child must differ from that of the slowminded, ungifted child.... Yet still more important are the differences between the individual tasks which the life after school will put before the individuals. To make the child willing and able to realize ideal values, means also to secure the subtlest adjustment to these later differences. The laborer and the farmer, the banker and the doctor all must help in building up the realm of values. But they are equally prepared for it only if they are prepared for it in very different ways.[1]

The existing division of labor *demanded* a particular educational process which would prepare unequals for that inequality. By so doing, schools inculcated into the working class a consciousness conducive to engaging cooperatively in production; they also conditioned the middle classes to seeking their measure of success through serving in the bureaucracies of modern capitalism. IQ tests, their content arranged in such a way as to reflect a continuum of intelligence, rationalized educational preparations that were very different for differing classes but nevertheless produced an education that fostered an ideology of individualism.

In the twentieth century the organization of the social order came to be rationalized upon intelligence; concomitantly the use of intelligence tests as a means of inculcating adherence to intelligence was introduced. If the masses were to believe that intelligence was the key to capitalism, the political problem of the survival of capitalism could be resolved (at least temporarily). Tests, rather than "proving" that differences existed, "proved" that intelligence was the basis of social and economic class—in the era of monopoly.

Intelligence testing, therefore, was indispensable in a socialization process the goals of which were the organic union of individuals. Many in the working class claimed that private property was the basis for the distribution of wealth, but the bourgeoisie claimed that a naturally ordained quality, intelligence, was the foundation for socioeconomic inequality. Since nature operated within laws outside of the area of human will, the effect of socializing children with a respect for intelligence paralleled the inculcation of a respect for an immutable human nature.

Through such techniques as IQ testing, the school acts as a gigantic inculcator of capitalism's ideological core: individualism and acceptance of the naturalness of inequality. Individualism is an ideological concept which at the level of consciousness tends to cement the various classes together. On the one hand, the emphasis placed upon the primacy of the individual consecrates private property and its concentration in the hands of a few. On the other, individualism places the responsibility for high or low socioeconomic status upon the individual. Through emphasizing inequality and the primacy of the individual, the principle of capitalist production, that is private property and social production, is strengthened. In the interest of the private owners of property, workers must have both a high degree of individualism and a low degree of individuality. The contradiction is only apparent. The entire society must, if production is to remain stable, be conscious of the primacy of the individual in an unequal society. The working class must also be expected to conform to the continual exigencies of a constantly moving system of production. Workers must conform to the cooperative principle. As individualism is fostered through such devices as IQ tests, individuality—that is, individual abilities, desires, and preferences—is destroyed, and a consciousness of inequality is constantly strengthened. Concomitantly the needs of private property are consistently met.

The objective of the education based upon the social theory of the organic society intrinsically stressed accommodation to a "success" which did not entail aspiring to become a property owner. The new individualism was not the individualism whose goal was the acquisition of property to be employed directly in production. The goal was an inward-seeking individualism which did not mean acquiring property so much as it meant having an occupation reflecting a respectable level of intelligence (and, of course, income). The individual was taught that one became a worker, not because of the absence of suitable or cheap instruments of production (such as land or tools), but because of the absence of intelligence. A stigma was implicitly attached to manual labor—now the respectable were the intellectual, not the industrious. The hard work of the labor force was not considered industriousness; indeed industriousness more than ever before came to mean the use of "brains."

Rather than viewing IQ tests principally as mechanisms for sorting, as many historians of education do, one must view them principally as powerful ideological weapons corresponding to the existing division of labor under monopoly capitalism. IQ testing functions not as an independent sorter, but as an ideological tool that faithfully sustains the existing inequality and the division of labor through teaching the primacy of intelligence and therefore of an individualism which is founded upon the monopolization of the means of production.

The only means through which the theory could be made effective in education would have been for the state to have acted forcefully in requiring the presence of all school-age children in the school. That mass education happened at all must be credited to monopoly capitalism—not that monopolies ordered children into schools, but organized production around extremely advanced levels of technology. The increasing mechanization of production made many workers, especially women and children, superfluous to production. As the economy grew in the early decades of the present century, mechanization insured that as the system of production extended itself, proportionately fewer workers would be employed. The idea that such a thing as the teen-age existed can be credited to the advanced technology, which displaced young workers and required their attendance in a state-run institution. Formerly, under nonmonopoly industrial capital, large numbers of workers were required to produce relatively small amounts of commodities. Gradually, mechanization took the place of many hands and increased productivity per laborer. Eventually a portion of the work force, children under sixteen, were unnecessary for the successful operation of production.

Mass education was unavoidable, but it also was a rich opportunity for the inculcation of Progressive ideology into the consciousness of the young. The history of education in the twentieth century has been governed by a content based upon monopoly production; however, education has been available only in proportion to the level of technology in a given area. Mass compulsory education became a reality only recently throughout the United States; its development occurred unevenly, with the more industrialized areas forging ahead. In the regions where such simple (and backward) productive technology as tenant farming or sharecropping or unmechanized harvesting in agribusiness obtained, whole families participated in production. Little time could be allocated to sitting unproductively in a schoolhouse. Gradually, as technology spread, mass-production techniques in urban and rural areas altered the need for labor. In the more industrialized areas, and this included most cities, mass compulsory education became a necessity.

Prior to mass education and mechanization, children of working-class parents became workers as soon as they were able, without the benefit of an IQ test. Their fate was sealed—with a school or without one, with an IQ test or without one. The principal purpose of mass education for the working class under monopoly capitalism was 1) to keep the future work force *out* of work until it was time to place them into production without the hiatus of the school years interfering and at the same time, 2) to prepare the work force ideologically for the "organic society," and 3) to impart general occupational skills such as reading, writing, mathematics, typing, home economics, auto mechanics, upholstery, wood shop, bookkeeping and similar subjects. I think it can be argued convincingly that little in the way of high degrees of manual skills are taught in schools; most of the essential training is done on the job, with the foundation for work and possible advance in skills laid in the school years. Occupational training has been second to ideological preparation. Schools found it too costly to keep up with constantly evolving production skills. The result was that very general skills were taught, but a keen respect for intelligence, and thus individualism, developed.

The purpose of vocational education and its incorporation into education was not so much to train for a specific job, but to provide general psychological preparation for the world of manual labor. Students in "shop" acquire few skills directly related to a specific job, but many "general" skills, including attitudes toward work, are stressed. High-school vocational courses have, generally speaking, seldom imparted high skills. Most course work remains general but very practical, so that employers can build upon the general training for specific on-the-job training.

Modern schooling in the U.S. has one principal task, and it is ideological. This ideological mission is the creation of individualism within the consciousness of students. By total immersion in an atmosphere in which anything but individualism is discouraged, children become proper citizens, either as productive workers or unmotivated unemployed. It is within this framework that instinct-centered techniques become valuable—for instinct-centered methods are really methods that imply that each child is biologically different. Instinct-centered technique ultimately evolved into the use of testing as *the* mechanism for creating individualism. Rather than offering an education that rigidly allows class lines, schools attempt to destroy any consciousness of belonging to a class and to destroy any belief in the possible existence of classes. However, schools under such circumstances cannot alter the class structure and cannot manipulate the distribution of property. Classes continue to be produced and reproduced in the daily process of production, and schools, like "little lumps of dough," are molded to exact specifications based upon production. The basic function of schools is to produce a *consciousness* or ideology within students that obscures the relationship between their lives and capitalist production. In this way, uninterrupted production can more effectively take place and therefore a constant reproduction of the social order can be maintained.

It is principally in the process of production that a reproduction of the relations of production occurs; the educational system reinforces and supports this reproductive process through ideological training. Education by itself does not *create* the relations of production. The process of production along with the socialization process accomplishes such a task. The purchase and use of labor power in production produces economic classes; they are converted into political actors according to their ideological conditioning. Schools therefore do not produce classes. No appropriation of labor, hence no creation of surplus value, is effected in the process of education (except perhaps in the case of the schoolteacher). It is important to bear in mind that children eventually become workers not principally because of the education they receive, but because they are of a class which owns no property and therefore has nothing but its labor power to exchange with the owners of the means of production.

The problem resolves itself once more into the question of the responsibility of the schools in the society. Do schools create inequality or are they institutions supportive of a process emanating in production? The thesis governing this study is that schools are "instruments" supporting the social order but do not determine that social order. The content of the mass educational process has been one means of attempting to resolve the manifest antagonisms between classes through ideological training but was not a means of creating or reproducing classes or of reproducing the unequal distribution of property. Its principal task was and is the creation of a political consciousness which predisposes the people to accept the existing social order, a social order whose basis is not the educational system but capitalist production. In the final analysis, private ownership of the means of production at a monopoly stage formed the need, not for the schools to create classes or the division of labor, which they could not do, but for them to inculcate a pragmatic ideology within the mind of each individual. The principal goal of such ideological indoctrination is the enhancement of uninterrupted production. Within capitalist production, there is a relationship between workers and capitalists which is reflected within the schools in the form of ideological preparation for an acceptance of that relationship. Schools are like an insurance policy. Being part of the state, they act to conserve and to reproduce ideologically the social relations created in the constant process of private production. It is the process of production and its social effects which mold the task of the school. The basis of Progressivism was monopoly capitalism; the essence of Progressivism in the schools was the ideological training of youth for the existing mode of production. Thus the constant reproduction of the relations of production could be insured in the process of uninterrupted production.

Finally, the principal political point established in this study is that the state is the medium through which the economically dominant class becomes the politically dominant class. Monopoly capitalism, as an economic system, would disintegrate without the political protection given to it by the state. The form of this protection varies: military force, ideological conditioning, economic planning, social planning. The class struggle is a "veiled civil war" which would erupt into a violent revolution without the intervention of the state in its various forms.

The state, then, is the shell within which monopoly capitalism survives. The question of democracy, that is, democracy for the majority, must confront the relationship of the state to oppression and exploitation. To establish a society in which full democratic rights are accorded equally to everyone demands the abolition of the capitalist state. The first step in the resolution of the antagonism between classes (i.e., in the creation of a democracy for the people) is the taking of state power by the people and the transformation of the state into an instrument for the destruction of oppressive and exploitative institutions and structures.

Currently the United States faces serious problems with its youth: twenty percent of high school students drop out before graduating; the rate of functional illiteracy, above twenty percent, is alarming and even higher among national minorities; reading and writing skills are dropping among entering college freshmen. It would be incorrect to blame the schools for all of these problems, many of which are caused by social conditions outside the schools. However, there are certain serious problems produced by the schools through particular kinds of practices which have evolved over the course of time. Perhaps the most distressing practice is the categorization of students into a hierarchy of intelligence. The consequence of this technique is to classify the majority as "average" and a significant minority as "below average." Schools automatically turn children away from learning, because they are taught to doubt themselves and their own abilities and potential. Schools perform their political task by teaching the majority of people to rely not on themselves, but on external authority. This kind of learning gradually undermines the self-confidence and motivation necessary to sustain individual effort and consequently to broaden and deepen learning.

Schools reproduce the despotism of the factories: a hierarchy of "managers and subordinates." Such an educational pattern results, not in a consciousness of equality, but in the acceptance of inequality, of unequal abilities, skills, and intelligence levels. The majority of children are easily led to believe in their own mediocrity, to practice self-doubt, and to limit the range of their interests and pursuits to their "level." Self-confidence is not one of the by-products of a capitalist education for the majority of students.

Education has a political task to accomplish, and in accomplishing it, it creates social problems manifested as dropouts, disinterest in formal learning, low reading and writing skills—all due to low self-esteem and negative self-concepts generated by educational techniques which emphasize individualism and inequality through tracking and curriculum differentiation according to levels of "intelligence" or "aptitude." Perhaps the most conspicuous aspect of education in the U.S. is not the high dropout rate or the functional illiteracy but the serious psychological damage perpetrated through teaching. Schools generally fail to develop confidence and motivation in students, because schools are responsible for developing a quiescent majority, politically manageable, if not apolitical. Elitism is fostered and this constantly divides students into the "thinkers" and "workers": the intellectually oriented and the practical or vocational student. The former is confident, able to study, learn, and discipline himself or herself, because this is what education has revealed; the latter is a second-class student, who has been placed in a lower educational level because of personal liabilities. Students quickly learn this categorization, and as they realize the social distinctions, the "smart" and "dumb" categories, they readily begin to define themselves accordingly. They define their selves as those selves have been defined for them.

Antidemocracy in the schools is a necessary political device to resolve the class struggle. One of the most obvious forms of antidemocracy has been the chauvinistic forms of education practiced against national minorities. Patterns of cultural discrimination, English as the "official" and exclusive language, and the denial of the nationalities' histories are but a few of the manifestations of antidemocracy. Despite the struggles and victories of the sixties, the schools remain entrenched in pursuing inequality in schooling. Many programs won by minorities in the sixties and seventies, such as bilingual education, and special higher education admissions programs, have been whittled down to the bare. The struggle for democratic education continues as one of the major objectives of the people of the United States. This is a struggle not only for the people of the communities, but also for the teachers, whose professional objectives must encompass democracy in every aspect of society.

Some writers have advocated the taking over of the schools as the solution to the antidemocratic educational system; others have proposed the taking over of the factories and offices as the first step. Neither of these programs for social change recognizes the importance of the state in perpetuating monopoly capitalism. Struggle for democracy within the schools, offices, and factories is an important tactical part of the process for fundamental social change, but making the schools, offices, or the factories themselves the principal objective can never bring political power and fundamental change. The solution to oppression and exploitation (to antidemocracy in general) has as its strategic objective the taking of political power away from the economically dominant class. The possibility for the real transformation of society will be realized when political power will reside in those people whose interests are served through democracy. These are the various oppressed and exploited classes, nationalities, and strata now dominated by the interests of monopoly capitalism.

Case Study:
EDUCATIONAL REFORM IN LOS ANGELES AND ITS EFFECT ON THE CHICANO COMMUNITY, 1900-1930*

The theme of equal educational opportunity was a major concern of the urban Chicano Movement in the late 1960s and early 1970s. Chicanos accused the entire school system of racism and insensitivity towards the Chicano community. Schools, declared the activists, used institutionalized techniques such as intelligence tests and a tracking system to insure that disproportional numbers of Chicano children would be placed in vocational education courses or in classes for the mentally retarded.

Chicano activists pointed to low reading scores, high dropout rates (with up to fifty percent of Chicano high-school freshmen dropping out before graduation), high enrollment of Chicanos in courses for the educationlly mentally retarded, and the exclusive use of English in the classroom as evidence that the educational needs of Chicano children were not being met. They demanded an end to IQ testing, tracking, discriminatory emphasis on vocational work, and to disregard for Mexican customs, traditions, and the Spanish language. Essentially, the demands recognized the viability of community control of schools. These democratic demands were intended to serve the immediate interests of the Chicano community. The activists demanded that

---

*Originally published in slightly different form in *Explorations in Ethnic Studies*, Vol. 1, No. 2 (1978), pp. 5-26.

schools be a means for achieving economic and political equality and overall community development.

What are the roots of the antagonisms between school and community? Only through a historical approach can the nature of the present relationship between the Chicano people and institutions of the dominant society be made clear. The study of the role of mass public education in the Los Angeles Chicano community during the period 1900-1930 can provide insights into the continuing conflict between the Chicano community and the schools, and illuminate the historical development of the inequality in the educational process which indisputably exists today. It is assumed here that there is no justification for an undemocratic educational system.

This study examines the curricular program of the Los Angeles City Schools during the 1920s and 1930s with special reference to the effect of this program upon Mexican children and, ultimately, upon the Mexican community. Education for the Mexican community in Los Angeles did not provide opportunities for "social mobility." In fact, the schools limited economic opportunities through an educational program that consciously reinforced the existing social relations, especially those critical relations between capitalist and worker that threatened to burst apart under the weight of monopoly capitalism.

1. Background for Educational Reform

The evolution of the organization of public schools in Los Angeles paralleled the industrial, demographic, and bureaucratic changes in the city. Using 1880 as a point of departure, we find that in the following fifty-year period Los Angeles underwent a radical transition. In 1880 Los Angeles contained 11,000 citizens; by 1930 the population stood at 1,250,000 inhabitants. In that fifty-year span Los Angeles had grown one hundred times. By the early 1920s Los Angeles was increasing its population at the rate of 100,000 per year.

This extreme growth rate necessitated a public bureaucracy to care for the sprawling population and expanding economy. Between 1910 and 1920 numerous municipal agencies were created. A Housing Commission and a Municipal Charities Commission were established and the bureaucracy of the public education system was developed. The social and economic changes naturally affected the educational system. The school population was nineteen times larger in 1930 than it was in 1900, although the population had grown only twelve times during that same period. The school population rose from 20,497 in 1900 to 404,351 in 1930. The massive increase in the pupil population pressured the city into devising means to cope with the situation.

The Los Angeles City Schools were faced with enormous problems in their function of socialization. Financial, physical, administrative, and educational matters could not be resolved with the old methods. Therefore, a process of school reorganization and reorientation became inevitable. Between 1900 and 1930 the increasing enrollment could only be accommodated through a steadily enlarging organization. As an example, in 1900 only one high school served the secondary educational needs of the city; by 1930 there were thirty-one.

Special schools, curricula, and course work were established between 1900 and 1930 for those unable to read and for foreign students unable to speak English. At the same time, the Department of Vocational Education began to administer a regular program. In 1917 and 1918 respectively, the Division of Educational Research and the Department of Psychology were founded, and in 1920 were merged into the Department of Psychology and Educational Research. It was this department which exerted the greatest influence in curricular and administrative reform affecting the Mexican community. It was also this department which was the nerve center of oppressive bureaucratic techniques in education.

The school district's educational system was directly affected by the general educational ideas being promulgated throughout the country. The district's associations of elementary and secondary teachers, as well as the counselors, principals, and central administration lobbied for the most up-to-date approach to education. District publications (prepared by the Department of Psychology and Educational Research) such as the biweekly *Educational Research Bulletin* usually carried a book review section which informed counselors and teachers of recent as well as past publications in psychology and guidance. There were, in addition, frequent excerpts from books and lectures of well-known educators, including Dewey, Bobbit, Thorndike, and Terman, from politicians such as Teddy Roosevelt and Wilson, and from the lesser-known superintendents of schools of various cities who repeated the messages of the "experts."

Not merely through indirect means were the "experts" instrumental in developing the educational program. In 1924 Dr. Franklin Bobbit of the University of Chicago was hired to direct the complete reorganization of the high-school courses of study. Bobbit, who had previously participated in the commission which reorganized the educational system of the Philippine Islands (to conform to U.S. imperialist ambitions), performed a similar task for Los Angeles while working out of the Department of Psychology and Educational Research.[1] Those teachers who participated in the reorganization of social studies courses were asked to use all pertinent materials "emanating from

Teacher's College, Columbia University, University of Chicago, The National Council, The Historical Outlook, etc., for study."[2]

In the process of developing an educational system to conform to social reality, the social sciences became a central element in the creation of a cooperative citizen. This reorganization of the curriculum resulted in a social studies program whose principal objective was to promote the:

> ability to think, feel, act, and react as an efficient, intelligent, sympathetic and loyal member of the entire social group— that group that is prior to and above differentiation and within which social differentiation occurs. Large-group or citizen consciousness, sense of membership in the total social group, rather than in some special class.[3]

That objective was in close correspondence with the expressed wishes of the businessmen and industrialists. In an article appearing in the *Los Angeles School Journal*, the Assistant Director of the Department of Psychology and Educational Research quoted a report of the American Management Association as an example of the broad purpose of education. Schools were urged to:

> prepare the new workers for a better understanding of mutual dependence that employees have upon each other . . . give the new worker those economic, historical and sociological facts which will enable him to judge the truth and soundness of the various doctrines, theories, nostrums, panaceas, etc., with which he may come in contact.[4]

As an example of a local school program designed for the interests of local capitalists, the December 10, 1923, issue of the *Los Angeles School Journal* is noteworthy. In an article discussing the forthcoming Teacher's Institute, the topics and speakers were presented. The following composed the vocational education section of that institute:

"Co-operation of Industry with the Schools"
    Sylvester Weaver, Los Angeles Builder's Exchange

"Training for the Building Trades"
    Godfrey Edwards, Los Angeles Builder's Exchange

"The King of Mechanics Wanted in Industry"
    John E. Van Zant, Paul S. Hoffman Company, Inc.

"Trade Extension"
    J.C. Greenburg, in charge of Trade Extension Work for the [Los Angeles] Sanitation Department

Local reform had designed a curriculum that sought to insure social stability and continued capitalist growth. In its most fundamental aspects, Los Angeles schools applied an educational theory that corresponded to the expressed wishes of employers of wage labor.

2. The Mexican Problem

Within the phenomenal economic spiral, the necessity for a sufficient labor force manifested itself, attracting a large movement of Mexican immigrants and descendants of Mexican immigrants into Los Angeles.[5] Mexican settlements developed mainly in the Eastside in an area known as Maravilla. According to the 1920 census, 30,000 Mexicans resided in Los Angeles, and by 1930 the number stood at nearly 100,000. Various estimates at the time placed the number much higher, from approximately 150,000 to 200,000. It is highly probable that Mexicans were undercounted. More important for this study than the exact number of Mexicans residing in Los Angeles is the number of Mexican pupils in Los Angeles schools. The school officials interpreted their roles in relationship to both Mexican pupils and the Mexican community. It was this relationship which conditioned the reform of school programs that ultimately affected Mexican children.

Throughout the 1920s the numbers of Mexican children enrolled in Los Angeles schools increased according to their settlement in the area. In 1923 the total enrollment of Mexican children was slightly above 14,000, or 8.8 percent of the total school enrollment.[6] In the next several years the rise in Mexican enrollment and their concentration in the East Los Angeles area would direct the interest of the educational profession to resolve the "Mexican problem."

In 1926 the Los Angeles school system enrolled 218,097 pupils in all areas of elementary and secondary education. The numbers of Mexican children had increased over 11,500 since 1923 so that in 1926 there were 25,825 Mexican children enrolled, or approximately 11.5 percent of the total. Mexicans were the largest minority by far, followed by Blacks (approximately 5,000) and Japanese (approximately 4,000).[7]

Each year brought new arrivals to the labor market so that by 1928 Mexican enrollment in Los Angeles schools had climbed to well over 32,000. This figure represented a major portion of the total "foreign" enrollment in the schools. Not only were Mexican immigrants attracted, but many other immigrant groups as well. In 1920 the city's population was 576,673, of which 112,057 were foreign-born white persons. Nearly 20 percent of the latter group (or 21,598) were born in Mexico. In comparison, in 1910 the foreign-born population numbered 60,584, of whom 5,611 were born in Mexico.[8] The overcrowded conditions that plagued the schools would surely reflect upon the attitudes of the educators. In 1922 the high schools, which were built to accommodate 13,134 pupils, had an enrollment of 17,770. In 1924 the elementary schools had 48,000 more pupils than they had seats.

Economic changes were bringing such increasing enrollments, but the cause was racially interpreted. In 1922 an editorial in the *Los Angeles School Journal* lamented the increase in foreign-born, especially the Mexican-born, population. The article noted that "during the decade, 1910-1920, while the total population increased 81 percent, the foreign population increased 85 percent, and the Mexican population 285 percent."[9]

Appearing in the same journal was an article written by the president of the Board of Education and entitled "Problems of the Los Angeles School Board," in which a description of the scope of the foreign-born problem was examined. It reported that "ten percent of the students in the Los Angeles schools are foreign born. The last state census of children in Los Angeles over three years of age and under eighteen revealed that twenty percent of the parents were aliens." Mexicans, by virtue of their number, became the focus of the attention of the school district's administration.

A strong stand in the Mexican enrollment issue was taken by the Superintendent of Schools, Mrs. Susan B. Dorsey, in a speech delivered before the Principals Club in 1923. She said: "The first duty of education is to equalize opportunities for every child." However, she continued:

> It is unfortunate and unfair for Los Angeles, the third largest Mexican city in the world, to bear the burdens of taking care educationally of this enormous group. We do have to bear a spiritual burden quite disproportionate to the return from having this great number of aliens in our midst. This burden comes to us merely because we are near the border.

She claimed that Mexicans came and went without establishing roots in the city, although depositing their "burdens." The superintendent further explained that the state and the nation should recognize this unusual problem and help shoulder the responsibility by providing state and federal aid. This sharing of responsibility is important, she continued, because if "we Americanize them we can live with them, but if we do not, crime will go on at an increasing rate."[10]

An assistant supervisor in the Department of Compulsory Education with special work among Mexicans wrote that the "Mexican problem in the Los Angeles School System is principally the product of poverty in the home which, in turn, is largely the appendage of the influx of immigrants from the Republic south of us." The administrator traced this poverty to the "original raciality of the Mexicans' ... Mongolian descent." He further explained this racial theory:

> The infusion of Spanish blood into Aztec and Maya veins has Latinized later generations since the sixteenth century. The mixture of the two is fundamentally responsible for the carefree, if not indolent, characteristic of the race. . . . The lofty spirit of independence of both races explains the composure of the present day Mexican under circumstances and conditions which would appall the Anglo-Saxon or American subject.[11]

The same assistant supervisor stated that such allegedly Mexican traits as lack of ambition, early sexual activities, and poverty could be resolved by "the establishment of a labor bureau of preferred applicants under the auspices of the school board." His suggestion does not seem to have been implemented; at least there is no evidence of the establishment of such an employment agency in the literature.

3. The Scientific Method: The Department of Psychology and Educational Research

The most important procedures put to use under mass compulsory education in Los Angeles were intelligence-testing devices. These procedures were a monumental obstacle to educational opportunity for the minorities and the poor in general. Testing did not initially appear in Los Angeles as a fully developed pedagogical technique. As with most innovations, tests were first employed on a small-scale experimental basis. Eventually, testing procedures became the core of the educational process.

Testing devices were first used in Los Angeles in 1917 under an experiment carried out by a hastily organized division within the school system called the Division of Educational Research. Its first task was to administer an "intelligence survey," using as the basis for the study administration of the Binet test to approximately 2,000 pupils.

How to deal with the variation of mental abilities became the task of another administrative body, the Department of Psychology, created in 1918 with the specific task of classifying tested pupils. The department estimated that, on the basis of the research, 5,000 elementary school pupils possessed an intelligence too low to profit by the methods used in regular and ungraded classes.[12] The Department was given further responsibilities encompassing three main areas. These were: 1) the "testing of children's mentality and school accomplishment, 2) devising materials for individual instruction, and 3) supervising the special schools and classes" for advanced and retarded pupils.

The two departments, Educational Research and Psychology, were merged into one department in 1920. Originally a staff of two managed the offices, but by 1924 the staff numbered fifteen, and by 1930 the twenty-six staff members administered perhaps the most influential department in the educational bureaucracy of Los Angeles. With each staff increment, the responsibilities of the division also seemed to grow. In 1930 the department had six major functions. These were:

> (1) high school research and guidance (counseling); (2) secondary school curriculum development; (3) elementary research and guidance; (4) special schools and classes; (5) psychological clinic; (6) statistics.[13]

Each area of responsibility was administered by a section within the department.

Testing, classification (or homogeneous grouping), curriculum development, and counseling were the four specific areas that reflected the basic core of principles of the entire department and, ultimately, of the city school system. Testing had become a monumental administrative procedure by 1929. In the school year 1928-29, a total of 328,000 tests were given to pupils of the elementary schools alone.[14] Largely on the basis of these tests, school children were placed in normal classes, gifted rooms, slow rooms, and/or classes for the "mentally retarded" (or "development" centers).

The correspondence between test scores and social class was dramatic. Significant correlations were drawn from intelligence surveys administered between 1926 and 1928. One such study, carried out under the direction of the Department of Psychology and Educational Research, compared the intelligence and achievement of Mexicans to white Americans. The study provides insight into the effect of school policy on Chicanos. In 1931 a group of 1,204 Mexican grade school children were compared to a control group of 1,074 white American children. It was found that the median intelligence quotient for the Mexican group was 91.2, a figure approximately nine points below the "normal" quotient of 100 for an unselected population. The median quotient for the white American group was 105, considerably above that of the Mexican children and five points above the normal for an unselected population. It should also be mentioned that the Mexican group averaged twelve months above the age of their white American counterparts. Grade for grade, Mexican children were one full year behind, or overage, compared to their white companions. The supervisor who directed the study concluded that the factors contributing to the low scores by Mexican children were: 1) language handicap, and 2) a "selection of a type of Mexican family who comes to Los Angeles." She added: "Most of the fathers of the children represented in the group belong to the laboring class."[15] Upon the basis of the test scores, it was found that approximately forty-eight percent scored below 90. These children would automatically qualify for the slow-learner rooms. Of the entire group, nearly eighteen percent qualified for classes for the mentally retarded.

Thus, there was a very high probability that nearly one-half of the Mexican children would find themselves placed in either slow-learner rooms or in classes for the mentally retarded. The remaining fifty-two percent had poor chances of ever being placed in an educational program other than for the manual vocations.

4. The Educational Technicians: The Counselors

Surveys such as the above only reflected the overall social levels of the school district. However, counselors, while they were concerned with homogeneous groupings within schools, were consciously focusing primarily on individual pupils. Each elementary school counselor's report furnished "three separate listings of those children who need ... special attention." First, there were those children with IQ levels above 125 who qualified for "gifted" rooms. These rooms were designed to give an enriched program to children of superior mental endowment. At the other end of the scale, children whose IQ was 70 or below were candidates for "mentally retarded" rooms. On the basis of IQ alone, the students were considered for the group or room which corresponded to their mental level. Once selected, the pupil was then given a series of tests designed to diagnose the interests and strengths upon which the teachers would base their approach to instructing the student.[16]

The segregation of children considered to be of abnormal mentality was founded upon three basic criteria: a) that the more intelligent pupils were to be accelerated; b) that the backward, or retarded, pupils restrained the superior pupils from progressing; and c) that the retarded formed a stagnant pool of constant failures. The consensus was that the brighter pupils were held back by the slower pupils, making the segregation of these groups desirable. Only the "average" pupil was left alone to seek achievement in the world of mediocrity.

The counselors tended to view themselves as objective, scientifically trained professionals whose work was central to the proper functioning of the educational process. Guided by a "scientific attitude," they saw their principal educational goal as the "satisfactory adjustment of the individual."[17] Under the mantle of a science, counselors assumed (and, in fact, were given) nearly absolute power and responsibility over the pupils with whom they came into contact through the medium of educational testing. When presented with the "scientific" results of the intelligence test, few could muster an opposing argument, and very few did in Los Angeles. All the evidence favored the scientific professionals. Indeed, the arguments appeared logical, well thought out, and progressive.

Not only did the Department of Psychology and Educational Research break with past methods of administration and education, it was also carrying out a crusade to convince the entire school system that the "scientific method" was the correct approach to education. The literature of the department reflected this crusading spirit imbued with self-righteousness and moral indignation at those who failed to recognize "science." In 1923 the director of the Division of High School Research of the department wrote that one of the duties of the counselor was to "sell his mission to the teachers and to act as a leader in the faculty in the cooperative study and solution of the modern problems of education."[18] Merely by being given a wide range of responsibilities, the scientific professionals enlarged their image. Their feelings of omnipotence can be understood by their functions, which were (according to their literature) to result in a "more accurate classification of pupils for purposes of instruction."[19]

The director of the department emphasized the importance of scientific techniques in an article appearing in the department's journal. She wrote:

> Every situation investigated, every child tested is, or should be, a research problem, and strictly scientific procedure should be observed. Data scientifically obtained and treated can, if properly recorded and evaluated, be used at any time as the basis of conclusions which may prove a genuine contribution to educational and psychological knowledge.[20]

A high-school principal exclaimed that it was "only with the advent of the counselor that we have had our thinking organized and set upon a scientific foundation." He added that not only was the counselor invaluable in the administration and program, but counselors also kept him "fresh in . . . educational philosophy and assisted me in presenting to the faculty those studies which get at the actual facts."[21]

It was not merely in the administration of tests and in the computing of quotients that counselors were involved. Counselors were told that their role was a means to an end, that is, they were to set "up the best possible educational and life career program for Johnny."[22] It was not simply a matter of formulas and data; counselors were using a means through which human beings could be more accurately socialized to the society in which they lived. The scientific method was only a means through which a socialization process could be more accurately and efficiently achieved. The recognition of individual differences was perceived to be a humanistic breakthrough. The ideological nature of the educational process was mystified in the numerous myths of the educational program—myths that were in essence part of the educational process itself. "The school counselor has developed in recognition of the individual differences existing among children," wrote the assistant director of the department. He added that for normal pupil growth to proceed the educational procedures must be modified so that the "school may be fitted to the child."[23]

The director was most emphatic in exclaiming that the recognition of individual differences "both in innate ability and in personality make-up" had resulted in the need to modify curricula and teaching methods. Guidance, she continued, "based on carefully collected and evaluated data, is our only hope of diminishing the enormous waste in human material which an inflexible school system necessarily produces."[24] The proclaimed ideology of the scientists was purported to be a mixture of the highly technical and the humanistic but was, in fact, a method of intensifying individualism with children in an orderly and efficient manner. The corresponding results were a social stratification of schools within the Los Angeles school system.

Only by examining the day-to-day work of counselors as outlined by the department's guidelines and reports can we accurately assess the importance of counseling in the school program. These operations involved four main areas: (1) testing, (2) school surveys, (3) classification, and (4) curriculum. The Report of the Committee on Analysis of High School Counseling in Los Angeles is an important source, because it reveals in detail the function and operation of counselors.[25]

Counselors became involved in their schools through a step process of "gathering . . . facts about the individual children and about the school as a whole." When these facts were tabulated, a "scientific guidance program" became possible. Each child was to have "a complete social case history." Information gathered included

> age, mental and chronological, the intelligence quotient, the nationality, the father's occupation, the amount of retardation or acceleration, the achievement status in the various subjects,

the physical defects, the outstanding character qualities, and the pupil's general attitude toward the school.

Once these facts were assembled, a "complete picture of the school as a whole" could be projected. The picture was referred to by counselors as the school survey, an analysis of the factors necessary for the counselors to carry out their assignments. This survey also assessed the schools' efficiency in the

> various subjects, the central tendencies of the individual mental abilities, the amount of retardation and acceleration in various grades, the opportunities for social development, the moral status as shown in the number of disciplinary problems occurring, and the physical vitality as manifested in the attendance and health records.

Several tasks occupied the major portion of the high-school counselors' time; two of these were student and school surveys and curriculum. The counselors had to be thoroughly knowledgeable about the courses offered in order for proper guidance to be given. However, guidance was still dependent upon the occupational opportunities available "in the community." Thus, counselors undertook surveys in cooperation with the Department of Vocational Education and "in cooperation with the occupations teachers of the city." Committees were formed from the cooperative effort which assembled "data concerning the various lines of work." This data included "a description of the job, the preparation required for entrance, the income, the opportunities for learning and advancement, and the number of workers in demand."

The occupational surveys were realistic in delineating occupations open to racial and ethnic groups. The report stated that

> some of the specific studies being undertaken by these groups include surveys of the occupations suitable to and firms employing Negro, Mexican, and Jewish help.

It was not unusual that Blacks, Mexicans, and Jews were singled out for special guidance consideration. Although it was "chiefly on the basis of test scores that pupils are classified into equal ability groups," teachers' recommendations, achievement test scores, and educational records were also used in the classification procedure. The report made clear that only "when there is strong evidence that a child is of very low potentiality, will the counselor suggest to him a vocation which is apparently within the range of his ability." Furthermore, the report added, it was good for the child to keep the curriculum at his or her level: "The counselors seek, with the help of tests, to free children from the possibility of attempting tasks far beyond their ability and to avoid the resulting pain, discouragement, and humiliation."

Thus, high-school students were placed at an "individualized" learning level corresponding to an occupational position waiting to be filled. The tests invariably selected the poorest students for occupations that were of the manual variety and, since these were not of high social value, counselors strove to raise their importance in the consciousness of the students.

> A great effort is made to overcome the traditional feeling that it is unworthy and ignoble to enter anything but the professions. . . . he need not feel disgrace that he is not preparing for one of the professions.

Through a bit of mental engineering, the real difference in income and social status between manual occupations and professional occupations was to be overcome. All one had to do was to "think" he was equal to another, and equality resulted. However, students were not given the opportunity to exercise their capabilities and desires fully. A number of techniques were used to distinguish mental levels of students. Some schools gave colored cards to each student admitting "them to the proper classes." These cards stated whether their work was "Honor College Recommended," "College Recommended," or "High School Graduation." In other high schools the teachers were given lists by the counselor indicating each child's group. In another school, the counselor prepared a directory with pertinent information on each student, such as IQ, "previous number of failures, and a group . . . in which he should be enrolled." The director of the High School Research Division of the department was much more blunt in his frank assessment of the role of counselors. He wrote that the job of the counselor was "that of the placement of the misfit."[26]

Teachers were urged by the department to "be conversant with the economic and social conditions in which they teach, so that they may the easier guide pupils towards selecting activities which the parents will consider worthy and will support." Thus, prior to the benefit of an IQ test, students were already categorized into educational areas corresponding to their socioeconomic level. In the counseling and guidance that followed, the categorization was reinforced until the schools became a microcosm of the society which they served. Children were placed into general occupational preparations through various pedagogical devices. That which concerns us here is vocational, or manual, training.

The first means of placing children into manual training was the development rooms and centers for the allegedly "mentally retarded" of the higher elementary grades. In 1928-29 a total 2,554 children, representing only one-fourth of the referrals, were enrolled in the program which was designed as an educational program for the mentally defective. Each child was "programmed" with due consideration to a great variety of factors, such as "the child's health and nutrition, his emotional stability, his social development, his chronological age, his mental age, his particular grade placement in the vocational or fine arts, and his particular industrial adaptability." Once these children were enrolled, there was no means for returning them to normal classes. Their problem and their social level became permanently fixed within the normal operation of the institution. The philosophy of the development centers was rigid: each child "must become a part" of the "industrial world." No alternatives were possible. The average IQ of the students was approximately 63.[27]

The limits of "successful accomplishment," or achievement, were external, or social, and impinged upon the classroom. The development centers and classes were "located in the sections of the city where there was greatest need for them." Thus in 1930, of the eleven centers, ten were located in areas characterized as "laboring class" communities. Enrollment figures clearly describe the social level of the students, since attendance varied with the agricultural work seasons:

> The children enter in Fall, due to the seasonal employment in the country, where the children and their parents are employed picking fruits and nuts. The enrollment reaches the peak in the Spring when many centers and rooms have to maintain waiting lists. The month of June usually brings an appreciable exodus when the children and their parents go out into the fields to harvest the onion crop.[28]

Each center's program was based upon some type of manual work. Each center had a "full-time manual education teacher and a full-time crafts teacher. The larger centers had a full-time agricultural teacher and the smaller centers had the service of an agricultural teacher two or three days a week." The centers divided the course work for boys and girls, reinforcing the existing sexual division of labor found in society. Centers were "equipped with a home economics unit" which consisted "of a cooking room, cafeteria, sewing room, and laundry." A manual education unit served the male students. It consisted of a "main workroom, a lumber room, a paint room, and a tool room; a hand-work unit with provision for loom weaving, clay-work, basketry, and miscellaneous types of craft work."[29]

The center's population was largely "from foreign homes" and was handicapped by a language "problem," according to a survey of nearly 1,600 children taken by the Department of Psychology and Educational Research.[30] Mexicans, Blacks, Russians, Asians, Jews, and Italians were represented among the children. Blacks were segregated into two centers; Mexican children constituted the entire population of one center, one-third in two others, and one-fourth in two more. In all, Mexican children were highly represented in five of the eleven development centers.

The development rooms produced no skilled labor for the economy, nor was there any appreciable relation between training and later occupation. Of the 325 who graduated from the development centers in 1928-29, 65 were working in agriculture as fruit pickers, 60 sold newspapers, and the remainder were scattered over a wide range of unskilled manual occupations. Even though there seemed to be no relation between the graduates' occupations and the training program, there was, nevertheless, a definite attempt to train the students for particular occupations. At times the plans were apparently successful. One administrator found that training girls in laundry work enabled them to hold positions in large laundries when they left school. In fact, he stated, "several employers have told us that a dull girl makes a very much better operator on a mangle than a normal girl." He also stated that "fitting the person to the job reduces the turnover in industry, and is, of course, desirable from an economic point of view."[31] That "perfect fit" was also a result of the psychological conditioning that the schools so eloquently struggled to inculcate.

5. *Curriculum Development and Vocational Education in the High Schools*

As industrialization proceeded, the labor needs of industry were reflected in the district's educational program. By 1930 the larger outlines of educational reform regarding testing, teaching, counseling, and curriculum development had already been institutionalized in Los Angeles. All that remained was to fill in the particulars, especially in curriculum development. It was made clear by the fledgling Division of Educational Research "that the demands of commerce and industry must be met so far as they represent the general need."[32]

The purpose of schooling was interwoven with and, ultimately, shaped by capitalism. The preparation of students to enter "the business and industrial world" was more than just an abstract preparation for "life." It was an education molded by the interests of capital. The Director of Vocational Education understood the responsibility of schools: "Since Los Angeles is more and more becoming a manufacturing city, the demand for men and women for industry is clearly evident." School administrators were quite disturbed, for example, that in a survey of eighth grade boys it was found that "[n]o one had determined to enter an automobile factory." Furthermore, the survey found that pupils' vocational aspirations and the needs for labor clearly did not correspond. This was found to be an unnecessary and inefficient barrier to the smooth transition from school to work. The solution to the problem was thought to be proper placing of students in school work commensurate with their aptitudes and abilities. "If the change of interest can be brought about during the school career," stated a report of the Los Angeles City Schools, "a large saving in time and energy for the pupils and their future employers may be saved." Moreover, the report continued, it

> is not uncommon for the labor turnover in business houses and in factories to exceed 200 percent per year. This is very expensive as each new employee must become accustomed to his new place before he is able to do his best work, and a large part of the labor turnover is due to dissatisfaction and unrest on the part of the employee.

By 1920 the Los Angeles School District had organized an efficient approach to balancing curriculum and labor needs. Teachers of vocational education held biweekly conferences "examining minutely the basic occupations listed in the U.S. Census Classification of Gainful Pursuits, to determine just what should be the definite content of class instruction."[33]

Vocational courses thus became arranged to suit the needs of the business and industrial world. Simultaneously, pedagogical goals were based upon these needs. Thus a boy or girl applying for a position and confronted with the embarrassing question, "What can you do?" posed a pedagogical problem. The schools were to prepare students so they might be spared the agony of the employer's question. "The employer," stated the school district's report, "expects immediate service and production."[34] The question "What can you do?" became a legitimate pedagogical problem resolved through the public school's program.

The question was not applied universally, since it was modified by IQ tests, achievement scores, teacher's assessments, and grades. Students were chosen for vocational courses primarily on the basis of the IQ test and other selected criteria. The results of these methods reflected the class structure of society. Students of low socioeconomic status, as well as those with low IQ's, were given far narrower choices for entering the wide range of education available.

School administrators held on to the belief that the individual "blossomed" within an individualized curriculum. One wrote that "education is merely the manner of training the mind and body that will enable the individual to best adjust himself to his environment, with the incidental advantages of economic independence, self-realization, and ... happiness."[35] However, he continued, as far as vocational education was concerned, it was the "dull pupil" who was particularly suited for such a self-fulfilling experience. Lack of mental ability was no longer a cause for failure, for somewhere along the line there was an individualized course of study that corresponded to one's IQ. Following Lewis Terman's "discovery" that an IQ score could indicate general occupational aptitude, courses of study were arranged along the lines indicated by the IQ score.

However, vocational courses were not entirely the result of the school district's initiative. The local Chamber of Commerce, as well as individual businessmen, not only supported the schools, but also worked closely with them.

The cooperative efforts of the schools and industry proceeded "upon very practical lines and registered remarkable success," wrote one administrator.[36] The manager of the Industrial Department of the Chamber of Commerce agreed:[37]

> The interest of the businessmen in the schools of Los Angeles is naturally keen, inasmuch as he helps pay the bills of the schools. But his interest does not end there in dollars and cents. Employees of his concern are the products of the public schools and their efficiency depends in large measure upon the methods employed in the schools.

The cooperative spirit produced positive results. Vocational education was placed on more equal terms with the regular school subjects, and a committee, formed of representatives of the Chamber of Commerce and the Board of Education, met on a regular basis to resolve pedagogical questions involving vocational work. It is not clear how long this committee operated, but what is clear is that a steadily enlarging scope of educational activities brought both the Chamber and the school district into quite close cooperation.

The Director of Vocational Education wrote in 1924 that "Los Angeles was fortunate in bringing about ... most wholesome cooperation in the schools ... from business and industry." He added:

> In this city we hold that for the normal child education should be liberal and general in the earlier years of the child and remain so until the senior high school. However, in a city so

large we find groups of children, usually of adolescent age, who more readily obtain their general education through actual participation in various shop activities. For those, vocational education often is of great advantage.[38]

Not only were the higher administrative levels in close touch with business and industry, counselors also regularly surveyed the employment possibilities in the school's immediate community. One principal urged that each colleague "be in close touch with the leading businessmen and women in his district, for through them he can sense the desires and needs of his people, at the same time gaining the confidence of the community as a whole."[39] A principal of a high school noted the cooperation and exclaimed that the "Chambers of Commerce and other similar organizations . . . have aligned themselves with the schools in carrying out educational programs and campaigns."[40] A teacher at a high school wrote:

Before sending boys and girls out to accept positions they must be taught that, technically expert though they may be, they must ever keep in mind that their employers carry the responsibility of the business and outline the work, and that the employees must be pliant, obedient, courteous, and willing to help the enterprise.[41]

Los Angeles schools were particularly boastful of their relationship to capital. An editorial appearing in the *Los Angeles School Journal* (1927) summarized the situation well: "Teachers and business people are alike in building the future. Such cooperation as exists in Los Angeles is a long step toward an amalgamation of education and life."

Each of the regular junior and senior high schools offered vocational courses for males and females, although the distribution of these courses was not equal. Some senior and junior high schools had extraordinary numbers of vocational courses, while others had only one or two. Not surprisingly, in the east side where the bulk of the foreign-born resided, a concentration of vocational courses was evident. The two east-side schools, Lincoln and Roosevelt, had unusually high numbers of vocational courses. Of the thirty-one high schools operating in 1932, only eight offered "class A" all-day vocational courses for males. Class A schools set aside "three clock hours for trade instruction." There were altogether thirty-one class A courses available at these eight schools. Lincoln and Roosevelt offered seventeen of these; Fremont, located in another predominantly working-class section of the city, offered nine class A courses. Thus, three high schools offered twenty-six of the thirty-one class A vocational courses. They were all in working-class sections of the city.

The number of non-class-A vocational courses for males clustered again around the working-class neighborhood schools. Lincoln had seventeen of these courses, Roosevelt offered eighteen, and Jefferson had eleven. University High School, on the west side, offered only one vocational course and one of the class A variety. The emphasis is more significant when it is recognized that only eighteen vocational subjects were made available.

The evidence strongly points to the heavy emphasis upon vocational work in certain sections of the city, particularly the east side where the bulk of the Mexican community resided. Virtually no vocational work was being done in at least half of the high schools in 1929; yet in that same year, Lincoln, Roosevelt (on the east side), and Jefferson (in the Mexican-Black central section) made available for their students forty-six of the seventy regular vocational courses taught in the entire city. Roosevelt and Lincoln alone offered thirty-five vocational courses.[42]

Vocational courses for girls were aided by state and federal funds and followed similar distribution patterns. For instance, homemaking was offered at only four schools: Lafayette Junior High (with an enrollment of 36 percent Black, 14 percent Mexican, and 30 percent Jewish), Belvedere Junior High (51 percent Mexican), Hollenbeck (Mexican and Jewish), and Jefferson (mixed working class). Lincoln offered dressmaking, millinery, and power sewing. Roosevelt offered dressmaking, sewing, power sewing, and personal hygiene. What this in fact meant was that of six vocational subjects for females, Lincoln offered three, Roosevelt four, and Fremont two. Only seven schools taught vocational courses for women. All of them were located in immigrant and poor neighborhoods.[43]

A very special example of the vocational emphasis for Mexican children was the case of the San Fernando Elementary School. The school principal requested that the school, "attended entirely by Mexicans" totalling 600 students, be officially changed "to become a Mexican Industiral School." The superintendent of schools and the board of education were favorably disposed to such a change in school purpose, which was to "better fit the boys and girls to meet their problems of life in the future years." The regular school work was thought to be appropriate for the lower grades, "but the older children will have a longer time to finish their academic work, and will have more vocational training." The latter was to consist of a pragmatic program:[44]

> The girls will have more extensive sewing, knitting, crocheting, drawn work, rug weaving and pottery. They will be taught

personal hygiene, home-making, care of the sick. With the aid of a nursery they will learn the care of little children. The boys will be given more advanced agriculture and shop work of various kinds.

It is not clear if the school actually operated as a Mexican Industrial School, since there is no further mention in any of the school's publications. What was significant was the continual emphasis upon vocational education for Mexican children, even to the point of creating a Mexican Industrial School.

6. Conclusion

The Los Angeles educational program in the 1920s and early 1930s was characterized by an adherence to general Progressive techniques and philosophy. Los Angeles had reached a stage in its development during the 1920s when educational reform had become necessary. These reforms insured that the Mexican community would be subjected to a narrow, one-dimensional educational program that stressed nonacademic vocational course work. Channelled into these courses by the counseling program, Mexican children became a major portion of the students in vocational course work and in slow-learner classrooms.

For these thousands of Mexican children in public schools, education was not an opportunity for social mobility. Instead, their education was designed to benefit the interests of capital. Mexican pupils were being trained in numbers far out of proportion to their percentage of the school population for predetermined occupations in the economy, usually in the lowest paying categories, which most of their fathers and mothers had entered upon immigrating.

Los Angeles was not alone in implementing such an educational program. A 1933 study by the U.S. Office of Education reported identical schooling programs in the Los Angeles, Denver, San Antonio, and El Paso school districts. Their common approach placed Mexican pupils "into a course of study suited to their needs," which was a nonacademic curriculum emphasizing manual training.[45]

Thus, the normal operation of free, mass, and compulsory education was one means by which the Mexican community supplied the capitalist economy with an "educated" labor force. The schools, agents of social stability, served the public, but only after that service had been molded to the specifications and the interests of monopoly capitalism.

The political objective of the schools would eventually become the cause of its opposition. The harvest of antidemocracy proved to be the urban Chicano Movement of the 1960s, which joined with the Black,

Asian, and Native American Movements in their focus upon inequality in education. Numerous democratic gains were forced upon the schools and many bilingual programs were instituted, although often watered down. In general, bilingual education was the teaching of English by way of Spanish. But even this was too democratic, and so in the eighties we are witnessing the return of English as the principal language in all curricular programs. We are returning slowly to the situation of the fifties.

At a recent immigration conference held in San Diego sponsored by the Chicano Civil Rights Organization, the workshop on education repeated the list of complaints which were voiced in the sixties. What was immediately apparent was that the major educational problems, rooted in the system of monopoly capitalism, were not resolved by the spontaneous Chicano rebellion of the sixties. The tasks remain to be completed: this time, however, accumulated experience and knowledge will guide the nationalities' movements of the eighties.

NOTES

Chapter 1: A Methodological Introduction

1. For Marxists, occupation, income, status, and psychological outlook are not the criteria for determining classes. The Marxist measure for classes is the relationship of individuals to the means of production, i.e., the social relations of production, the distinction between exploiters and exploited.
2. See, for example, Louis Hartz, *The Liberal Tradition in America* (New York: Harcourt, 1955).
3. Marx defined two forms of proletarian consciousness. The first is a class consciousness manifesting itself in purely economic trade-union struggles—expressed through strikes, boycotts, and agitation for higher wages, shorter work hours, and increased work benefits. As such, a class-conscious working class recognizes that it must organize and struggle if it is to better its material level of living. The second form of consciousness Marx defined as a *political* class consciousness. This form is the organization and struggle of the working class for its political interests. The highest expression of this political consciousness is the capturing of state power. This political consciousness is revolutionary, and implies that the proletariat (to the extent that it is conscious of its political interests) is prepared to become the class in control of the state. Both forms of consciousness are necessary for any revolutionary activity; however, if a political consciousness is lacking, there will be no revolutionary struggles for state power. Both forms of consciousness imply a class struggle: the first is an economic class struggle; the second is a political class struggle.
4. The question of proof has occasionally been raised in connection with Marxist methodology, and especially in relation to Lenin's theses on monopoly capitalism. However, if criticism begins with whether Marxism or Lenin's contentions have been *proved* empirically, we must then answer with a book on methodology. Marxists (in general) do not see theory mainly as an academic or scholarly tool with which a hypothesis is verified empirically. Marxist theory is not proven in the library or in books. If it were such, it would remain a theory; Marx and Lenin did not apply dialectical and historical materialism for the sake of empirically proving that such and such was a fact—and then on to the next point. Marxism, by its own standards, is a tool not only for interpreting the world, *but for changing it*. Thus, the viability of Marxism can be seen in the successful completion of several major socialist revolutions. It is in the application of Marxism to social practice that one tests the mettle of Marxism—not in its halfway application, e.g., to the educational process.

    Lenin's theses *do* stand up to the rigorous test of empirical validity. Most critics of Marxist methodology do not realize the tremendous amount of research which Lenin completed before writing *Imperialism, the Highest Stage of Capitalism*. Lenin, however, was not concerned with merely *proving*; his purpose was linked to the practice of the Russian socialist revolution. If we were to concede that Lenin's theses were correct in social practice but that nevertheless it is not a sufficient criterion for historical proof, we would still have to acknowledge the massive and detailed research which Lenin carried out to prove his point. Harry Magdoff cogently argues this

point: "Those who think that all Lenin did was to pull together a few strands of thought then floating about, or those who imagine that useful theory on social matters comes from intuition or pure deduction from other theories, would do well to consult the extensive notebooks Lenin wrote in preparation for his brief essay on imperialism. His notes on his research in this field constitute the over 800 page volume 39 of his *Collected Works*." Source: Harry Magdoff, "How to Make a Molehill Out of a Mountain," *Monthly Review*, 28, 10 (March 1977), pp. 1-18.
5. V.I. Lenin, *Imperialism, the Highest Stage of Capitalism* in Lenin, *Collected Works*, 22 (Moscow: Progress Publishers, 1964), p. 266.
6. Karl Marx, *Capital*, I (Moscow: Foreign Languages Publishing House, 1966), 170-171.
7. Marx said, "One capitalist always kills many. Hand in hand with this centralisation, or this expropriation of many capitalists by few, develop, on an ever extending scale, the cooperative form of the labour process, the conscious technical application of science, the methodical cultivation of the soil, the transformation of the instruments of labour into instruments of labour only usable in common, the economising of all means of production by their use as the means of production combined, socialised labour, the entanglement of all peoples in the net of the world-market, and with this, the international character of the capitalist regime. Along with the constantly diminishing number of the magnates of capital, who usurp and monopolise all advantages of this process of transformation, grows the mass of misery, oppression, slavery, degradation, exploitation; but with this too grows the revolt of the working class, a class always increasing in number, and disciplined, united, organised by the very mechanism of the process of capitalist production itself. The monopoly of capital becomes a fetter upon the mode of production, which has sprung up and flourished along with, and under, it. Centralisation of the means of production and socialisation of labour at last reach a point where they become incompatible with their capitalist integument. [This] integument is burst asunder. The knell of capitalist private property sounds. The expropriators are expropriated." *Capital* (New York: International Publishers, 1967), I, 763.
8. Lenin, *Imperialism*, p. 206.
9. *Ibid.*, p. 205.
10. *Ibid.*, p. 197. Has concentration continued? The figures made available by the federal government show that monopolization continues; the Studies by the Staff of the Cabinet Committee on Price Stability (Washington, D.C., 1968) demonstrate Lenin's argument.

Concentration of Assets and Profits in Manufacturing, First Quarter, 1968

Corporations having assets of:	No. of companies	% of co.	$ of manu. assets	% of manu. profits
$1 billion or more	78	0.04	43 million	49
$250 million to $1 billion	194	0.1	21 million	20
$10 million to $250 million	2,165	1.2	22 million	19
Under $10 million	185,000	98.7	14 million	12

Thus in 1968, less than 1% of all industrial corporations owned 64% of all corporate industrial capital. (Quoted in *Dollars and Sense*, Dec. 1974, p. 4).
11. Marxists define the state as an institution of society with a set of functions designed principally to enforce, regulate, legitimize, and preserve existing social, political, and economic relations within society. The capitalist state performs its specific tasks through its various agencies: the military, executive, legislative, judicial, educational, and regulative (economic and social) agencies. As such, the state is the totality of those local, state and federal agencies which constitutes the "public power." Each has a portion of the total power, although in the era of monopoly capitalism, the central state (the federal government) has a greater share of total power than local and state governments. In effect, the latter under conditions of monopoly capitalism are dominated by the federal government. Under conditions of competitive capitalism, the peripheral local and state governments had wider latitude in enforcing the will of local dominant interests. Under monopoly, there are economic interests which span the nation and these therefore predominate over smaller local interests. The point, however, is that the state is the political institution of the dominant class through which this class, or the powerful fraction of the class, expresses its social, political, and economic interests.
12. Robert A. Lively, "The American System: A Review Article," in Richard M. Abrams and Lawrence W. Levine, *The Shaping of Twentieth Century America* (Boston: Little, Brown, 1965), pp. 4-23.
13. The change in the military from that of a small inefficient militia, to that of a permanent, massive, highly complex but centralized military apparatus is a noteworthy example. On the eve of the Spanish-American War, the military had only 26,000 men, with "no adequate plans, equipment, or supplies" to carry out the war. Furthermore, the "War Department was crippled by antiquated methods [and] incompetent administration." See John Blum, ed., *The National Experience* (New York: Harcourt, 1968), p. 529. By the middle of the twentieth century, the military held leases throughout the "Free World" permanently occupied by hundreds of thousands of soldiers. But more importantly, the economy became heavily dependent upon federal military expenditures.

Economists E.K. Hunt and Howard J. Sherman conclude that close to fifteen percent of the GNP during the 1960s was derived from military spending. They further document the importance of the military for employment. Only "five key military-related industries accounted for 7.9 percent of all employment in New York, 12.3 percent in New Jersey, 13 percent in Texas, 14.6 percent in Massachusetts . . . 31.4 percent in California . . . 34.8 percent in Washington," etc. (E.K. Hunt and Howard J. Sherman, *Economics* [New York: Harper, 1972], pp. 148-149). The gigantic stature of the military in the economy and society at midcentury is totally different from the situation in the latter nineteenth century when at one time the United States could muster only three warships for its Navy.
14. Lenin, *Imperialism*, pp. 22-23. The relationship, and power, of the financiers vis-a-vis industrial enterprises (as well as small banking corporations) was shown by the Pujo Committee in 1912. The J.P. Morgan interests and the Rockefeller-controlled National City Bank and Baker's First National Bank held a total of 341 directorships in 112 corporations with a total capitalization

of $22,245,000,000. (Leo Huberman, *We, the People* [New York: Harper, 1947], p. 245). Lenin noted that this was about one-third of the total wealth in the United States. (V.I. Lenin, *On the United States* [New York: International Publishers, 1970], p. 609).

15. Daniel Fusfeld, *The Age of the Economist* (Glenview, Illinois: Scott, Foresman, 1972), p. 58. Freedom did not include the right to revolution, or the destruction of property. The police power was employed whenever any acts, or social formations (e.g., Native Americans) threatened capitalist property. The really distinctive feature of the state under monopoly capitalism is the gigantic extension of bureaucratic police power into the personal lives of citizens. For example: welfare, taxes (local, state, federal), compulsory education, spy agencies, loyalty oaths, state certification of all kinds and so on.
16. Cited in V.I. Lenin, *Selected Works* (New York: International Publishers, 1971), p. 270.
17. V.I. Lenin, "The Caricature of Marxism and Imperialist Economism," in *Collected Works*, 23 (London: Lawrence and Wishart, 1960), 42-43.
18. Herbert Marcuse, *Negations: Essays in Critical Theory* (Boston: Beacon Press, 1968), p. 203.
19. *Ibid.*
20. Benjamin Constant once stated, "I have defended for forty years the same principle: liberty in everything, in religion, in literature, in philosophy, in industry, in politics; and by liberty, I understand it to mean the triumph of individuality, with respect to the authority which pretends to govern through despotism, as well as over the masses that claim the right to subjugate the minority." Aron's rejection of classical democrary is illuminating. He argues that there is no such thing as government "by the people, for the people, and of the people." His position is that only a minority rule, composed of those who are most capable. This managing elite, however, must govern wisely lest it either become corrupted or create discontent. One means of achieving this balance is the circulation of elites. Thus, according to Aron, a representative government is the circulation of elites, which is the negation of popular representation. Schumpeter's conception of democracy is similar to Aron's. See Raymond Aron, "Social Structure and Ruling Class," *The British Journal of Sociology*, 1 (Mar.–June 1950) and Joseph Schumpeter, *Capitalism, Socialism and Democracy* (New York: Harper, 1942).
21. Herbert Marcuse, "Repressive Tolerance," in Robert P. Wolff et al., *A Critique of Pure Tolerance* (Boston: Beacon Press, 1965), p. 95.
22. V.I. Lenin, "The Caricature of Marxism and Imperialist Economism," in *Collected Works*, vol. 23, p. 43.
23. Samuel P. Hays, "The Politics of Reform in Municipal Government in the Progressive Era," *Pacific Northwest Quarterly*, 55 (Oct. 1964), 169.
24. Charles Forcey, *Crossroads of Liberalism* (New York: Oxford Univ. Press, 1961), pp. 40, 297.
25. John R. Commons, *Social Reform and the Church* (New York: Crowell, 1894), p. 77.
26. Gabriel Kolko, *Triumph of Conservatism* (Glencoe, Ill.: Free Press, 1963), p. 290.
27. *Ibid.*, p. 2.
28. *Ibid.*
29. Kolko undeniably upholds the primacy of politics in U.S. history: "By

effectively ignoring the role of the state in modern capitalism, Marxism lost sight of the possible resilience in capitalism, a resilience made possible by political rather than economic power. But if the state could determine the direction of the economy, an entirely new situation might be created, and in fact was" (*ibid.*, p. 294). Even though Kolko rejects Marx theoretically, his empirical data correspond with Lenin's theory of imperialism. Kolko, strangely enough, follows a path which Lenin probably would have followed in a similar study of Progressivism. The difference is in the theoretical conclusions. Again, I emphasize that Kolko's book has a Marxist content (empirical data) but with a non-Marxist theoretical conclusion. Kolko interprets Marxism to be a mechanical "one-way street"—strictly from economics to politics. Marx and Engels never formulated their theory of politics in such a manner. They concluded that politics has an important role to play (occasionally an independent one), but that it cannot be separated from economic considerations in the long run. "According to Marx, the state is an organ of class rule, an organ for the oppression of one class by another; it is the creation of 'order,' which legalizes and perpetuates this oppression by moderating the conflict between classes" (Lenin, *Selected Works* [New York: International Publishers, 1971], p. 268). The state, Engels wrote, is "as a rule, the state of the most powerful, economically dominant class, which, through the medium of the state, becomes also the politically dominant class" (*ibid.*, p. 271). Engels further noted that in the U.S. the largest capitalists exercised "its power indirectly, but all the more surely, by means of the direct corruption of officials" (*ibid.*, p. 272). The role which capitalists play in each particular case of national capitalism can be empirically determined, but nevertheless the state is the medium through which wealth asserts itself politically. Thus, Marxists would agree with Kolko's study of the state control exerted by big capitalists in the progressive era. Kolko has misread Marx and Engels, and ignored Lenin, who systematically developed a comprehensive theory of the relationship of the state to the economically dominant class. Kolko attacks not Marx, but the mechanical, dogmatic misinterpretation of Marxist materialism, i.e., economism.
30. *Ibid.*, p. 5.
31. G. Stanley Hall, *Morale* (New York: Appleton, 1920), p. 216.
32. Lawrence Cremin, *The Transformation of the School* (New York: Vintage-Knopf, 1964).
33. See, for example, the following works: Gerald Gutek, *An Historical Introduction to American Education* (New York: Crowell, 1971); M. Blaug, ed., *Economics of Education* (Middlesex, England: Penguin, 1974); Richard Hofstadter and Wilson Smith, *American Higher Education: A Documentary History* (Chicago: Univ. of Chicago Press, 1961). For an exposition on similar approaches on international development, see: George F. Kneller, *The Education of the Mexican Nation* (1951; repr. New York: Octagon, 1973); Eugene Staley, *The Future of Underveloped Countries* (New York: Praeger, 1961). These works take a macroperspective; however, there are abundant books which take a complementary microperspective focusing on the psychology of children: for example, Arthur T. Jersild, *The Psychology of Adolescence* (Toronto: Macmillan, 1963); Frank Reissman, *The Culturally Disadvantaged Child* (New York: Harper, 1962); Ronald J. Samuda, *Psychological Testing of American Minorities: Issues and Consequences* (New York: Dodd, Mead, 1975).

34. Part of the reason Cremin writes so one-sidedly is that he is defending educators from the reactionary criticism against schools leveled by the right during the fifties. Cremin struggles to show (and correctly so) that the anarchistic Greenwich village "free schools" were not the typical form of Progressivism. Further, Cremin emphasizes that Dewey was much better than critics would allow. He is trying to place Progressivism in education within a framework acceptable to those critics.
35. R. Callahan, p. 152.
36. *Ibid.*
37. *Ibid.*
38. Introduction to Clarence Karier, Paul Violas, and Joel Spring, *Roots of Crisis* (Chicago: Rand McNally, 1973), p.6.
39. Karier, "Liberal Ideology and Orderly Change" in *Roots of Crisis*, p. 105.
40. *Ibid.*, pp. vii-ix.
41. Colin Greer, *The Great School Legend* (New York: Basic Books, 1972), p. 154.
42. Michael B. Katz, *Class, Bureaucracy and Schools* (New York: Praeger, 1975), p. 144.
43. See Paul Violas, "Progressive Social Philosophy: Charles Horton Cooley and Edward Alsworth Ross" in Karier et al., *Roots of Crisis*, pp. 40-65.
44. Not all of these radical critics shy away from showing the relationship between schools and business and industry. However, when the relationship is made, it is presented as one of many possible relationships that the school could possibly have. Thus, only arbitrary policies would be implemented in schools.
45. Samuel Bowles and Herbert Gintis, *Schooling in Capitalist America* (New York: Basic Books, 1976), p. 44.
46. *Ibid.*
47. Samuel Bowles and Herbert Gintis, "Capitalism and Education in the United States," *Socialist Revolution*, Vol. 5, No. 3, p. 121.
48. Bowles and Gintis, "Capitalism and Education in the United States," p. 125.
49. Bowles and Gintis, *Schooling in Capitalist America*, p. 46.
50. *Ibid.*, p. 62.
51. *Ibid.*, p. 44.

Chapter 2: The Roots of Progressive Education: Educational Theory and the Rise of the Bourgeoisie

1. This brings to mind the very strong bond, nearly indivisible, between methods and ends in education. The recent emphasis upon individualized learning is a confirmation of the ideal of the individual as the basis for society's development. In employing the method, the goal is realized. Methods appear neutral but in reality encase the goals. If the goals are political, as they inevitably are, so also are the methods.
2. See Marc Bloch, *Feudal Society*, Vols. I and II (Chicago: Univ. of Chicago Press, 1964); and Maurice Dobb, *Studies in the Development of Capitalism* (New York: International Publishers, 1963).
3. *John Locke on Education*, ed. Peter Gay (New York: Teachers College Press, Columbia Univ., 1964), p. 43.
4. *Ibid.*

5. John Locke, *On Politics and Education*, ed. Howard R. Penndman (New York: Van Nostrand, 1947), pp. 88, 90.
6. *Ibid.*, pp. 84-85.
7. *Ibid.*
8. John Locke, *On Politics and Education* (New York: Walter J. Block, 1974), p. 59.
9. The law of property, a natural law, is "given up" by each member of society to the state to enforce and regulate. Life, liberty, and rights of property, given to each person through birth, are institutionalized in the hands of the state. The state is entrusted with conserving and recognizing "the law of nature" and cannot alienate it without consent of the governed. It is in society that the individual rights to private property are commonly protected, " . . . and it is not without reason that he seeks out and is willing to join in society with others who are already united, or have a mind to unite for the mutual preservation of their lives, liberties and estates, which I call by the general name–property" (*ibid.*, pp. 138-139).
10. H.R. Fox Bourne, *The Life of John Locke* (London: Henrys King, 1876), II, 378.
11. *Ibid.*
12. *Ibid.*, p. 381.
13. *Ibid.*, p. 384.
14. *Ibid.*, p. 385.
15. J.J. Rousseau, *Emile*, (London: Everyman's Library-Dent, 1966), p. 5.
16. *Ibid.*, p. 7.
16. *Ibid.*, p. 7.
17. *Ibid.*, p. 62.
18. *Ibid.*, p. 152.
19. *Ibid.*
20. Adam Smith, *An Inquiry into the Nature and Causes of the Wealth of Nations*, (Edinburgh: Adam and Charles Black) p. 352. Not more than eighty years previously, Locke broke with tradition and proposed that reading, writing, and accounting be part of the practical education of the bourgeoisie. Out of practical considerations as well Smith finds them useful for the working class.
21. *Ibid.*, p. 589.
22. *Ibid.*, p. 352.

Chapter 3: Monopoly Capitalism and Progressive Reformism

1. Michael Katz, *The Irony of Early School Reform* (Cambridge, Mass.: Harvard Univ. Press, 1968), p. 43.
2. *Ibid.*, p. 93.
3. *Ibid.*, pp. 102-103.
4. *Ibid.*, p. 87.
5. *Ibid.*, p. 45. Educational theory within the history of capitalism has had a thread of continuity. The Puritan communities had similar ideas towards education; promptness, orderliness, industry, and frugality were all good bourgeois virtues. This, too, characterized the writings of Locke and Smith. That it appears during the educational reform movement in Massachusetts should not surprise us. However, my purpose is not principally to show

that reform in the 1840s and 1850s was characterized by "the inculcation of habits of industry and class unity," but to show that these characteristics of education appear throughout the history of capitalism, from Locke to the Progressives.

6. C.D. Wright, *The Industrial Evolution of the United States* (1895; rpt. New York: Russell, 1967), pp. 141-142.

7. E.K. Hunt and Howard J. Sherman, *Economics* (New York: Harper, 1975), p. 251.

8. Agrarian discontent was pervasive during the initial period of labor-capital conflict. The injection of this instability into society along with urban labor agitation posed a critical political problem for the government. Farmers were steadily losing their farms to either banks or creditors, or merely going broke and selling out to other farmers, while labor disputes arose elsewhere. These two phenomena—rural and urban discontent—stemmed from the steady monopolization in the economy. Labor agitation was more serious because the tendencies in the economy were more severely affected by independent labor organization and strikes than by radical rural discontent, which did not severely hold back economic development. Moreover, populists appear to have been small producers who were losing out to larger competitors. Walter T.K. Nugent observes that populists were commonly "yeoman farmers" who suffered from the vagaries of the market place and were attempting to protect "their personal arrangements." Nugent further observes that Populism was not a movement of ideologues. It seems clear that populists were small property holders who correctly saw the coming demise of their economic and social condition. See Walter T.K. Nugent, "Some Parameters of Populism," *Agricultural History*, 40, No. 4 (Oct. 1966). I therefore make a distinction between rural discontent and the urban labor movement. The urban laborer was far more a threat to social stability than the farmer, and therefore reformism in the late nineteenth and early twentieth centuries was much more conscious of the political consequences of reform toward labor than toward farmers. See also Introduction in Theodore Saloutos, *Populism: Reaction or Reform* (New York: Holt, Rinehart, 1968), p. 1.

9. Philip F. Foner, *History of the Labor Movement in the United States*, I (New York: International Publishers, 1947), 108. Foner also notes the great change in labor activity that occurred in the 1880s. A contemporary observer, quoted by Foner, reported, "The year 1886 has witnessed a more profound and far more extended agitation among the members of organized labor than in any previous year in the history of our country." (Foner, *History of the Labor Movement of the United States*, II [New York: International Publishers, 1955], 11). See also C.D. Wright, *The Industrial Revolution in the United States*, chapters 24, 25.

10. Labor historian Samuel Yellen writes, "The great railroad strikes which broke out spontaneously and spread with the speed of a plague in the summer of 1877 were the expression of a deep and accumulated discontent. Labor outbreaks had been common in the United States before this time, but had been confined to separate localities. Never before had industry and commerce been confronted with a nation-wide uprising of workers, an uprising so obstinate and bitter that it was crushed only with great bloodshed" *(American Labor Struggles:* 1877-1934 [1934; rpt. New York: Monad Press, 1974], p.3). The Pennsylvania state legislature appointed a committee

to investigate and report upon the 1877 Railroad Strike. Their report stated that "there was a sort of epidemic of strikers running through the laboring classes of the country, *more particularly those in the employ of large corporations, caused by the general depression in business, which followed the panic of 1873"*(emphasis mine). Report of the Committee appointed to Investigate the Pennsylvania Railroad Riots in July, 1877, Legislative Document No. 29, Harrisburg, 1878, p. 46. Quoted in Richard O. Boyer and Herbert M. Morais, *Labor's Untold Story* (New York: United Electrical Radio and Machine Workers of America, 1972), p. 59.

The rise to prominence of the railroad in the nation's economy created the material basis for the Great Railroad Strike of 1877. In 1830 only twenty-three roads were in operation in the United States with only a few workers. By 1893 there were 173,000 miles of rails and 750,000 workers on those rails. Along with the increase in size and labor force there was a concomitant tendency towards concentration. The post-Civil War period saw the consolidation of two-thirds of the nation's railroads into the remaining third. "In 1880 alone, 115 companies lost their identity, and between 1880 and 1888 some 425 companies were brought under the control of other roads. The Pennsylvania Railroad by 1890 was an amalgamation of 73 smaller companies and some five thousand miles of rail." See John Blum et al., *The National Experience* (New York: Harcourt, 1968), p. 441. In 1885 *Poor's Manual of Railroads* needed twenty-five pages to "list [the] railways in the United States which . . . merged in other lines." See David A. Wells, *Recent Economic Changes* (New York: Appleton, 1889), p. 96. This is indicative of the greater concentration and socialization of production and distribution occurring in nearly all aspects of the economy.

11. Yellen, p. 3.
12. Boyer and Morais, p. 61.
13. Boyer and Morais, p. 143.
14. Jeremy Brecher, *Strike!* (San Francisco: Straight Arrow Books), p. 58.
15. Sidney Lens, *The Labor Wars* (Garden City, N.Y.: Anchor-Doubleday, 1974), p. 127.
16. Boyer and Morais, pp. 78-79.
17. *Ibid.*, p. 184.
18. *Ibid.*, p. 140.
19. *Ibid.*, p. 106.
20. *Ibid.*, p. 179.
21. *Ibid.*, p. 144.
22. *Ibid.*, p. 83.
23. *Ibid.*, p. 139.
24. It might be claimed that Roosevelt, Taft, Wilson, and Brandeis differed fundamentally on the trust question. To say that Roosevelt, Taft, Wilson, or Brandeis had unanimous agreement on every issue is absolutely false. To say that they broke rank in relation to monopoly capitalism is likewise false. For example, some splits over specific issues are clear. In 1910 Taft and Roosevelt held opposing views on American financial investments in China. Taft favored those investments, whereas Roosevelt opposed them (because of the possibility of upsetting the Japanese sphere of interest there). However, neither man opposed the export of finance capital, establishing financial enclaves abroad. This is the essential point: both used the power of the federal government in the exporting of finance capital (which

is one form of monopoly capitalism). How to employ that power, for which interest, and at what risks were the real bones of contention.

Some historians claim that the four men held different views on the trust question, either against monopoly or for cooperation with financial and industrial magnates. I argue that such points are irrelevant. Gabriel Kolko has shown that antitrust court decisions did not alter the pattern of monopolization; see *The Triumph of Conservatism* (Glencoe, Ill: Free Press, 1963). Furthermore, the economic historian Alfred D. Chandler, Jr., has concluded that antimonopoly legislation in effect preserved *oligopoly* — the very form which most commonly characterizes monopoly capitalism ("The Beginning of 'Big Business' in American Industry," *Business History Review* [Spring 1959], pp. 1-31). This fact led the political scientist Murray Edelman to conclude that "trust-busting" has historically been symbolic, rather than real. See Murray Edelman, *The Symbolic Uses of Politics* (Urbana, Ill.: Univ. of Illinois Press, 1964), Chapter 2. Thurman Arnold described the function of antitrust legislation and court decisions on trusts in a similar fashion:

> The actual result of the antitrust laws was to promote the growth of great industrial organizations by deflecting the attack on them into purely moral and ceremonial channels . . . every scheme for direct control broke to pieces on the great protective rock of the antitrust laws. . . .
>
> The antitrust laws remained as a most important symbol. Whenever anyone demanded practical regulation, they formed an effective moral obstacle, since all the liberals would answer a demand that the antitrust laws be enforced. Men like Senator Borah founded political careers on the continuance of such crusades, which were entirely futile but enormously picturesque, and which paid big dividends in terms of personal prestige (quoted in Edelman, p. 40).

Evidence warrants placing Wilson not among the opponents of monopoly as is commonly done among many historians, but among its staunchest allies. Before the American Bar Association in 1912 Wilson echoed Roosevelt's (and Taft's) meaningless distinction between good and bad trusts (good as far as the future of monopoly capitalism was concerned):

> Nobody can fail to see that modern business is going to be done by corporations. The old time of individual competition is probably gone by. It may come back; I don't know; it will not come back within our time, I dare say. We will do business henceforth, when we do it, on a great and successful scale, by means of corporations. I am not afraid of any corporation, no matter how big. I am afraid of any corporation, however small, that is bad, that is rotten to the core, whose practices and actors are in restraint of trade (Kolko, pp. 206-207).

Louis Brandeis, who worked closely with Wilson, is often made out to be an opponent of monopoly. However, if we look closely at Brandeis, we see an excellent example of the symbolic uses of politics described by Edelman and Arnold. Shortly after the Pujo committee squabble, Brandeis wrote a very biting critique of finance capital, "Other People's Money and How the Bankers Use It" (1914). Some have interpreted such stands as evidence of his antimonopoly position. However, Brandeis never proposed reforms which would have endangered the well-being of monopoly; on the contrary, his proposals were consonant with the interests of monopoly. He "strongly favored price-fixing and fair-trade laws"; however, it should be noted that price-fixing was not opposed by the major monopolists (Kolko, p. 208). That a person with the education and political training of Brandeis could support such measures and publicly oppose monopoly gives credence to Thurman Arnold's statement: "Men . . . founded political careers on . . . such [antimonopoly] crusades." One simply does not pose as an antimonopolist and then hold positions which were beneficial to monopoly. We can infer that Brandeis posed no danger ideologically or theoretically to monopoly. I cite one more example concerning Brandeis. He was outraged (at least publicly) at the findings of the Pujo committee—but advocated, as a solution to the power of banks, the very reform measures the largest banks wanted. Gabriel Kolko has shown conclusively that bankers had a central role in shaping the banking reform measures passed in the aftermath of the Pujo committee's findings (during Wilson's first term in office). Carter Glass, who played a vital role in shaping the Federal Reserve Act (supported by Brandeis), remarked in 1916:

> The proponents of the Federal reserve act had no idea of impairing the rightful prestige of New York as the financial metropolis of this hemisphere. They rather expected to confirm its distinction, and even hoped to assert powerfully in unwresting the scepter from London and eventually making New York the financial center of the world (Kolko, p. 254).

Thus, if one wishes to focus on the "differences" between Roosevelt, Taft, Brandeis, and Wilson, the fundamental similarities of their outlook and political practice are obscured. Their differences, in essence, pale in comparison to the key roles they played in establishing the integration of the federal government with monopoly capitalism.

25. Sidney E. Mead, "American Protestantism Since the Civil War," in Richard M. Abrams and Lawrence W. Levine, *The Shaping of Twentieth Century America* (Boston: Little, Brown, 1965), p. 107.
26. *Ibid.*, p. 116.
27. See Richard Hofstadter, *Great Issues in American History* (New York: Vintage Books, 1958), II, 179; C. Vann Woodward, "The Urban Society"; John Blum et al. *The National Experience* (New York: Harcourt, 1968), p. 475.
28. See Robert H. Wiebe, *The Search for Order 1877-1920* (New York: Hill and Wang, 1967), pp. 44-45; John R. Commons, *Social Reform and the Church* (New York: Crowell, 1894). Commons expresses most of the main ideas which Strong stated in *Our Country*, although he is more sophisticated and places greater emphasis on social science. In addition, Richard T. Ely wrote a most supportive introduction to Commons' little book.
29. Josiah Strong, *The Twentieth Century City* (New York: Arno Press, 1970), p. 139.
30. Josiah Strong, *Our Country* (New York: Independent Press, 1885), p. 78.
31. David Ward, *Cities and Immigrants: A Geography of Change in Nineteenth Century America* (New York: Oxford Univ. Press, 1971), p. 51.
32. Strong, *The Twentieth Century City*, (New York: Baker and Taylor, 1898).
33. *Ibid.*, p. 117.
34. Strong, *Our Country*, p. 100.
35. *Ibid.*, p. 180.
36. *Ibid.*, p. 185.
37. *Ibid.*, p. 198.

38. *Ibid.*, p. 175.
39. Strong, *The Twentieth Century City*, p. 121.
40. *Ibid.*, pp. 122-213.
41. *Ibid.*, p. 142
42. Strong, *Our Country*, p. 215.
43. Jeremy Felt, *Hostages of Fortune: Child Labor Reform in New York State* (Syracuse, N.Y.: Syracuse Univ. Press, 1965), p. 45.
44. Jacob Riis, *The Peril and Preservation of the Home* (Philadelphia: George W. Jacobs, 1903), p. 175.
45. *Ibid.*, p. 56.
46. *Ibid.*, p. 174.
47. Jacob Riis, *How the Other Half Lives*. With an Introduction by Sam Bass Warner (1890; rpt. Cambridge, Mass.: Harvard Univ. Press, 1970), pp. 198-199.
48. Riis, *The Peril and Preservation of the Home*, p. 6.
49. Riis, *How the Other Half Lives*, p. 181.
50. *Ibid.*, p. 54.
51. Riis, *The Peril and Preservation of the Home*, p. 19.
52. *Ibid.*, pp. 122-123.
53. Riis, *How the Other Half Lives*, p. 191.
54. Riis, *The Peril and Preservation of the Home*, pp. 129-230.
55. *Ibid.*, pp. 41-42.
56. Richard T. Ely, *The Labor Movement in America* (New York: Crowell, 1886), pp. 321-324.
57. Richard Hofstadter wrote: "Edward A. Ross, the vigorous professor of sociology at the University of Wisconsin and one of the former advisers of Governor La Follette's regime, was among the foremost academic thinkers who participated heartily in the Progressive movement" (*The Progressive Movement* [Englewood Cliffs, N.J.: Prentice-Hall, 1963], p. 73).
58. J.O. Hertzler, "Edward Alsworth Ross: Sociological Pioneer and Interpreter," *American Sociological Review*, 16 (Oct. 1951), 597-198.
59. Edward A. Ross, *Sin and Society* (Boston: Houghton-Mifflin, 1907).
60. Edward A. Ross, *Social Control: A Survey of the Foundation of Order* (New York: Macmillan, 1912).
61. Quoted in Paul Violas, "Progressive Social Philosophy," in Karier, *Roots of Crisis*, p. 46.
62. Albion Small, *General Sociology* (Chicago: Univ. of Chicago Press, 1905), p. 623.
63. Franklin Giddings, like Cooley and Ross, also argued that the more complex the division of labor, the greater "definite aim to life" and "definite discipline" insuring that each "fulfill the duties that pertain to his position." See Giddings, *The Principles of Sociology* (New York: Macmillan, 1896), pp. 396-397. He was in complete agreement with Ross's theory of "Social Control": "The phrase 'social control' is especially valuable because it is comprehensive." Giddings' definition of a progressive society is illuminating: "A population that has only a few interests, which, however, are harmoniously combined, is conservative in its choices. A population that has varied interests, which are as yet unharmoniously combined, is radical in its choices. Only the population that has many, varied and harmoniously combined interests is consistently progressive in its choices." Quoted in Clarence H. Northcutt, "The Sociological Theories of Franklin Henry

Notes for Chapter Three

Giddings: Consciousness of Kind, Pluralistic Behavior, and Statistical Method," in Harry Elmer Barnes, *An Introduction to the History of Sociology* (Chicago: Univ. of Chicago Press, 1948), p. 760.
64. Ross, *Social Control*, p. 1.
65. *Ibid.*, p. 2.
66. Cooley agreed with Ross on this important point. Cooley wrote: "We need, then, a system of social groups, corresponding to the system of functions in society, each group having esprit de corps, emulation and standards within itself, and all animated with a spirit of loyalty and service to the whole . . . competitive spirit would be cherished, but could not degenerate into irresponsible individualism" (*Social Process* [New York: Scribner's, 1918], p. 143).
67. Again, the similarities between Ross and Cooley are obvious: Cooley advised the specialization of function within an interdependent system of roles: "We must be taught to do something well and never allowed to lose sense of the relation of that one thing to the general endeavor" (Quoted by Violas, p. 45).
68. Ross, *Social Control*, p. 2.
69. *Ibid.*, p. 5.
70. Small's conception of education, summarized here by Lawrence Cremin, parallels that of Ross: "Education . . . must place the upcoming generation in contact with the three great realities of modern life: Interdependence, the realization that in the industrial world no man liveth unto himself; cooperation, the correlative of interdependence; and progress, the realization that new men and events forever necessitate new social arrangements" (*The Transformation of the School* [New York: Vintage Books, 1964], p. 99). Note the similarity with Ross's emphasis upon the unification of the social elements.
71. Ross, *Social Control*, p. 164.
72. *Ibid.*, p. 177.
73. *Ibid.*, p. 384.
74. *Ibid.*
75. *Ibid.*, p. 402.
76. *Ibid.*, p. 403.
77. The capitalist state has always been involved in economic matters and it is wrong to assert that under monopoly capitalism the state suddenly participates in the economy. What differentiates the laissez-faire state from the state under monopoly capitalism is the quantity and quality of state intervention. Moreover, that sharp upsurge of state activity is mirrored by a theoretical system legitimizing existing practices. As the practice of increased state intervention comes into being the theories of state intervention follow closely on its heels. See, for example, the Constitution of the American Economic Association (1885), authored by Richard T. Ely. Here is an example of a clear theoretical statement prescribing a high degree of state intervention in the economy as well as in the social process. See John A. Garraty, *The Transformation of American Society, 1870-1890* (New York: Harper, 1968), pp. 244-253.
78. Ross, *Social Control*, p. 403.
79. *Ibid.*
80. Theodore Roosevelt, *The Roosevelt Policy*, ed. William Griffith (New York: Current Literature Publishing Company, 1919), I, 146-147.

81. *Ibid.*, p. 153.
82. *Ibid.*, pp. 279-280.
83. *Ibid.*, pp. 282-285.

Chapter 4: John Dewey, Theoretician of Progressive Education

1. See Clarence Karier, "Liberal Ideology and Orderly Change" in Karier et al., *Roots of Crisis*.
2. Martin Carnoy, *Education as Cultural Imperialism* (New York: David McKay, 1974), p. 254.
3. Bowles and Gintis, "Capitalism and Education in the United States," p. 121.
4. *Ibid.*, p. 126. Bowles and Gintis claim that Progressivism was never implemented in the schools. How they arrive at such a conclusion is not clear. Here is what they say: "In short, the history of twentieth century education is the history not of Progressivism but of the imposition upon schools of 'business values' and social relationships reflecting the pyramid of authority and privilege in the capitalist system." In essence, the authors contend that a pluralist contention of forces ended in the victory of businessmen over progressive reformers. Bowles and Gintis claim, therefore, that Progressive education was never given a chance: "A historian of Progressivism in education might well echo Gandhi's assessment of Western Civilization: 'It would be a good idea.'" (*Schooling in Capitalist America*, p. 44).
5. Bowles and Gintis, *Schooling in Capitalist America*, p. 46.
6. John Dewey, *My Pedagogic Creed* (Washington, D.C.: Progressive Education Association, 1929), p. 17.
7. *Ibid.*, p. 16.
8. *Ibid.*, p. 17.
9. William James, *Principles of Psychology* (New York: Dover Publications, 1950), I, 76. A critical question not specifically focused upon in this study is the role Pragmatism played within the contradictions existing between capital and labor. Did it ignore the questions which Ross, Strong, and Riis confronted? This study does not dissect the philosophical attributes of Pragmatism but it does examine what effect it had in practice. A longstanding debate has gone on between the defenders of Pragmatism and Marxist scholars who have attacked it. Even though I do think that Pragmatism was the philosophical face of monopoly capitalism, I shall not attempt to show the connection between it and the contradiction between capital and labor, but rather to show how the Pragmatic psychological principles of William James were used within the educational scheme of Dewey and (in chapter 5) within the conceptualization of IQ testing. I shall examine how Pragmatism functioned practically.

   Pragmatism stripped of all of its technicality was regarded by James and Dewey as a method for achieving social stability. James said, in a lecture on his philosophy for everyday living:

   > We are suffering today in America from what is called the labor-question; and when you go out into the world, you will each and all of you be caught up in its perplexities. I use the brief term labor-question to cover all sorts of anarchistic discontents and socialistic projects, and the conservative resistances which they provoke. So far as this conflict is unhealthy and regrettable . . . the unhealthiness

> consists solely in the fact that one-half of our fellow countrymen remain entirely blind to the internal significance of the lives of the other half. They miss the joys and sorrows, they fail to feel the moral virtue, and they do not guess the presence of the intellectual ideals. They are at cross-purposes all along the line. . . . Each in short ignores the fact that happiness and unhappiness and significance are a vital mystery; each pins them absolutely on some ridiculous feature of the external situation; and everybody remains outside of everybody else's sight.
>
> Society has, with all this, undoubtedly got to pass toward some newer and better equilibrium. . . . But if, after all that I have said, any of you expect that they will make any genuine vital difference on a large scale, to the lives of our descendants, you will have missed the significance of my entire lecture. The solid meaning of life is always the same external thing. . . . [N]o outward changes of condition of life can keep the nightingale of its eternal meaning from singing in all sorts of different men's hearts. That is the main fact to remember. If we could not only admit it with our lips, but really and truly believe it, how convulsive insistencies, how our antipathies and dreads of each other would soften down! If the poor man and the rich could look at each other in this way . . . how gentle would grow their disputes! What tolerance and good humor, what willingness to live and let live would come into this world! (*On Some of Life's Ideals* [New York: Holt, 1976], pp. 89-94).

Dewey also considered the relationship of his philosophy with the social conflicts of the period. Writing in 1948, Dewey compared his then pessimistic attitude to his earlier optimism concerning social harmony:

> The First World War was a decided shock to the earlier period of optimism, in which there prevailed widespread belief in continued progress toward mutual understanding among peoples and classes, and hence a sure movement to harmony and peace. Today the shock is almost incredibly greater. Insecurity and strife are so general that the prevailing attitude is one of anxious and pessimistic uncertainty (*Reconstruction in Philosophy* [Boston: Beacon Press, 1960], p. vi).

Dewey urged a reconstruction of philosophy with "new ends and standards, new moral principles "so that harmony and order can be achieved." Our philosophers of Pragmatism did not hide from the principal practical considerations of the era—and, it will be most instructive to see how Pragmatism appeared practically: in the educational theory of Dewey and in the development of intelligence testing.

10. *Principles of Psychology*, II, 295-296.
11. John Dewey, *School and Society* (Chicago: Univ. of Chicago Press, 1943), p. 76.
12. James, *Principles*, I, 76.
13, *Ibid.*, II, 409-410.
14. Dewey, *School and Society*, p. 135.
15. James, *Principles*, II, 385.
16. John Dewey, *Reconstruction in Philosophy* (Boston: Beacon Press, 1960), p. 86.
17. James, *Principles*, II, 402.
18. *Ibid.*
19. *Ibid.*, p. 422.
20. *Ibid.*, p. 121.

21. John Dewey, *The Philosophy of John Dewey*, ed. J. Ratner (New York: Holt, 1928), p. 288.
22. James, *Principles*, II, 423.
23. *Ibid.*, p. 422.
24. John Dewey, *Quest for Certainty* (New York: Martin Balch, 1929), p. 26. Dewey added: "All that we can safely say is that human nature, like other forms of life, tends to differentiation, and thus moves in the direction of the distinctively individual."
25. Dewey, *School and Society*, p. 27.
26. Dewey, *Experience and Education* (New York: Macmillan, 1938), p. 4.
27. *Ibid.*, p. v.
28. *Ibid.*
29. *Ibid.*, p. 9.
30. Dewey, *School and Society*, p. 12.
31. *Ibid.*, p. 96-97.
32. Quoted in Horace M. Kallen, "John Dewey and the Spirit of Pragmatism" in Sidney Hook et al., *John Dewey, Philosopher of Science and Freedom* (New York: Dial Press, 1950), p. 34.
33. Dewey, *The Philosophy of John Dewey*, p. 406.
34. *Ibid.*, p. 418.
35. Dewey, *School and Society*. p. 29.
36. Dewey, *The Philosophy of John Dewey*. p. 434.
37. *Ibid.*, p. 385.
38. *Ibid.*, p. 419.
39. William James, *Principles*, II, 398.
40. *Ibid.*, p. 401.
41. Dewey, *School and Society*, p. 125.
42. *Ibid.*
43. John Dewey, *Liberalism and Social Action* (New York: Putnam, 1935), p. 58.
44. John Dewey, *My Pedagogic Creed* (Chicago: A. Flanagan, 1910), p. 4.
45. *Ibid.*
46. Dewey, *School and Society*, p. 22. Instinct theory was pervasive among leading Progressive scholars. Thorstein Veblen's theory of culture was based upon instinct theory. Morton White has written, "Veblen subscribed to the instinct psychology and postulated an original instinct . . . He called it 'the instinct of workmanship.' Because man is an agent who seeks the accomplishment of ends, he develops a taste for effective work and a distaste for futile effort." White concluded that this conception was the core of Veblen's discussion of the leisure class. It is most interesting to see the parallels between Dewey's and Veblen's conception of instinct. Both were deeply affected by James's psychology.
47. Dewey, *The Philosophy of John Dewey*, p. 385.
48. John Dewey, *Experience and Education* (New York: Macmillan, 1938), p. 8.
49. Dewey, *School and Society*, p. 16.
50. *Ibid.*, pp. 14-15.
51. *Ibid.*, pp. 99-100.
52. Dewey, *School and Society*, pp. 23-24.
53. Dewey, *Experience and Education*, p. 52.
54. *Ibid.*

55. *Ibid.*
56. John and Evelyn Dewey, *Schools of Tomorrow* (1915; rpt. New York: Dutton, 1962), p. 225.
57. Dewey, *My Pedogogic Creed*, p.6.
58. *Ibid.*
59. John Dewey, *Individualism: Old and New* (New York: Minton, Balch, 1930), pp. 85-86.
60. John Dewey, *Education Today* (New York: Putnam, 1940), p. 330.
61. Dewey, *Individualism: Old and New*, p. 36. Dewey counseled an acceptance of things as they were: "By accepting the corporate and industrial world in which we live, and by thus fulfilling the precondition for interaction with it, we, who are also parts of the moving present, create ourselves as we create an unknown future" (*ibid.*, p. 117). Dewey, however, saw the end (organicism) as the real. He therefore denied the instability in society as a product of the mode of production and instead considered the ideal functioning of society as the natural, and universal form of social intercourse.
62. *Ibid.*, pp. 49-50.
63. *Ibid.*, p. 118.
64. John and Evelyn Dewey, *Schools of Tomorrow*, p. 177.
65. *Ibid.*, p. 181.
66. *Ibid.*, p. 177.
67. *Ibid.*, p. 178.
68. *Ibid.*, p. 177.
69. *Ibid.*, p. 180.
70. *Ibid.*, p. 124.
71. *Ibid.*, p. 125. Dewey also said, "the existing state of society, which the schools reflect, is not something fixed and uniform" (*Education Today*, p. 349.
72. John Dewey, *School and Society*, p. 29. In that same vein, Dewey wrote that "there are plenty of real connections between the experiences of children and business conditions which need to be utilized and illuminated. The child should study his commercial arithmetic and geography, not as isolated things by themselves, but in their reference to his social environment. The youth needs to become acquainted with the bank as a factor in modern life, with what it does, and how it does it; and then relevant arithmetical processes would have some meaning" (*ibid.*, pp. 77-78).
73. John and Evelyn Dewey, *Schools of Tomorrow*, pp. 125-126.
74. *Ibid.*, p. 102.
75. *Ibid.*, p. 121.
76. Dewey, *Individualism: Old and New*, pp. 32-34. Dewey added, "A stable recovery of individuality waits upon an elimination of the older economic and political individualism, an elimination which will liberate imagination and endeavor for the task of making corporate society contribute to the free culture of its members" (p. 71). The revolt against laissez-faire individualism is common in the literature of the Progressive era. For example, Frederick Jackson Turner's famous paper to the American Historical Association in 1893 included a careful attack upon laissez-faire individualism:

> The frontier is productive of individualism . . . The tendency is antisocial and particularly to any direct control.

and later

> The democracy born of free land, strong in selfishness and individualism, intolerant of administrative experience and education, and pressing individual liberty beyond its proper bounds, has its dangers as well as its benefits. Individualism . . . rendered possible the spoils system and . . . lack of highly developed civic spirit . . .

The alternative was to move on to a "New Frontier," i.e., a new individualism that would be characterized by a "civic spirit." See George Rogers Taylor, *The Turner Thesis Concerning the Role of the Frontier in American History* (Boston: Heath, 1956), pp. 14-15.

Jane Addams expressed similar thoughts from a different perspective: "If, as many times stated, we are passing from an age of individualism to one of association, there is no doubt that for decisive and effective action the individual still has the best of it. He will secure efficient results while committees are still deliberating upon the best method of making a beginning. And yet, if the need of the times demands associated effort, it may easily be true that the action which appears ineffective, and yet is carried out upon the more highly developed line of associated effort, may represent a finer social quality and have a greater social value than the more effective individual action. . . . The individual acts promptly, and we are dazzled by his success while only dimly conscious of the inadequacy of his code. Nowhere is this more clearly illustrated than in industrial relations, as existing between the owner of a large factor and his employers."

A growing conflict may be detected between the democratic ideal, which urges the workmen to demand representation in the administration of industry, and the accepted position, that the man who owns the capital and takes the risks has the exclusive right of management. It is in reality a clash between individual or aristocratic management, and corporate or democratic management. A large and highly developed factory presents a sharp contrast between its socialized form and individualistic ends. (*Democracy and Social Ethics* [Cambridge, Mass.: Harvard Univ. Press, 1964], pp. 137-138). See also, Paul C. Violas, "Jane Addams and the New Liberalism" in Karier, *Roots of Crisis*. Violas argues persuasively that Addams' main concern was the attainment of organic society.

77. Dewey, *Education Today*, p. 180.
78. John and Evelyn Dewey, *Schools of Tomorrow*, p. 129.
79. *Ibid.*, p. 195.
80. John Dewey, "Industrial Education: A Wrong Kind," *The New Republic*, 2, 16 (Feb. 20, 1915), 72-73.
81. John and Evelyn Dewey, *Schools of Tomorrow,* p. 150.
82. *Ibid*.
83. Dewey, *School and Society*, p. 27.
84. In one instance Dewey depicted the school system as "founded in the name of equality of opportunity for all, independent of birth, economic status, race, creed, or color . . . in order that each individual may become what he, and he alone, is capable of becoming." In another breath, Dewey acknowledged "managers and subordinates, . . . natural divisions of labor "within the classroom, and a general emphasis upon vocational education in poor districts." Thus Dewey defined schools as an open institution within which the natural abilities of children were arranged in a hierarchical structure corresponding to the true social relations within society. See "Dewey on Education," *The Social Frontier* (May 1937).

85. John Dewey, "Education vs. Trade Training . . . Dr. Dewey's Reply" *The New Republic* (May 15, 1915), pp. 42-43.
86. Dewey, *Individualism: Old and New*, p. 109.
87. *Ibid.*, p. 118.
88. *Ibid.*, p. 119.
89. John and Evelyn Dewey, *Schools of Tomorrow*, p. 95.
90. *Ibid.*, p. 58.

Chapter 5: The Rise of Intelligence Testing

1. Leon J. Kamin, *The Science and Politics of IQ* (Potomac, Maryland: Lawrence Erlbaum, 1974); Bowles and Gintis, *Schooling in Capitalist America*; Clarence Karier, *Shaping the American Educational State* (New York: Free Press, 1975). Bowles and Gintis use statistical analysis (as does Kamin) to break down the credibility of IQ testing. As an empirical tool, statistical analysis is quite effective; it bypasses, however, the underlying theoretical system upon which IQ testing is constructed. Bowles and Gintis write:

    > We conclude that a family's position in the class structure is reproduced primarily by mechanisms operating independently of the inheritance, production, and certification of intellectual skills. How do we support this proposition? The correct way of posing the question is to ask the following: To what extent is the statistical association between socio-economic background and economic success reduced when childhood IQ is held constant? If the proponents of IQism are correct, the reduction should be substantial. . . . The way to test this is to . . . use linear regression analysis.

    In their argument, therefore, the concept of intelligence remains unscathed despite the substantial critique of its specific use.

2. See Kamin, *The Science and Politics of IQ*; and "Heredity, Intelligence, Politics and Psychology," in Karier, *Shaping the American Educational State*, pp. 367-393. Kamin is generally known for his statistical attacks on the late charlatan Cyril Burt, arch defender of innate intelligence. See, for example, "An Epitaph for Sir Cyril?" in *Newsweek*, December 20, 1976. See also Noam Chomsky, "IQ Tests: Building Blocks for the New Class System," in Karier, *Shaping the American Educational State*, pp. 393-406; Clarence J. Karier in his *Shaping the American Educational State*, pp. 161-164; and "Testing in the Corporate Liberal State," in Karier et al., *Roots of Crisis*, pp. 108-137.

    Numerous critics and psychologists have taken the "nurture" side in the debate over "nature vs. nurture," without, however, challenging the concept "intelligence" and its ideological function in society. No matter which side is defended, either innate intelligence or environmentally conditioned intelligence, the concept "intelligence" remains unscathed.

    The testing debate between Walter Lippmann and Lewis Terman during the early twenties is an example. Lippmann's environmentalist arguments challenged the viability of general IQ testing, but not the viability of specific testing (such as aptitude tests for engineers, doctors, or lawyers) as a factor for increasing social efficiency. Terman, however, stood fast for *innate* intelligence and for the viability of an IQ test as a guide in future educational training. Thus both the defender and opponent of IQ testing and innate intelligence could have easily supported the concept of intelligence. The debate was finally resolved through the eventual dominance of the culture concept, the nurture side of the argument. See Hamilton Cravens and John C. Burnham, "Psychology and Evolutionary Naturalism in American Thought, 1890-1940," *The American Quarterly*, 23 (Dec. 1971), 635-657.

The decline of instinct intelligence signaled the rise of cultured intelligence. Thus the question of success in society was determined to be the outcome of the cultural makeup of the population. This is the position of Daniel Moynihan and Nathan Glazer, *Beyond the Melting Pot* (Cambridge: University Press, 1963) and Frank Reissman, *The Culturally Disadvantaged Child* (New York: Harper, 1962) and dominated the thought of the Great Society's poverty programs.

Other critics of IQ testing, such as Noam Chomsky, acknowledge the legitimacy of an intelligence quotient for any given individual, but reject the racial and social conclusions of certain experimenters. See Chomsky, "IQ Tests: Building Blocks for the New Class System." This position attacks the racial interpretations of testing and argues for a laissez-faire function of intelligence in the population.

3. See John Locke, *On Politics and Education*; H.R. Fox Bourne, *The Life of John Locke* (London: Henrys King, 1876), II, 378ff.
4. Joseph Peterson, *Early Conceptions and Tests of Intelligence* (1929; rpt. Westport, Conn.: Greenwood Press, 1969), pp. 45-46.
5. *Ibid.*
6. *Ibid.*, pp. 81-86.
7. Francis Galton, *Hereditary Genius*, introd. C.D. Darlington (New York: World, 1962).
8. *Ibid.*, pp. 77-78.
9. *Ibid.*
10. See Joseph Peterson, *Early Conceptions and Tests of Intelligence*, p. 78.
11. See William James, *Psychology* (New York: Dover, 1950), I, 92.
12. James, *Principles*, I, 91.
13. *Ibid.*, p. 141.
14. *Ibid.*, p. 230.
15. *Ibid.*, p. 233.
16. James, *Principles*, I, 235-236.
17. *Ibid.*, p. 286.
18. Dewey, *Experience in Education*, p. 51.
19. James, *Principles*, I, 287.
20. *Ibid.*
21. James, *Principles*, I, 287.
22. *Ibid.*, I, 23.
23. Dewey, *School and Society*, p. 27.
24. *Ibid.*
25. See Karier, *Shaping the American Educational State*. Karier selected representative articles by leading proponents of intelligence testing. His volume is a useful source of the central ideas of the principal figures in the development of IQ testing.
26. See Joseph Peterson, *Early Conceptions and Tests of Intelligence*, pp. 81-85.
27. Alfred Binet and Thomas Simon, *The Development of Intelligence in Children*, trans. Elizabeth S. Kite (Vineland, N.J.: Vineland Training School, 1916).

28. *Ibid.*, p. 251.
29. *Ibid.*
30. *Ibid.*, p. 328.
31. *Ibid.*
32. *Ibid.*, p. 324.
33. *Ibid.*, p. 262.
34. *Ibid.*, p. 305.
35. Quoted in Karier et al., *Roots of Crisis*, pp. 122-123.
36. Edward L. Thorndike, *Human Nature and the Social Order* (New York: Macmillan, 1940), pp. 579-582; 721.
37. *Ibid.*, pp. 960-962.
38. *Ibid.*, pp. 699-700.
39. See Thomas R. Garth, *Race Psychology, A Study of Racial Mental Differences* (New York: McGraw-Hill, 1931), and Otto Klineberg, "An Experimental Study of Speed and Other Factors in 'Racial' Differences," *Archives of Psychology*, Vol. 15, No. 93 (1927-1928), 1-111.
40. Lewis M. Terman, "The Conservation of Talent," *School and Society*, 19 (Mar. 29, 1924) 363.

Chapter 6: Mass Education and the Forces of Production

1. See Michael B. Katz, *The Irony of Early School Reform* (Cambridge, Mass.: Harvard Univ. Press, 1968).
2. Jeremy Felt, *Hostages of Fortune, Child Labor Reform in New York State* (Syracuse, N.Y.: Syracuse Univ. Press, 1965), p. 7.
3. *Ibid.*, p. 25.
4. *Ibid.*, p. 45.
5. *Ibid.*, p. 75.
6. *Ibid.*, p. 84.
7. Amber Arthur Warburton, Helen Wood, and Marian M. Crane, "The Work and Welfare of Children of Agricultural Laborers in Hidalgo County, Texas," U.S. Department of Labor, Children's Bureau Publication No. 298 (Washington, D.C.: U.S. Government Printing Office, 1943), p. 4.
8. *Ibid.*, p. 10.
9. *Ibid.*, p. 15.
10. *Ibid.*, p. 20.
11. *Ibid.*, p. 39.
12. *Ibid.*, p. 31.
13. *Ibid.*, Table 12, p. 33. Another federal study found that in Zavala County, Texas, only 17 percent of children aged 7 to 10 years and about 40 percent of those from 11 to 13 years attended school for the full year in 1938. Selden C. Menefee, "Mexican Migratory Workers of South Texas" (Washington, D.C.: U.S. Government Printing Office, 1941), p. 44.
14. Selden C. Menefee and Oren C. Cassmore, "The Pecan Shellers of San Antonio" (Washington, D.C.: U.S. Government Printing Office, 1940), p. 47.

Conclusion

1. Hugo Munsterberg, *Psychology and the Teacher* (New York: Appleton, 1909), p. 71.

Case Study: Educational Reform in Los Angeles and Its Effect on the Chicano Community, 1900-1930

1. *Los Angeles School Journal*, 5 (Dec. 19, 1921).
2. *Los Angeles Educational Research Bulletin*, 4 (Dec. 15, 1924), 5.
3. *Ibid.*, 3 (Oct. 29, 1923), 3.
4. *Los Angeles School Journal*, 9 (Oct. 19, 1925), 28.
5. For an excellent analysis of the political economy of Mexican migration to the United States see: Rosalinda M. Gonzalez and Raul A. Fernandez, "U.S. Imperialism and Migration: The Effects on Mexican Women and Families," *Review of Radical Political Economy* (Winter/Spring, 1980).
6. *School Journal*, 6 (May 21, 1923), 9.
7. *Los Angeles School District Publications*, No. 36 (1926), 4.
8. *School Journal*, 5 (Dec. 19, 1921), 23.
9. *Ibid.*, 5 (Jan. 16, 1922), 17.
10. *Ibid.*, 16 (Feb. 1923), 59.
11. *Ibid.*, 11 (May 14, 1928), 154.
12. *School District Publications*, No. 211 (1931), 3.
13. *Ibid.*, p. 7.
14. *Ibid.*, No. 185 (1929), 12.
15. *Ibid.*, pp. 90-92.
16. *Ibid.*, p. 12.
17. *Educational Research Bulletin*, 4 (Apr. 15, 1925), 13.
18. *Ibid.*, 3 (Oct. 29, 1933), 1.
19. *Ibid.*, 4 (Jan. 15, 1925), 1.
20, *Ibid.*, 5 (Sept. 5, 1925), 2-3.
21. *Ibid.*, 6 (Feb. 1926), 2.
22. *Ibid.*, 5 (Sept. 27, 1925), 3.
23. *Ibid.*, p. 5.
24. *Ibid.*, 6 (June 14, 1926), 1.
25. *Ibid.*, pp. 2-6.
26. *Ibid.*, 3 (Oct. 29, 1923), 1.
27. *School Publications*, No. 185 (1929), pp. 71, 80.
28. *Ibid.*, No. 211 (1931), p. 116.
29. *Ibid.*, p. 115.
30. *Ibid.*, p. 122.
31. *Ibid.*, No. 185 (1929), pp. 89-90, 87.
32. *Ibid.*, No. 13 (1918), p. 5.
33. *School Journal*, 4 (Sept. 20, 1920), 7.
34. *School Publications*, No. 41 (1922), p. 5.
35. *School Journal*, 4 (Sept. 20, 1920), 7.
36. *Ibid.*, 5 (Jan. 3, 1921), 3.
37. *Ibid.*, 5 (Jan. 16, 1922), 16.
38. *Ibid.*, 7 (May 12, 1924), 41.
39. *Ibid.*, 9 (Feb. 15, 1926), 13.
40. *Ibid.*, 5 (Nov. 6, 1922), 6.
41. *Ibid.*, 10 (Feb. 14, 1927), 16.
42. *Ibid.*, 10 (May 2, 1927), 9.
43. *Ibid.*, p. 10.
44. *Ibid.*, 6 (June 4, 1923), 23.
45. U.S. Department of the Interior, Office of Education. *The Education of Spanish Speaking Children in Five Southwestern States* (Washington, D.C.: U.S. Government Printing Office, 1933).

INDEX OF NAMES

Abbot, Lyman, 131
Abrams, Richard M., 175, 183
Addams, Jane, 36, 64, 66, 190
Altgeld, John P., 63
Arnold, Thurman, 182-83
Arons, Raymond, 25, 176
Bailyn, Bernard, 31
Baldwin, William H., 131
Barnard, Harry, 63
Berlowitz, Marvin J., 105
Binet, Alfred, 112-15, 192
Block, Marc, 178
Blum, John, 175, 181, 183
Bobbit, Franklin, 153
Borah, William E., 182
Bourne, H.R. Fox, 179, 192
Bowles, Samuel, 32, 34-36, 86, 106, 178, 186, 191
Boyer, Richard O., 181
Brandeis, Louis, 181-83
Burnham, John C., 192
Burt, Cyril, 191
Callahan, Raymond, 31-32, 36, 178
Carnegie, Andrew, 65
Carnoy, Martin, 85-86, 186
Cassmore, Oren C., 136, 193
Cattell, James McKeen, 109, 112
Chandler, Alfred D., Jr., 182
Chapman, Frank E., 105
Chomsky, Noam, 106, 191-92
Comenius, I.A., 43
Commons, John R., 26, 37, 64, 66, 68, 176, 183
Constant, Benjamin, 176
Cooley, Charles H., 34, 37, 64, 77-79, 178, 184-85
Crane, Marian M., 193
Cravens, Hamilton, 192
Creel, George, 132
Cremin, Lawrence, 30-32, 177-78, 185
Croly, Herbert, 25-26, 63
Cubberly, Ellwood, 31

Debbs, Eugene, 62
Dewey, Evelyn, 189-91
Dewey, John, 30, 34, 36-37, 64, 68, 78, 80, 82, 85-104 passim, 124, 140-41, 153, 186-89, 190-91
Dobb, Maurice, 178
Donnelly, Samuel B., 131
Dorsey, Susan B., 156
Durkheim, Emile, 13, 78, 86
Edelman, Murray, 182
Ely, Richard T., 64, 68, 76-77, 184-85
Engels, Frederick, 14, 23, 177
Felt, Jeremy, 72, 131, 184, 193
Fernandez, Raul A., 194
Foner, Philip, 54, 180
Forcey, Charles, 176
Franklin, Benjamin, 108, 116
Fusfeld, Daniel, 176
Galton, Francis, 108, 109, 116-17, 192
Gandhi, Mahatma, 36, 186
Garraty, John A., 185
Garth, Thomas R., 193
Gay, Pater, 178
Giddings, Franklin, 77, 184-85
Gilbert, J.A., 112
Gintis, Herbert, 32, 34-46, 86, 106, 178, 186, 191
Glass, Carter, 183
Glazer, Nathan, 192
Goddard, Henry H., 111, 115
Gompers, Samuel, 66
Gonzalez, Rosalinda M., 194
Grant, Madison, 125
Greer, Colin, 30-31, 33, 35, 178
Griffith, William, 185
Gutek, Gerald, 177
Hall, G. Stanley, 29, 177
Handlin, Oscar, 31
Hartz, Louis, 30, 173
Hays, Samuel P., 26, 176
Herrnstein, Richard J., 111
Hertzler, J.O., 184
Hobbes, Thomas, 107
Hofstadter, Richard, 32, 68, 177, 183-84

Index of Names

Hook, Sidney, 188
Huberman, Leo, 176
Hunt, E.K., 175, 180
Illich, Ivan 31-33
James, William, 37, 64, 87-90, 92-93, 109-10, 124-140, 186-88, 192
Jensen, Arthur R., 111
Jersild, Arthur T., 177
Kallen, Horace M., 188
Kamin, Leon J., 106, 191
Karier, Clarence, 31-32, 34-45, 85, 106, 178, 184, 196, 190-93
Katz, Michael, 31, 33, 127, 178-79, 193
Kelley, Florence, 131, 137
Kite, Elizabeth S., 192
Klineberg, Otto, 125, 193
Kneller, George F., 177
Kolko, Gabriel, 26-28, 176-77, 182-83
Lenin, V.I., 9-10, 17-18, 20-21, 23, 25-28, 173-77
Lens, Sydney, 61
Levine, Lawrence W., 175, 183
Lindsay, Benjamin B., 132
Lippmann, Walter, 25-26, 66
Lively, Robert A., 22, 175
Locke, John, 37, 40-41, 43-49, 51, 89-90, 106, 126, 178-79, 192
Lodge, Henry Cabot, 68
Macy, V.E., 131
Magdoff, Harry, 173-74
Mahan, Alfred T., 68
Mann, Horace, 54-55, 100
Marcuse, Herbert, 24-25, 176
Markham, Edwin, 131
Marx, Karl, 9-11, 14-15, 18-19, 23, 26-27, 173-74, 177
Mead, Sidney E., 67-68, 183
Menefee, Selden C., 136, 193
Montaigne, Michel de, 43
Moody, Dwight L., 68
Morais, Herbert M., 181
Moynihan, Daviel, 192
Munsterberg, Hugo, 112, 141, 193
Northcutt, Clarence H., 184
Nugent, Walter T.K., 180
Parsons, Talcott, 25
Peabody, Francis G., 67

Penndman, Howard R., 179
Perkins, Charles, 65
Perkins, George W., 140
Peterson, Joseph, 192
Phipps, Henry, 66
Ratner, J., 188
Reissman, Frank, 177, 192
Rhoades, John H., 131
Riis, Jacob, 37, 40, 67, 72-75, 81, 131, 184, 186
Roosevelt, Theodore, 37, 68, 77, 81-83, 90, 140, 181-83, 185
Ross, Edward Alsworth, 34, 37, 64, 68, 76-83, 90, 97, 100, 102, 122, 140, 178, 184-86
Rousseau, Jean Jacques, 37, 40-41, 47-49, 51, 89, 92, 119, 179
Saloutos, Theodore, 180
Samuda, Ronald J., 177
Schiff, Jacob, 72, 131
Schlesinger, Arthur, 30
Schumpeter, Joseph, 25, 176
Sherman, Howard J., 175, 180
Shockley, William, 111
Simon, Thomas, 112, 192
Small, Albion, 77-78, 80, 184-85
Smith, Adam, 37, 40, 48-51, 56, 125, 179
Smith, Wilson, 177
Spencer, Herbert, 108, 126
Spring, Joel, 31-36, 178
Staley, Eugene, 177
Straight, Willard, 67
Strong, Josiah, 13, 37, 67-71, 73, 75, 78, 81, 183-84, 186
Taft, William Howard, 181-83
Taylor, Frederick, 36
Taylor, George Rogers, 190
Terman, Lewis, 108, 111, 122, 125, 141, 167, 191, 193
Thorndike, Edward L., 30, 111, 118-19, 122, 141, 153, 193
Veblen, Thorstein, 188
Violas, Paul, 34, 178, 184-85, 190
Warburg, Paul, 131
Warburton, Amber Arthur, 193
Ward, David, 183
Weber, Max, 24, 77
Weinstein, James, 65
Wells, David A., 181

Index of Names

White, Morton, 188
Wiebe, Robert J., 183
Wilson, Woodrow, 181-83
Wolff, Robert P., 176
Wood, Helen, 193
Woodward, C. Vann, 183
Wright, C.D., 54, 62, 180
Yellen, Samuel, 180-81
Yerkes, Robert, 122

STUDIES IN MARXISM

STUDIES IN MARXISM is a series of books providing discussions of important issues in all fields of knowledge from the dialectical-materialist perspective.

Conference proceedings volumes:

Vol. 1: **MARXISM AND NEW LEFT IDEOLOGY.** Proceedings of the First Midwest Marxist Scholars Conference, 1976. *Ed. by Ileana Rodríguez and William L. Rowe. 1977.*

Vol. 2: **SOCIAL CLASS IN THE CONTEMPORARY UNITED STATES.** Papers from the Second Midwest Marxist Scholars Conference, May 1977. *Ed. by Gerald M. Erickson and Harold L. Schwartz. 1977.*

Vol. 4: **THE UNITED STATES IN CRISIS: MARXIST ANALYSES.** Papers from the Third Midwest Marxist Scholars Conference, March 1978. *Ed. by Lajos Biro and Marc J. Cohen. 1979.*

Vol. 6: **THE UNITED STATES EDUCATIONAL SYSTEM: MARXIST APPROACHES.** Papers from the Fourth Midwest Marxist Scholars Conference, March 1979. *Ed. by Marvin J. Berlowitz and Frank E. Chapman, Jr. 1980.*

Vol. 12: **STUDIES IN LABOR THEORY AND PRACTICE.** Papers from the Fifth Midwest Marxist Scholars Conference, May 1980. *Ed. by William L. Rowe. 1982.*

Volumes on special topics:

Vol. 3: **THE SOCIALIST COUNTRIES: GENERAL FEATURES OF POLITICAL, ECONOMIC, AND CULTURAL LIFE.** *By Erwin Marquit.* Theory and practice of socialism. Useful for reference or as introductory text. Includes extensive statistical information. 1978.

Vol. 5: **NICARAGUA IN REVOLUTION: THE POETS SPEAK.** *Ed. by Bridget Aldaraca, Edward Baker, Ileana Rodríguez, and Marc Zimmerman.* Poems in Spanish, and in English translation, portraying long struggle against Somoza regime and imperialism. 1980.

Vol. 7: **PHILOSOPHICAL PROBLEMS IN PHYSICAL SCIENCE.** *By Herbert Hörz, Hans-Dieter Pöltz, Heinrich Parthey, Ulrich Röseberg, and Karl-Friedrich Wessel.* First publication in English of outstanding text from the German Democratic Republic. 1980.

Vol. 8: **PROGRESSIVE EDUCATION: A MARXIST INTERPRETATION.** *By Gilbert G. Gonzalez.* Includes special section on harmful consequences of application of Dewey's theories to Chicano community in Los Angeles. 1982.

Vol. 9: **THE PHILOSOPHY OF MARXISM: AN EXPOSITION.** *By John Somerville.* Well-known introductory text again available. Unmatched excellence for classroom use. Popular style. Reprint of 1967 edition. 1981.

Vol. 10: **DIALECTICAL CONTRADICTIONS: CONTEMPORARY MARXIST DISCUSSIONS.** *Ed. by Erwin Marquit, Philip Moran, and Willis H. Truitt.* Unique international collection deals with the theory of dialectical contradictions and its applications in various fields. 1981.

Vol. 11: **CRISIS CONSCIOUSNESS IN CONTEMPORARY PHILOSOPHY.** *By Andras Gedo.* Comprehensive Marxist study of crisis consciousness in contemporary life philosophy and bourgeois futurology by outstanding Hungarian philosopher. 1982.

Order from: MARXIST EDUCATIONAL PRESS, c/o Anthropology Department, 215 Ford Hall, University of Minnesota, 224 Church Street S.E., Minneapolis, Minnesota 55455.